History of
Nineteenth-Century Russian Literature

Volume II. The Age of Realism

History of Nineteenth-Century Russian Literature

Volume II. The Age of Realism

by

Dmitrij Čiževskij

Translated by
Richard Noel Porter

Edited, with a Foreword, by
Serge A. Zenkovsky

1974
Vanderbilt University Press
Nashville

Library of Congress Cataloguing-in-Publication Data

Chyzhevs'kyi, Dmytro, 1894-
  History of nineteenth-century Russian literature.

  Translation of Russische Literaturgeschichte des 19. Jahrhunderts.
  Includes bibliographies.
  CONTENTS: v. 1 Romantic Period.—v. 2. The Age of Realism.
  1. Russian Literature–19th cent.–History and criticism. I. Title.
PG3012.C513   891.7'09'003   72-2878
  Vol. I. ISBN 0-8265-1187-2 (cloth)
           ISBN 0-8265-1188-0 (paper)
  Vol. II. ISBN 0-8265-1189-9 (cloth)
           ISBN 0-8265-1190-2 (paper)

Printed in U.S.A.

Contents

Editor's Foreword

Literary historians have coined special terms of distinction for two outstanding periods of nineteenth- and twentieth-century Russian literature. One, the "Golden Age," included the years of the blossoming of romantic poetry (1815–1840), the time of Puškin, Baratynskij, Lermontov, and Tjutčev. The other, the "Silver Age," was the modernistic period in poetry, that of the Symbolists, Acmeists, and Futurists.

Amazingly enough, however, the half-century 1840–1890, the interval between these two periods dominated by poetry—the era of the great Russian realistic novel—was never labeled with any particular name other than the purely technical term, the "time of realism" or of "critical realism." Yet Russian prose of these five decades received undisputed recognition abroad, becoming extremely popular with foreign readers and literary critics and exercising considerable impact on other literatures.

Perhaps in the eyes of the genuine lover of Russian letters, the age of realism does not particularly merit being placed above the other periods of prerevolutionary literature. For him it may be difficult to say who, exactly, is greater, Puškin or Dostoevskij, Blok or Tolstoj, Majakovskij or Turgenev. For the foreign reader, however, it is precisely the realistic novels that represent the acme of Russian literary achievement. This results from the fact that, for the person unfamiliar with the Russian language and, in general, for anyone who does not command the native language of a particular poet, it is difficult, if not impossible, to render due honor to the verse that must be read in translation. The whole beauty of the musicality, the rhythm, the fine metaphoric imagery and the subtle allusions of poetry all remain largely hidden from him. On the other hand, a translated prose work—with its ideas, heroes, and structure, whether it be a novel by Turgenev or Dostoevskij or a story by Čexov—often adheres quite closely to the original text and can be duly appreciated, even in translation. This is obviously the main reason that the Russian novel, primarily, and not Russian poetry, has been so popular and widely read abroad, and why the novel became Russia's main contribution to the world's treasury of letters.

While in the earlier periods of their literary history and even in the time of romanticism, Russians followed the main Western literary movements, with certain time gaps, this was not so in the case of the realistic school. Although some features of realism can be discerned in such early works as those of Chaucer, Villon, Rabelais, Swift, and, in Russia, in the works of Avvakum (late seventeenth century), and, later, in the poems and prose of Puškin, Lermontov, and Gogol', realism as a definite literary school came into being only in the late 1830s and 1840s. Yet, it should be kept in mind that the term *realism* has various definitions and not always the same lifespan in the different Western countries. The very word *réalisme*, as a literary term, was expressed for the first time in 1826 on the pages of the French literary periodical, *Le Mercure du XIX siècle*.[1] On these same pages, there was also provided a basic and still largely viable definition of realism as a new literary movement predestined to replace the then dominant romantic school. It was pointed out that realism should treat models and themes suggested by nature and life and would be capable of producing *la littérature du vrai*. A decade later, Honoré de Balzac became one of the first leading exponents of this realistic trend in the literature of Western Europe. After the publication in 1836 of his *Le Mèdecin de Campagne*, he came to the idea of writing *La Comédie Humaine*, a series of novels intended to present the entire panorama of contemporary French society. In Balzac we find still very strong romantic coloration, but his intentions were clearly stated in 1842 in his *avant-propos* to the *Comédie Humaine*, in which he announced his purpose of studying the human species in the same way that a zoologist studies the animal ones. He saw in his series of novels a social study and an artistic mirror of French society of his time. Almost simultaneously with Balzac, Dickens initiated the era of the realistic novel in England, and in his work, likewise, some strong romantic elements could be observed. Like Balzac, Dickens clearly regarded his literary work not only as art

---

1. "Avant propos le treizième volume," by an anonymous author, probably C. G. Étienne, *Le Mercure du Dix Neuvième Siècle*,XIII (1826), 5-7.

for art's sake or an exercise in *belles-lettres*—as literature was
viewed by many romantic writers—but as a truthful presentation of his contemporaries.

As readers of this new volume by Professor Čiževskij will see,
Russian realistic literature came into being just a few years after
the appearance of realistic literature in the West. To some extent,
the first manifestation of Russian realism developed in the so-
called natural school, which paid particular attention to the life of
the "downtrodden and injured," usually overlooked by the romantic writers. (The Russian "natural school" is not to be confused with
French "naturalism.")

Professor Čiževskij's new book on Russian realism is actually
the third volume of his history of Russian literature. The first volume, *History of Russian Literature from the Eleventh Century to the
End of the Baroque*, appeared in 1960 (Mouton and Co.,
S'Gravenhage). The next volume, *History of Russian Literature of
the Nineteenth Century: The Romantic Period*, was published in
1974 by Vanderbilt University Press. The present volume differs
slightly in some respects from the two preceding works, but the author still applies the same basic methodology: first, he studies the
philosophical background of the literary movement; then he determines and evaluates its main features and achievements; finally, he investigates the individual writers. It is expected that the
fourth and final volume of Čiževskij's history of Russian literature
will include the writers of the end of the nineteenth century (for
instance, Čexov and Gor'kij, and those of Russia's Silver Age) and
will appear in the near future. That volume will offer an extensive
bibliography on the nineteenth century, from the 1840s to the
revolution of 1917; therefore no bibliography is included in the
present volume.

Vanderbilt University Press was fortunate to have had this
third volume, as well as the preceding one on romanticism, translated by Professor Richard Porter—who, besides being a specialist
on Russian literature, has an excellent command of German, the
language in which Čiževskij's work was originally written.
Thanks to Professor Porter, many difficult passages of the original,
saturated with German and Russian literary terminology, become
easily accessible to English-language readers. Professor Porter, as
well as this editor, has taken the liberty of correcting some mis-

prints and minor errors in dates and names that occasionally occurred in the original edition. The editor also would like to express his gratitude to Martha I. Strayhorn, editor, of Vanderbilt University Press, for her painstaking checking of the manuscript and her extremely careful reading of galley and page proofs, as well as for the numerous suggestions she made in the process of preparing this work for publication.

SERGE A. ZENKOVSKY

Vanderbilt University
December 1973

PREFACE

Because of the scope of the material to be covered, I have had to divide this second part of my literary history into two volumes. In the third volume, I shall discuss late realism (with which Čexov and Gor'kij are associated), symbolism, futurism, and the various other literary currents of that time.

Unfortunately, I shall have to append the bibliography and my suggestions for independent work to Volume III.

Independent research by the reader seems to me of great importance. My suggestions deal with questions that presuppose a knowledge of Russian, something that I cannot assume, of course, for all my readers. I especially regret that the bibliography for Volume II is not immediately available, since there is no European literature, the other Slavic literatures not excepted, that has a greater need for bibliographies than has Russian. An example of the trouble with present bibliographies is the work of K. Muratova, which appeared at the same time as the first volume of this history and is good in some respects, but which lists six hundred entries, without any evaluation, for Gogol', Turgenev, and L.N. Tolstoj. At times, twenty or more works are included under a single entry, and almost all the works mentioned are in Russian. There is still no *critical* bibliography of Russian literature. But in my bibliography I have tried to offer the reader a selection of useful works.

The third volume of this work, with bibliography and my suggestions for further study, will, I hope, be ready soon.

I would like to express my thanks to my students Ute Dransfeld, Inga Lancon-von Schlick, Dr. Gabriele Selge, and expecially to Ursula Fritsche and Dr. Horst-Jürgen Gerigk, who helped me in the preparation of this volume. I would also like to thank the Fink Verlag for its valuable assistance.

Heidelberg
December 1966

DMITRIJ ČIŽEVSKIJ

History of
Nineteenth-Century Russian Literature

The Age of Realism

I
Realism

1. Realism is a vague concept in Russian literary scholarship. There have been literary historians who have called almost all Russian literature realistic.[1] In defining realism, one usually resorts to empty formulas and deals more with social and political affairs than with literary concerns. The realists and the critics and literary historians partial to them have been most to blame for the inadequate research done on realism. In their exaggerated opinions of themselves, the realists thought that they had reached an unprecedented plateau of achievement. It was said that most of what was valuable in the literature of the past merely anticipated realism and that everything worthwhile in world literature could be thought of as realistic.

In Russia, there has been a particularly high opinion of realism and a particular dearth of authoritative works on the essence of realism. Since the realistic period was the greatest period in Russian literature and since the leading realistic writers, L. N. Tolstoj, Dostoevskij, and Turgenev, were strikingly individual, it has been extremely difficult to generalize about the period as a whole. Consequently, it has been the rule to use broad and empty formulas, which Western European scholars and popular writers have unfortunately taken over. In order to give an idea of the realistic style, one must deal at least briefly with this primitive characterization.

2. The usual, and completely unsatisfactory, explanation of realism is that realism portrays the world as it is in reality. In Russian, this sounds somewhat better: *"Realizm izobražaet dejstvitel'nost'*

---

1. The realistic period in Russian literature encompasses, broadly, the years from the 1850s to the 1890s. Realism supplanted romanticism as a general writing style and was in turn superseded by the rise of symbolism, toward the end of the nineteenth century.—EDITOR

tak, kak ona est' na samon dele"; but a literal translation shows that this is inadequate: "Realism portrays reality as it really is"—that is, as it is in reality. Since, in the Russian definition, there are two expressions for the idea of reality, one does not at first notice that the definition is a tautology.

The main difficulty is the vagueness of the concept of *reality*. Most realistic critics and literary historians have their own idea of reality, an idea that is open to question. The principal feature of this idea is that reality exists on only one level, that there is no hierarchy of levels of being, no higher or lower strata of being that operate according to their own laws and can attack, do battle with, and destroy *reality* as it really is. The great writers L. N. Tolstoj, Dostoevskij, and Turgenev are especially typical of the realistic period; but their views of reality are totally different from those of the Russian radical, liberal—and, later, Marxist—critics and literary historians, who are responsible for the usual interpretation of reality in Russian literature. Dostoevskij's reality includes the depths of the human soul, other worlds from which God sends the seeds of men's thoughts to this world, and God and the Devil, who war in the human soul. Tolstoj's reality includes God and the whole religious sphere; his idea of the life of the soul has little in common with the primitive psychology of Enlightenment used by other realists. And during almost all Turgenev's writing career, he was aware that life was governed by a merciless fate, a concept that hardly fits the realists' theory of reality.

A portrayal of reality presents only part of reality; language is incapable of presenting all of it. The point of view of the narrator, the perspective of a work, determines the scope, size, and character of this portrayal. In addition, the writer's view of reality is conditioned by various subjective as well as objective factors, such as the society in which he lives. Artistic devices can create the illusion of a complete portrayal of reality. Among these devices is an emphasis on details, suggesting that the writer knows everything and simply does not have space to tell it all. Instead of a complete description of reality, realistic works portray a part of it, a portion viewed from a certain perspective.

Naturally, all writers take the details of their works from the reality around them, as admirers of realism always manage to demonstrate. Where else would the material for literature come from? The quality of the realistic style is therefore not determined by its means of expression—that is, by any objective factors, but rather by the way in which they are put to use.

3. Among the typical features of the realistic style are metonymic devices, as Roman Jakobson indicates; devices that could be called metaphoric seldom or never appear. The metaphors traditional in romanticism and the Natural School had lost their suggestiveness, since every writer had the same store of metaphors, or because new, original metaphors were considered strained. Karolina Pavlova was largely, if not entirely, correct in saying that Stepan Ševyrev's romantic poetry was unpopular because he was fond of metaphors. (I use the word *metaphor* in a broad sense and intend that it include the various kinds of comparisons.)

Realism is the first antimetaphoric style in the history of European literature. Of course, literature cannot free itself entirely of metaphors, because language is full of them. Metaphors live on in realism, but in concealed form; and one can speak of the antimetaphoric tendency in realism and of the realists' aversion to metaphor.

The reasons for this aversion to metaphor go deep. The use of metaphor requires one to connect different levels of being. Object A is replaced by Object B; B must come from a different sphere if the metaphor is to be effective. Various worlds cross in a metaphor, the material world and the intellectual, ideal world, past and present, that which is and that which should be, tradition and revolution. But realists seek to deal with everything on a single plane, as elements of the same realm of being. Some of these realists, such as the materialists and positivists, do not believe in "other worlds." Idealists among the realists attempt to portray ideal being in the reality accessible to everyone, as Dostoevskij does, or are forced to show this everyday reality out of fear of losing their audience. No one has demonstrated to what extent the Russian realistic style was determined by the writers' view of the world and to what extent by the demands of readers and by purely stylistic considerations.

In other words, the romantic, metaphoric style is aware of various levels of being, above and below; but the realistic style is aware of only what is around it, on the same plane. It deals only with movement on that plane and makes use of this movement in various ways. As a result, much attention is paid to environment, a fundamental concept of Russian realism. Environment can be interpreted in different ways. First of all, it can be thought to consist of the people and things around the character that one is treating. The character's relationships with his friends and acquaintances are explored or, if the writer does not believe that men are dependent on their surroundings, these relationships at least stand as a symbol of the inner condition of the principal character. Dostoevskij's ethical statement that "everyone is guilty for everyone and of everything" is evidence of the same conviction that men are dependent on one another, only in an idealistic sense. The Russian positivists, who believed in the complete dependence of an individual on his environment, often spoke of a bad man's having been corrupted by his environment (the Russian expression is *sreda zaela*—"the environment had eaten on the man"); here too is a conviction that man and his environment are intimately related, although in a different sense from that expressed by Dostoevskij.

This tendency explains the realists' preference for long forms, such as the novel, which eventually developed into the empirical or experimental novel (cf. Émile Zola). Other genres were also usually broad, especially the reflective lyric, a favorite form of the period. Most genres typical of romanticism disappeared completely or were considerably modified: the fairy tale (although there were still satirical fairy tales), the mystery, the "numinous," or fantastic, ballad. The historical ballad was also less important in the realistic period than in the romantic.

4. The metonymical quality of realism led writers to try to explain the personality and actions of their characters. These explanations usually center on the backgrounds of the characters (and this practice results in false conclusions: *post hoc, ergo propter hoc*). It is assumed that a character is determined or at least influenced by his childhood, education, and heredity, and so writers such as Turgenev talk about the family histories of their characters. The romanticists also discuss their characters' families, not to explain the characters and their actions, but rather to suggest that some kind of fate hangs over them, as in the

case of the accursed family in Gogol's *Terrible Vengeance*. In romanticism, events are often attributed to two kinds of causes: those of this world and the human psyche, and those of a higher or ideal world. There is little of this dual causality in realism. It is most pronounced in Dostoevskij, whose characters are intended to stand for real people and for ideal qualities as well (see chapter VI, sec. 10). It was not until after the realistic period, in the time of symbolism, that writers again turned to dual causality.

What one does find in realism is the motivation for actions. That is the final step in the development of the novel, a process that goes back to the baroque, when characters in a novel were maneuvered like chessmen to make the story interesting. To some extent, actions in classicist novels depend on the caprice of the author. In romanticism, the pattern is the same. Characters are capricious and are driven by the mysterious "night side of the soul," by factors of which they are not conscious, and by fate and the destiny of their families. In realism, motivation must be credible above all else, even when there is only a pseudomotivation. The use of detail is a popular and often convincing method of accounting for motivation, as in the works of Turgenev. Detail is even more important in portraying characters.

Morbid states of mind and the unconscious can serve as motivations, as they do in the work of Dostoevskij. Some realists, such as Turgenev, still subscribe to the concept of mysterious forces in the world. The element of surprise in a work requires some actions to be at least seemingly unmotivated, as is evident in the work of Leskov. Among the paradoxes of motivation is the apparent or real incommensurability between motive and act, a basic feature of the psychology of realists such as Čexov. In any event, the psyche or inner life of man is the medium through which the realists show sin, evil, and the religious sphere. Motivation, or the causal explanation of the inner life, almost completely replaces the other way of looking at the inner life, that is, interpreting the meaning of it. The causal explanation replaces the interpretation of life and the world; it is not the meaning, but the cause, that must be shown. Some writers, such as Dostoevskij and, to some extent, L. N. Tolstoj, are not confined by this requirement.

One kind of motivation that appeared early in Russian literature was the practice of telling what social or political group
a character belongs to. Some realists offer no further explanation
of why a person acts as he does; it is assumed that one always
acts typically of his group.

5. The demand for motivation, or pseudomotivation, in realism
places great importance on verisimilitude. Since reality cannot
be drawn or photographed, a realistic work can only seem
plausible. The romanticists did not think, of course, that plausibil-
ity mattered. They gave fantastic explanations—something is
described as being the devil's fault, for instance—or they gave
no explanation at all, as in Gogol's *The Nose*: "Here the whole
business becomes shrouded in mist, and nothing is known of what
happened next"; or deliberately improbable explanations are
offered as in Puškin's *The Snowstorm,* of which one critic rightly
said: "Every step is unlikely: Who would marry a stranger passing
through town? Why did the witnesses not realize that the groom
was the wrong person? How could the priest have mistaken the
stranger for the actual bridegroom? One could ask thousands of
such questions." The demand for credibility is often thought of
as the demand to present the "typical." If one attempts consciously
to present that which is typical, one does gain a certain freedom;
but creative fantasy is encroached upon. In Russian realism, there
is an unresolved conflict between two tendencies. On the one hand,
writers such as Turgenev, the politically radical realists, and,
to some extent, Čexov sought to portray typical phenomena, that
which does or could happen often in life. On the other hand, writers
such as Dostoevskij and Leskov were interested in unusual people
and events, in the atypical. The conflict between these two tendencies is especially clear in historical fiction, which was not,
however, an important genre in the realistic period.

6. By and large, realism attempted to avoid literary devices
typical of romanticism, devices that the Natural School had also
used. These devices are, primarily, hyperbole and grotesquery.
Whether hyperbole exaggerates the good or the bad, it removes
the work in question from the single level on which a metonymical
writer can operate. Grotesquery depends on destroying the normal
relationship of things. It joins dissimilar things and things from

different spheres; it often uses hyperbole, and it is not at all a metonymical device.

Realism does employ these devices, in one kind of writing: satire. The most gifted Russian realistic satirist, M. E. Saltykov-Ščedrin, is a master of the grotesque and is not afraid to include the unrealistic in his work. His grotesquery often borders on fantasy and sometimes crosses into the realm of the fairy tale (see chapter XII). Other realistic writers also make use of satire; there is satire in Dostoevskij and Turgenev and especially in Leskov.

Realistic writers typically play down the euphonic devices of language, a practice that may reflect the disdain of these empirically oriented writers for language not used in "real life" (euphony and, especially, verse).

7. Writers' fondness for detailed descriptions of surroundings lent comprehensive portrayals of life and nature in the longer forms of realistic literature a value and meaning all their own. Turgenev's very long depictions of nature, the frequent use of folklore by P. I. Mel'nikov-Pečerskij and Leskov, and Tolstoj's treatment of history are examples of detailed description typical of realism. This use of description required special stylistic devices; and to some extent old situations returned (*loca amoena,* storms, markets, and so on), although they were put to new uses.

Russian realism inherited its fondness for description from the Natural School. But the realists, even those who had begun writing in the Natural School, doing "physiological sketches" and pages of scenes without plots, declined to use the typical devices of the Natural School. Hyperbole and grotesquery were less popular with realists than they were with the Natural School; and realists turned away from portraying reality as dirty, low, meaningless, and absurd. Ragged characters who live outside society, morbid, crippled, animallike men with red eyes and awkward, impaired speech, incapable of expressing their thoughts—these people do not appear in realism, or, if they do, only as secondary, comic characters. One should not assume that realistic descriptions are very exact. There is, of course, a considerable difference between romantic portrayals of the common people, such as Gogol's ethnographic scenes, which aim only at a general impression of fidelity, and the careful reports of Mel'nikov-Pečerskij or even Leskov. By and large, however, Turgenev's idealized account of the peasants and other writers' typical treatment of revolutionaries (more noticeable in lesser, "reactionary" novelists than in the work of Leskov and Dostoevskij) are factual only on the surface. The personality and opinions of the author come through in his conception of the whole.

There were writers (see chapter V, sec. 2) who retained much of the stylistic and structural tradition of the Natural School, but they are a minor group.

8. Realism, then, did not require of writers a particular view of the world. Although social and political forces were especially influential at the time—throughout the last half of the nineteenth century—(one has only to remember the emancipation of the serfs and the other reforms then current), realistic writers differed in their attitudes toward these social and political matters; and at times they disagreed completely with each other. They represented all possible points of view on life and the world, from primitive materialism and naive positivism to idealism and a consistently Christian position. Russian and foreign philosophers were occasionally influential; Schopenhauer had some effect, as did Nietzsche toward the end of the century, although he was usually misunderstood.

Almost all realists admired learning, especially in the social and natural sciences. All too often, writers turned to scientific sources that were biased and that gave rise to a false picture of reality. Nevertheless, many writers sought to work as scientists did, to collect material and to set up definitions and theses; that was particularly true of didactic poetry, a popular form of the time.

9. Other interesting problems of realistic theory should be touched on, among them typology. A certain neglect of the ideal of beauty is also typical of realistic literature and of realistic art in general. It was thought that a writer should deal chiefly with current issues. The problem of language is one of the most important in realistic theory; here writers tended toward uniformity, which led not to an impoverishment of language but to an acceptance of all levels of language, even in poetry. Colloquial language, vulgarisms, professional jargon, and a modest amount of dialect came into the literary language. Foreign words, scholarly terms, and bureaucratic language were used without

hesitation. This change was reflected in the language of poetry, which acquired a new wealth of rhymes and many morphological archaisms and elements, such as participles, that were foreign to the spoken language. These usages varied, of course, from poet to poet.

10. A typical undercurrent of literary realism was impressionism. I call impressionism an *under*current because the impressionists did not form a separate literary school but merely wrote in an "original" style. The impressionists were writers who based their metonymical descriptions on details that seem at first unimportant and fortuitous but that have actually been selected with great care, as is evident in the work of Čexov, Fet, and on occasion L. N. Tolstoj.

The difficulty in describing reality is the endless scope involved as soon as one goes beyond finite objects. A description must therefore be limited to certain features of an object. In other words, all realism is actually impressionism. Writers who naively believe that they have completely reproduced or described reality are often bad writers, and writers who deliberately use impressionistic devices are able to create more striking and effective literature. Even writers who did not approve of impressionism often made use of carefully selected details. An example is Turgenev, who critized and rejected the obvious impressionism of L. N. Tolstoj but who did the same thing, in effect, with his device of typology.

II

Backgroung of Realism: The Natural School; Herzen

1. In Volume I of this work, the Natural School was discussed as a late stage in the development of romanticism and as an innovation leading to realism. After the period lasting from 1855 to 1860, a number of writers of the Natural School became outstanding realists, among them Turgenev, Grigorovič, Gončarov, and Nekrasov. In moving from the Natural School to realism, these writers set aside most of the distinguishing features of their early work, especially the extreme dreariness, negative hyperbole, and grotesquery, and turned away from the neglect of plot that had often marked their "physiological" sketches.

A list of works that Turgenev planned in his early years suggests that all the pieces were to have been physiological sketches, such as "One of the larger houses on Goroxovaja Street, etc.," "Physiognomy of St. Petersburg by night (the coachman, etc.; here a conversation with a coachman can be introduced)," "Some large factory . . . ," "On the Nevskij Prospekt, its visitors, its faces, its horsecars, the conversations in them, etc." At the time, Turgenev called these themes plots. His early tales, *A Sportsman's Sketches,* were essentially plotless, in keeping with the style of the Natural School, a style that Turgenev later referred to as his "old manner."

The plots of the Natural School are meager or insignificant. The plots of Dostoevskij's first novellas are also meager, but his subject matter is somewhat different from that of the Natural School (see chapter VI, sec 3).

Works of that kind filled such anthologies as *Fiziologia Peterburga* [The Physiology of St. Petersburg] (two volumes, 1844-45) and *Peterburgskij Sbornik* [St. Petersburg Collection] (1846).

Among the sketches were Nekrasov's *Peterburgskie ugly* (1845), Grigorovič's *Peterburgskie šarmanščiki* [The Organ Grinders of St. Petersburg] (1845), Vladimir Dal's *Peterburgskij dvornik* [St. Petersburg Janitor] (1842), Ivan Panaev's *Peterburgskij fel'etonist* [St. Petersburg Feuilletonist] (1841), and Evgenij Grebenka's *Peterburgskaja storona* [St. Petersburg Side] (1845). Even Faddej Bulgarin (see volume I), who had not yet achieved a genuinely romantic style, tried his hand at physiological sketches.

Few writers of this period are remembered for belonging to the Natural School. Among those who are are Jakov Petrovič Butkov, who died in 1856; Ivan Ivanovič Panaev (1812–1862); and Ivan Timofeevič Kokorev (1825-1853). All of them died early and were unable to take a stand on the new realistic literature.

2. Ivan Ivanovič Panaev published several poems and novellas between 1834 and 1840. In some of them, he attempted to do what V. F. Odoevskij had done and present the Russian nobility in a critical light, as in *Ona budet sčastliva* [She Will Be Happy] (1836). By 1838, Panaev had written *Sceny iz Peterburgskoj žizni* [Scenes from Life in St. Petersburg] and *Košelek* [The Purse], which have many features of the Natural School.

In the novella *Scenes from Life in St. Petersburg,* Panaev portrays a young St. Petersburg official similar to Gogol's Xlestakov. The official lives modestly with his aunt, whose young ward, Liza, falls in love with him. But he is intent on enjoying St. Petersburg. Through a colleague, he is introduced in the salons of people of some means, people dominated by officials and their society-conscious wives. The young official goes to balls, masquerades, and the theater. He is not so empty as Xlestakov, and he comes to realize that this society world is futile. In the end, it is not clear whether his engagement to Liza will result in a happy marriage. These *Scenes* have a deliberately loose construction. The language is colorful; and in the dialogue, Panaev uses the idiom of the circles he portrays. Occasionally, the narrator speaks out and makes ironic or critical remarks about the principal character or pretends to chat with the reader: "The department head Evgraf Matveevič—what is his last name? It's on the tip of my tongue. No, I forget."

The next year, Panaev published the novella *Doč' činovnogo* čeloveka [The Daughter of a High Official] (1839); and from 1841 on, he brought out more novellas in the same vein as his *Scenes*. These novellas deal with the St. Petersburg demimonde, with its fops and girls of easy virtue, its theaters, balls, and fashionable salons (*Onagr* [The Onager], *Akteon* [The Dung Beetle], 1841, 1842); the novellas also portray the uncultured, uneducated landowners who lead parasitic lives in large cities (*Barynja* [The Lady of the Manor], 1841). The form of the loose sketch, of scenes not connected by a plot and primarily concerned with portraying social types, is typical of most of Panaev's further work. From 1854 to 1857, he brought out his novellas *Xlyšči* (*xlyšč* is a vulgar word for "fop"), which present various kinds of fops: *A Fop in High Society*, 1854; *A Fop from a Small Town*, 1856; *A Fop de la haute école*, 1857. In the 1850s, Panaev continued an early sketch, *St. Petersburg Feuilletonist*, with the subtitle *A Zoological Sketch* (1841), in the feuilletons of the ideologically radical magazine *Sovremennik*, under the pseudonym "*Novyj poèt*" ("new poet"). In 1860, these feuilleton pieces were carefully edited, shortened, and collected in two volumes.

Panaev's first sketches have all the typical features of the Natural School: prevailing gloom, hyperbole, extreme grotesquery, caricatures, skillfully individualized dialogue, and base, filthy principal characters. In Panaev's later work, these features are less evident; there is a serious narrative tone, especially in the author's remarks, and an irony that does not always seem natural. In the later sketches, his human types and his brief stories about them are usually presented against a background of different sections of St. Petersburg, with typical people and scenes. For example, a novella about a girl who has been seduced and commits suicide is set in the waterfront district (*Galernaja gavan'* [1856]). Earlier, Turgenev had planned to depict this same poor district: *Galernaja gavan'* was on his list of proposed sketches. The social and political motives behind Panaev's later sketches are clear: the high officials, early Russian capitalists, and landowners who lead an easy life in St. Petersburg are the targets of a frontal attack. Later in his career, Panaev returned to verse and parodied, at times cleverly, what was left of romantic poetry. Often these parodies are not, properly speaking, literary parodies, which exaggerate certain features of literary works, usually in order to make them appear ridiculous. Literary parodies are different from travesties or simple burlesques and are of interest to the literary historian, since they show what contemporaries noticed in the works they parodied. But Panaev's parodies are often simple burlesques, lampooning good works for no particular reason.

The high quality of Panaev's style is most evident in his justly famous *Literary Reminiscences* (1860 f.). His smooth but acute style makes his account of the thirties, forties, and fifties particularly readable, although one must allow for his prejudices. Panaev was well thought of by important contemporaries and was esteemed by intellectuals interested in political and social issues. Although Panaev's collected works were brought out in 1888 and 1889 and in 1912, his sketches seemed dated, and he has been largely forgotten. His development from the style of the Natural School to a style close to that of realism deserves more study.

3. Another writer of the Natural School, whose works are available in a three-volume edition, is Ivan Timofeevič Kokorev, who died before he had turned thirty, in 1853.

For the most part, Kokorev's works are also sketches, which occasionally contain short novellas. A longer work, *Savvuška* (1852), which the author called a novella, includes a number of sketches in the biography of the poor tailor Savva Savvič. Kokorev's sketches appeared in Mixail Pogodin's magazine *Moskvitjanin,* and it is difficult to say how much the themes of the works were influenced by Pogodin's interests. Some of the sketches are reportage, such as *The Markets of Moscow* and *Small Industry in Moscow,* both of which contain facts—the first sketch even has tables of statistics. Another sketch, *The Cook,* appears in places to be a kind of novella, but it does not maintain the form or portray a particular person, attempting instead to give a collective picture of the cooks of Moscow. This deliberate neglect of form is typical of the Natural School.

Kokorev's style is also typical. It is distinguished by a deliberate alternation between a serious, informative narrative tone and the use of awkward, popular idiom in the speech of the characters and the text connected with them. Kokorev addresses the reader, writes in broken sentences, and uses anacoluthon. He is primarily interested in imitating the style of oral narrative: "But let's skip over that . . . ", "Let's turn our attention instead to . . . " He seeks to do away with the distinction between the thoughts and feelings of his characters and his own observations, and he makes use of various forms of stream of consciousness. These monologues differ lexically and stylistically from his own speech and include frequent vulgarisms and instances of argot and thieves' cant.

The lexical richness of Kokorev's language is striking. He describes very different walks of life and frequently explains words the reader may not know.

Kokorev uses words that have changed through folk etymology, such as *obliz'jana, mamzel,* and *takcija* ("official charge"); popular neologisms, such as *čugunka* (("railroad"); incorrect forms, such as *bratyj* for *vzjatyj* (("taken"); technical terms and expressions, such as *ostatok* ("remainder," in a special sense); expressions used without any explanation, such as *xmyl vzjal* ("all is lost") and *busil'nik* ("tea"); and derivations of uncertain origin, such as *molodjatinka* (in literary Russian, *molod), deševiz (deševizna), magazejščik, cajničať, okuxariťsja, stukmanka,* ("a blow"), and *živčejšij izvoščik.* Kokorev may also have borrowed words from other contemporary writers, such as *onagr* ("onager," in this sense, "dandy," cf. Panaev), *Vedrin* (presumably his boss, Pogodin, borrowed from a parody by Herzen), *literaturnye ostatki* (taken from a bookdealer whose name we do not know); foreign words used by the uneducated, such as *raceja, monšery, rezon, bonžur, mersi;* and words and expressions from thieves' cant, such as *lafa* ("good life"—the word later made its way into the literary language), *strema* ("failure"), *petux* ("watchman"), *šmeľ* ("purse"), and *na kon' kamurku busať* ("to drink in a dive").

Apparently, Kokorev also coined words. He made suggestions for Russian words to replace foreign words. For *vint* ("screw"), he recommended *červjak* (today one finds *červjačnyj xod,* but that is a technical expression and hardly goes back to Kokorev); for *biblioteka,* Kokorev suggested *knigoxranilišče;* for *miraž, marevo;* for *masštab, mernik;* for *pejzaž, kraevid* (which is now usual in Ukrainian); for *portret, podoben'* or *poličie;* for *sistema, čin;* for *fantazija, domysl;* for *xroničeskaja bolezn', slegaja bolezn';* and for *stiľ, pošib* (which is occasionally still used). Among the neologisms he offers are *besserdečnyj* ("heartless") and *bessmyslica* ("nonsense"), both of which were probably already in use. He also formed new antonyms, such as *dolgovat'* to *korotat'* and *letov'e* to *zimov'e*.

Kokorev collected linguistic curiosities, store signs and the like. He borrowed numerous proverbs from popular speech and invented some himself. These proverbs occur in the same passages in which he quotes Russian poets. His use of lexical and stylistic ornamentation goes back perhaps to his wish to "beautify the language euphonically."

Like so many writers of the Natural School, Kokorev had an ideological bent; he was attracted to the problem of poverty. Although the novella *Savvuška* ends happily, the reader senses that that is due to inexplicable good luck. All men are driven by poverty and want, whether they are tailors, cooks, cabmen, or the enterprising men from Yaroslavl willing to do any kind of work. Poverty excuses their conflicts, usually minor, with morality and the law. Kokorev knew the secrets of the good "Russian heart" (as he wrote in his notes). His short pieces of reportage and his discussion of books, in which he deals with the same themes, are interesting. He is a forerunner of later realistic writers who thought that poverty excused much and that, if wealth were not exactly a vice, it could soon lead to one. He connects his characters closely with their financial means.

The list of works that Kokorev planned to write is interesting. They are mostly physiological sketches, the themes of which are found in the work of other writers of the Natural School. Kokorev also intended to write novellas about educated people.

4. Poverty is the problem that dominates the works of Jakov Petrovič Butkov. Occasionally, he wrote physiological sketches to explain the lives and troubles of his characters. An official who goes mad when he wins a hundred rubles in a lottery and another who dies of joy when a job opens up for him are no exceptions in Butkov's gallery of characters plagued by hard luck. He takes a keen interest in the distinctive features of his characters, some of whom are desperately poor. Often his characters seem to disappear behind their accessories, their clothes, shoes, and furnishings, or they are at least less conspicuous than their accessories. This practice is not new; Gogol' uses it in his late work. But whereas Gogol's characters have arrived at their nadir

through spiritual emptiness (*pošlost'*), Butkov's characters have been driven by poverty (although there are, of course, instances of poverty in Gogol', as in *The Greatcoat*). In Butkov, poverty destroys what is left of human dignity. His characters are not concerned about morality, but about finding a way out of their plight. One man follows the funeral processions of strangers every day to take part in the funeral feast that is served afterward in accordance with Moscow custom (*Gorjun*). Another is given a good job when his wife yields to the advances of his boss (*Xorošee mesto*). A stroke of good fortune plunges her into senseless adventures (*Nevskij prospekt*).

Butkov's portrayal of people is particularly typical of the Natural School.

A figure with a violet face and bristling beard entered the room. . . . It had on a rather worn *čujka*, that item of aboriginal clothing. . . . In addition to this clothing there was a small varnished basket that the new arrival held in his hands and that did not resemble a hat or a cap. . . . Boots appeared beneath the long *čujka*. One boot was modest, unpolished, but in any case a real boot of the ultimate genus boot. . . . The other boot had obviously been created accidentally, at the whim of fate, to be a companion to the first boot. That was a foppish, varnished boot and shone like a mirror but had already a number of cracks in it, which showed that it was no more than a poor dandy, without character, and merely reflected a bit of glitter from the world of high society.

This grotesque, primitive portrayal of poverty is told in the traditionally humorous vein that was about to lose its sway.

5. The typical features of the Natural School were overworked and lost their appeal through constant repetition (see volume I—it must be emphasized that the style of the Natural School is not the same as the "naturalistic style"). Among these features of the Natural School are grotesque portrayals; the tendency to present the lower areas of human life, the dirty side of prosaic reality, unattractive landscapes, dismal, desolate backgrounds; the overemphasis on details of clothing; extensive description of everyday "physiological" acts, such as eating, drinking, and smoking; the awkward speech of the characters, and frequent use of stream of consciousness; a breakdown in composition as a result of the oral, reportorial style of narration (*skaz*), or for no apparent

reason, or because of the nature of these sketches, which had become fashionable in prose; the mixing of the high and low styles; a change in the central character, who is led astray not by his passions but by his whims and moods; the meekness of the characters; and the stylization, or disguise, of the narrator as someone not far above his characters in rank.

In addition to the ideological romanticists among the original writers of the Natural School—the first of them was Gogol', who founded the school without really intending to—writers now appeared who had no romantic illusions and who shared the radical political and social views of the new generation. It was not these writers who led literature out of the blind alley of the Natural School, but others—in particular, Dostoevskij and Herzen.

6. Fedor Mixajlovič Dostoevskij, whose work will be discussed later, began as a writer of the Natural School. He was enthusiastically hailed by other writers of the school and by Vissarion Belinskij, the critic who had given the school his blessing. These supporters turned away from Dostoevskij, however, as soon as he sought to go his own way, a way that was to lead to the psychological novel. They did not understand what he was trying to do. Dostoevskij was one of the first true realists, although, at first, he merely broke with the social, political, and naturalistic elements in the "natural" style (see chapter VI).

7. The most important step toward the realism of Turgenev, Gončarov, and Pisemskij was taken by a man who, unfortunately, soon gave up belles lettres, although he remained an important writer: Aleksandr Ivanovič Herzen (1812–1870), whose name in Russian was "Gercen." Herzen was one of the great Russian stylists of the nineteenth century. He soon turned to political journalism; but his writings as a journalist demonstrate his incomparable artistic style, brilliant despite his themes and views.

Herzen was the illegitimate son of a rich Moscow nobleman named Jakovlev and a German woman, Luise Haag. As a love-child, or *"Kind des Herzens,"* he was named Herzen at his father's wish. It is an unusual name in Russian, since the language has no *h* sound. At home, Herzen received an excellent education, which he continued at Moscow University. In 1834, he and his friend Nikolaj Ogarev (see chapter VII) were arrested for their political radicalism and socialistic leanings. Herzen was exiled to Vyatka in the northeastern part of European Russia and forced to serve three years there as an official. Then he was moved to Vladimir, in central Russia, but he was not allowed in Moscow. After a long stay in St. Petersburg and a new exile in Novgorod, Herzen was permitted to return to Moscow in 1842. There, he was close to the circle of Moscow Hegelians, with which he had previously been in touch. In 1847, during the first skirmishes between Slavophiles and Westernizers, he was allowed to go abroad, where he made many friends and acquaintances and took part in the revolution of 1848. He lived in France, Switzerland, and Italy, but remained longest in England. He managed to have a large part of his fortune sent abroad and was able to live independently. In 1857, Herzen founded the weekly paper *Kolokol* [The Bell], which was distributed, illegally, even in Russia and which played an extremely important part in Russian political journalism. Herzen lost much of the sympathy of Russian liberals through his support of the Polish revolt of 1863 and of young radicals. By and large, his life abroad was not happy. He died in Nice in 1870.

In Russia, Herzen's works were not permitted to be published for a long time, and his name could not be mentioned. It was not until 1905 that the first edition of his works appeared in Russia, in seven volumes, severely censored. An edition of his works was published in Geneva, from 1875 to 1879, but was banned in Russia. The third edition of his work, in twenty-two volumes, was brought out between 1919 and 1925 by M. Lemke. The fourth edition of Herzen's work began coming out in 1954 and was completed in 1965.

8. Herzen felt a great need to put his thoughts and feelings in writing. He started writing in 1829, mainly for himself. It was not until 1836 that he published a work, an essay on E. T. A. Hoffmann. In the forties, Herzen's writings came out in Russia and abroad. He wrote in a polished, pointed style and dealt with historical and philosophical questions, as well as journalistic themes. His memoirs, *Byloe i dumy* [My Past and Thoughts] (1852 ff.), told with all the brilliance of his style, is a remarkable work. It did not appear in its entirety until the twentieth century. It is an inexhaustible source of information

on Russian intellectual history, particularly in the 1840s; but critical judgment should be exercised in using the book. Herzen's diary is also literary, and his considerable correspondence is evidence of the care he always took in expressing himself.

In his younger years, Herzen tried his hand at fiction. In 1835–1836, he wrote *A Legend,* the story of a nun, Feodora, who disguises herself as a man, lives in a monastery, and conceals her sex, even when she is accused of fathering an illegitimate child. Herzen then wrote several novellas: *Vstreči* [Encounters] (1836); *Elena* (1836 ff.); *O sebe* [Concerning Myself] (1838), a fragment to which Herzen did not give a title; *Rimskie sceny* [Roman Scenes] (1838); *William Penn* (scenes in verse, 1839). The partly autobiographical novella *Zapiski molodogo čeloveka* [Memoirs of a Young Man] (1838, published in 1840) was the first of Herzen's fictional works to appear in print. His notes and letters tell of his further literary plans.

In his early work, Herzen was inspired by foreign literature, especially German—there are echoes of Schiller, Hoffmann, Goethe, and Heine. Despite his enthusiasm for E. T. A. Hoffmann, Herzen seems to have been influenced by the romantic novella only in his partly autobiographical novella *Elena,* where ideal and worldly love are contrasted. The *Memoirs of a Young Man* is reminiscent of Gogol's *Inspector General* and of Heine. The style of the work is close to that of the sketches of the Natural School, which were just beginning to come out. Much of the caricaturing style of these sketches appears in Herzen's satirical accounts of social life in Vyatka, called Malinov in the novella, and in his character portraits, such as that of the Polish skeptic Trenzinski, an antiromantic whom he liked. But Herzen makes only modest use of the style of the Natural School. In most of his early works, Herzen is not just a writer but a thinker as well, strikingly so in comparison with his contemporaries. In *Russian Nights* (see volume I, chapter IV, sec. 1), Prince V. F. Odoevskij places philosophical discussions between scenes, in the conversations of friends who are reading novellas to one another. In Herzen's first, autobiographical chapters of his *Memoirs* (I, "Childhood," II, "Youth") and in the portrayal of the town Malinov, the emphasis is on the author's observations. Herzen's conversations with Trenzinski are devoted to history and philosophy. From the *Memoirs,* one might have guessed that Herzen would not remain a writer of imaginative literature.

In the 1840s, Herzen still wrote essays, such as the contrasting description of St. Petersburg and Moscow (written in 1842, published in 1857), which is reminiscent of Belinskij and of Gogol' (whose notes of 1836 attracted attention) and *Kaprizy i razdum'e* [Moods and Thoughts] (1843–1847). But Herzen's main works were philosophical (*Dilettantism in Science,* 1843, and *Letters on the Study of Nature,* 1845–1846, the latter of which was well thought of by Dostoevskij) and purely journalistic (such as his humorous polemic in 1843 against Mixail Pogodin's magazine, *Moskvitjanin).*

In 1845–1846, Herzen published his novel *Kto vinovat* [Whose Fault?], one of the first works, if not the first, to go beyond the flourishing Natural School and show the way to realism. The novel deals with an unhappy marriage. Dmitrij Kruciferskij, a Moscow student and son of a doctor, is appointed tutor to the family of a patriarchal, coarse, and uneducated general. There he falls in love with Ljubov' Aleksandrovna, the illegitimate daughter of the general and a peasant woman; Ljubov' Aleksandrovna has been reared as a member of the general's family. Kruciferskij marries her and goes to teach in the city, where he meets a likable elderly doctor, Krupov. Under Krupov's wing, Kruciferskij lives happily for four years with his wife and son and teaches in a high school. Meanwhile, the second principal character of the novel, the landowner Bel'tov, comes back to town. Bel'tov has had a good eduction, first with a Swiss tutor and then at Moscow University, and he has been immensely disappointed by his work as a government official and by society life. He has made unsuccessful attempts to study medicine and to become a painter. In Europe too, Bel'tov has searched in vain for some meaningful activity. After visiting his former tutor in Switzerland, he has decided to return home and serve Russia. But even in his district town, he has kept his distance from everyone except his affectionate widowed mother; he does not feel that he fits into society.

Krupov introduces Bel'tov to Kruciferskij; it turns out that they have studied together at Moscow University. Bel'tov's fellow noblemen do not appoint him to an office, and Kruciferskij and

Krupov are the only men in town whom Bel'tov sees. His noble character comes out in his conversations with them, and it is clear that it is not entirely his fault that he has not found a meaningful place in life. In addition to his other misfortunes, Bel'tov falls in love with Kruciferskij's wife. Her diary reveals that she has grown fond of Bel'tov. Their love is not discussed, but it upsets the weak Kruciferskij. When Krupov advises Bel'tov to take a trip, it is too late. The family's happiness has been destroyed. Bel'tov goes abroad. His lonely mother and Ljubov' Aleksandrovna console one another with talk of Bel'tov. Kruciferskij seeks solace in drink.

9. As a result, three good people are unhappy. Who is at fault? Herzen was, of course, particularly interested in Bel'tov. Why could an able, educated man with noble desires and sentiments not find something meaningful to do in Russia? How did he become superfluous? Literary historians have called Onegin, Pečorin, and other characters in Russian literature superfluous men, although they could hardly have been expected to make an important contribution to Russian intellectual and political life. But it is clear that in another environment, in other social conditions, perhaps in another country, Bel'tov could have been an active and useful member of society.

Herzen asks the question "Who is at fault?" of the other characters in the novel, of the innocent, naive, weak Kruciferskij and of Ljubov' Aleksandrovna's father, General Negrov—"In him too there were possibilities, which life suppressed and destroyed." Negrov is frivolous and debauched (*razvraten*); "idleness, wealth, poor upbringing (*nerazvitost'*), and bad company had left their dirt on him . . . ; but the dirt did not stay." There are other characters in the novel who, sometimes at least, follow the "impulse of their hearts, which is always good." Who is to blame that these people lead useless lives and torture and destroy themselves and their fellow men?

This question occupied Herzen in his political journalism and, in his novel, causes him to go into theoretical discussions, to write in maxims, and to present a social-philosophical treatise; but, as a work of art, the novel does not suffer.

10. Since Herzen wrote his novel before the prime of the Natural School, those features of his style that recall the Natural School

come mostly from Gogol'. He uses these features sparingly, as do such writers as Turgenev and Grigorovič, who emerged from the Natural School. Even Herzen's satirical chapters, on the family of a marshal of nobility (*predvoditel'*) and the teachers of the district capital (part II, chapters III and VI), have none of the accumulation of artistic devices typical of the Natural School. There are humorous descriptions of characters (an old countess looks like a crow with a hood) and odd clothing (a maid in a calico dress with linen sleeves and a dressing gown the color of a frog's back); but these are isolated instances. Herzen emphasizes the surroundings of his characters. Provincial society is best portrayed through details, such as those of the elections, in which only the nobility can vote. Some of these details are humorous ("peculiar frock coats with velvet collars that have changed color but maintained their audacious form") and are reminiscent of Gogol'.

This emphasis on typical details is a feature Herzen shares with the realists; and like the realists, Herzen is given to telling about the life of his principal characters. This background information explains why Bel'tov is superfluous, why Kruciferskij is weak, and why Ljubov' Aleksandrovna's and Bel'tov's mothers are stronger in character than the men around them. This last attribute is typical of a number of realists, such as Turgenev and Gončarov. Herzen appears to have ascribed the strength of his women at least partly to their peasant origins. Kruciferskij's wife is the illegitimate daughter of General Negrov and a serf woman, and Bel'tov's mother was born a serf.

Although Herzen's novel is obviously tendentious, even in its title, the great artistry of the work cannot be denied. It is excellently constructed and narrated and contains only a few theoretical passages, primarily on Russia and the question of who is at fault. The fault, Herzen decides, lies with the lack of intellectual tradition. As a result, one wanders about as on "a vast steppe—one can go wherever one will . . . one never gets anywhere. That is the essence of our versatile idleness, of our active laziness." Among the merits of the novel is its excellent language, which contains only occasional instances of argot and whimsical vocabulary.

In 1847 and 1848, Herzen published two short novellas, *Doctor Krupov* and *The Pilfering Magpie*. *The Pilfering Magpie* tells of the tragedy of a serf actress. *Doctor Krupov* comments on the insanity of everyday life, which has nothing to do with creative madness as V. F. Odoevskij understood it (see volume I, chapter IV, sec. 1). The insanity that Herzen refers to is the lazy obtuseness that stands in the way of all progress, makes men's irrational behavior seem purposeful to them, and enables them to continue existing according to absurd traditions. This second novella contains the pathetic but artistic kind of journalism to which Herzen was to devote the rest of his life. He is of interest here as the first important and consistent realist in Russian literature.

11. Like Byronism and other radical literary currents, the Natural School met with opposition. Examples of this hostility are two comedies with almost identical titles, P. A. Karatygin's *Natural'naja škola* and N.I. Kulikov's *Škola natural'naja,* both of them written in the 1840s. In the plays, the writers of the Natural School are portrayed as "geniuses of the backyard" and "empty-headed hacks," who have no morals (*"bez pravil nravstvennyx"*) and no command of language (*"bez pravil jazyka"*). All they do is create "low and dirty scenes," the life "of beasts amid garbage and filth"; their characters come from the "lowest strata of mankind," peasants, footmen, tramps, and janitors, "riffraff from the slums of St. Petersburg." In his comedy of 1847, Karatygin accuses the writers of the Natural School of seeking to stir up "social reform." He senses the ideas and the spirit that are to come.

Without going into detail, K. N. Leont'ev calls the language of the Natural School a cacophony and the psychology of its characters a "cacopsyche." Neither of these qualities is present in the realists, who also dropped the use of foreign words, popular in the 1840s, and in so doing proved an exception. Since the eighteenth century, innovators in Russian had been accused of littering (*zasorit'*) the language with foreign words.

III

Turgenev

1. Ivan Sergeevič Turgenev (1818–1883) came from the province of Orel, in southern Great Russia, a region that produced a number of nineteenth-century writers. He was the second son of a wealthy, propertied noblewoman, who was apparently a stern and unloving mother. Turgenev's father played a less important part in his life. In 1827, Turgenev's parents moved to Moscow and then abroad; the two sons were left in private schools. In 1834, Turgenev went to St. Petersburg University, where the teachers were not very good. During this time, Turgenev was encouraged in his first literary efforts, in verse, by his literature professor, P. A. Pletnev (see volume I, chapter III, sec. 24) and was able to publish two of his poems. In St. Petersburg, Turgenev saw a number of important writers, including Puškin on two occasions.

On graduating from the university in 1838, Turgenev went to Berlin to study classical philology. There he got to know the young Russian Hegelians (see volume I, chapter VII, sec. 4). After returning to Berlin from vacation in 1840, he dedicated himself mainly to the study of Hegel. He was probably less influenced by the lectures of Professor Werder than by his discussions with the Moscow Hegelians, who made up a close circle in Berlin. Among them were Nikolaj Stankevič, Timofej Granovskij, and Mixail Bakunin. They visited the home of Bettina von Arnim, where they met Varnhagen von Ense and Alexander von Humboldt. Few of the German students who were friends with the Russians seem to have become well known. On a trip to Italy, Turgenev saw Stankevič, who was soon to die there. After another semester in Berlin, Turgenev returned to Russia in 1841.

Turgenev took a master's degree in philosophy. In his examination, which has been preserved, he writes mainly of Hegel and alludes to Ludwig Feuerbach. But his attention later turned more and more to poetry. During this period, he wrote his lyrical poems, which he later almost forgot, and his verse narratives, among them *Paraša* (a girl's name), which received excessive recognition, mainly from Belinskij. Belinskij already knew Turgenev, who was still close to the Moscow Hegelians. Later in Turgenev's works, there are ironic references to this circle; but his relations with them had a pronounced effect on his political, historical, and philosophical views.

In 1843, the famous young singer Pauline Viardot-Garcia, a French woman of Spanish descent, sang in Russia; and Turgenev met her. This relationship developed into a love that was to be fateful for Turgenev. We need not go into Mme. Viardot's feelings; for that matter, they are still not clear. Turgenev's private life was considerably affected; and in the 1840s, he traveled abroad to meet her, to Paris in 1845 and 1847 and to Berlin in 1847.

In the meantime, Turgenev wrote and published his first important prose works, among them the novellas *Andrej Kolosov* and *Tri portreta* [Three Portraits]. In writing on Turgenev's prose, Belinskij demonstrated his own lack of literary taste. Just as he criticized the best novellas of the young Dostoevskij (see chapter VI), Belinskij found Turgenev's novellas weak and decided that the author had "no creative gift" (*"tvorčeskij dar"*)!

From 1847 to 1849, Turgenev lived with Pauline Viardot and her husband at their home in Courtavenel, near Paris. In 1847, Nekrasov and Panaev began a new magazine, which ran a number of Turgenev's novellas that he was later to collect as *Zapiski oxotnika* [A Sportsman's Sketches]. Abroad, Turgenev met with Russians who had left Russia to escape the oppression of Nicholas I, among them Herzen. In Paris, Turgenev witnessed the revolution of 1848. By 1850, he was again in Russia; and in 1852, when Gogol' died, he wrote an obituary that was passed by the Moscow censorship after it had been refused in St. Petersburg. The times were difficult, and Nicholas I saw in the revolution that had swept Europe the collapse of his political ideals. Poets such as Schiller and Goethe seemed to him the cause of political unrest. As a result, Taras Ševčenko, the Ukrainian poet, an artist by profession, was sent to the army in Central Asia and forbidden to write or paint; Dostoevskij was sentenced to prison in Siberia. Turgenev fared better. Arrested for his article on Gogol', Turgenev was jailed and then banished to his estate. In the fall of 1853, he was pardoned and allowed to return to the capitals. In 1855, he wrote his first novel, *Rudin* (an earlier attempt at a novel was not published).

With the death of Nicholas I, in 1855, an era came to an end. In 1856, Turgenev received permission to leave Russia; and from that time on, he lived mainly abroad, as near the Viardots as possible. The rest of his life is largely the story of his writing, of his literary successes and failures. Despite his permanent residence abroad, he visited Russia every year. In 1863, he moved to Baden-Baden, where the Viardots were living (Pauline Viardot was already forty and no longer singing publicly). In 1871, after the Franco-Prussian War, the Viardots returned to Paris. Turgenev sold the house he had just built in Baden-Baden and went to Paris, once more to be near the Viardots.

In 1875, Turgenev moved with the Viardots to Bougival, near Paris. In the garden of the Viardots' villa, Turgenev built himself a small summer house, where he spent the last years of his life. He visited Paris at least once a week and received many Russian visitors in his home. He continued to take brief trips to Russia and was esteemed there. In 1879, he was awarded an honorary doctorate by Oxford. In 1880, along with Dostoevskij, he delivered a speech at the dedication of the Puškin Monument in Moscow. French and German critics considered Turgenev one of the most important contemporary writers. In 1882, he fell sick; after a difficult and painful illness, he died in the autumn of 1883.

2. Turgenev was the first Russian writer to be recognized as a European writer in his own lifetime. A full account of his fame has, unfortunately, not been written. His associations with German writers and critics were mostly superficial, although his relations with the influential critic Julian Schmidt were interesting. Turgenev was much closer to French writers. Before settling in Paris, he knew Mérimée, George Sand, and Sainte-Beuve; and Flaubert was an old friend. In Paris, Turgenev was a friend of Théophile Gautier (who died in 1872), Hippolyte Taine, Joseph Renan, and especially the group around Edmond Goncourt. Turgenev was close to Daudet, Maupassant, and Zola, and he considered Flaubert his master; but he was rather critical of other contemporary French writers, whose work he knew thoroughly.

3. Appreciation of Turgenev's work has changed considerably with time. Contemporaries had a much higher opinion of him than they did of the "odd" and devious Dostoevskij and of the "reactionary" Leskov, but critics and the reading public now place Turgenev at least behind Dostoevskij and Gogol', and perhaps even further back, behind Čexov. Until about 1905 or 1910, it was thought that Turgenev's novels were his most important works. Since then, his novellas have come to be valued more; and the Russian theater has staged Turgenev's plays, which had been neglected. His novels were once regarded as historical documents, as a history of Russian society from the 1840s to the 1870s; and attempts were made, for example, by D. N. Ovsjaniko-Kulikovskij and R. V. Ivanov-Razumnik, to write a history of the Russian intelligentsia on the basis of his novels. Only later were his novels approached as literary works of art, and then they were appraised quite differently. Turgenev's best novels are now often thought to be the unpolitical *Vešnie vody* [Torrents of Spring]—Turgenev called the work a *"povest',"* that is, a long novella—and *Dvorjanskoe gnezdo* [A Nest of Gentlefolk].

Emphasis here will be on the nature of the artistic devices in Turgenev's novellas, novels, and plays.

4. After *A Sportsman's Sketches* came out in book form, in 1852, Turgenev was considered a leading Russian writer. The book faced opposition, based partly on political objections and partly, as in the case of Stepan Ševyrev, on the critic's total rejection of the Natural School. Despite opposition, however, Gogol' came to the conclusion that Turgenev possessed a "remarkable (*'zamečatel'nyj'*) talent." Tjutčev, Gončarov, and L. N. Tolstoj (in 1852 and 1853) had equally high opinions of the book, and later the work was recognized abroad.

In 1852, Turgenev included in *A Sportsman's Sketches* twenty-two stories that had been written between 1846 and 1852. In the 1860 edition, he put in two later stories but dropped them from the 1865 edition. In 1874, Turgenev added to *A Sportsman's Sketches* three stories written between 1872 and 1874; and the work took on its present form.

Some of the novellas in the collection should probably be called sketches (*očerki*), in the sense of the Natural School. But most of them differ from the stylistic tradition of physiological sketches and are genuinely realistic novellas; in some stories, the styles are mixed.

There is no doubt that Turgenev was dealing with serfdom in these novellas. For all the variety of the stories, there is an ideological consistency. The peasants are presented as positive characters, conscious of their human dignity, and they are contrasted with the landowners, who are much less attractive and are not close to their serfs. This contrast caused the thinking reader to wonder whether the serf owner had a right to own and command human "souls" (as serfs were then called; see Gogol's *Dead Souls*). Turgenev portrays peasants without sentimentality, as, for instance, Grigorovič does. There are no tyrants among his landowners and no instances of cruelty (although one could have found them in reality); Turgenev emphasizes the indifference and negligence of masters in dealing with their serfs and shows the morally impossible position of people treated like chattels. The reader readily understands that it would be "better and more agreeable" for the serfs to live in freedom, as one censor put it.

There is great variety in the subject matter of the stories. Several sketches have no plot, among them some of Turgenev's best-known novellas, such as *Xor' i Kalinyč,* the first novella published in the series. This work describes two peasants who represent two human types, the practical, efficient Xor' and the visionary, aesthetically inclined Kalinyč. Kas'jan of *Kas'jan s Krasivoj Meči* [Kas'jan of Fair Springs] resembles Kalinyč but is a sectarian (this was a dangerous theme, only alluded to), and he lives apart. The landowners in *Dva pomeščika* [Two Landowners] are both equally unpleasant. Another landowner, Tat'jana Borisovna, a simple, likable woman, is contrasted with her nephew, a good-for-nothing who considers himself an artist, and with a woman neighbor who is enthusiastic about the philosophy of Hegel. Another sketch is *Odnodvorec Ovsjannikov* (an *odnodvorec* is a landowner who has no serfs and who works his own land); Ovsjannikov merely tells stories about neighboring landowners. Among the most attractive plotless novellas in the book are *Bežin Meadow* and *A Living Relic*. *Bežin Meadow* is about peasant children tending horses and sitting around a fire at night telling tales. *Živye mošči* [A Living Relic], written later, contains conversations with a peasant girl who has been crippled but who bears her situation with brave resignation. The sketch *Smert'* [Death] deals with the manner in which Russians die.

A few of the novellas are short stories and treat episodes in the lives of the characters, as in both accounts of peasants unhappy in love, *Ermolaj i mel'ničixa* [Ermolaj and the Miller's Wife] and *Svidanie* [The Tryst]. Some sketches contain miniature novellas, in which someone's life is told in a few lines. There are also genuine novellas with definite plots, although the emphasis is on character portrayal. Among these stories are *Uezdnyj lekar'* [The District Doctor], with whom a hopelessly sick woman falls in love, and *Petr·Petrovič Karataev,* who wishes to marry a peasant woman. Since the woman who owns the girl is not willing to give her up, Karataev must abduct her and accept the consequences; the girl must pay more dearly. In 1872, Turgenev wrote, and included in *A Sportsman's Sketches, Konec Čertopxanova* [Čertopxanov's End], which provides a conclusion to *Čertopxanov i Nedopjuskin.* Together, the two stories make a novella on a romantic hero from the provinces (in the style of Marlinskij [A. A. Bestužev]; see volume I, chapter IV, sec. 2). *Gamlet Ščigrovskogo uezda* [A Hamlet of the Ščigrov District] is a novella based partly on Turgenev's reminiscences and deals with a provincial Russian who admires Hegel, has studied in Berlin, and must live out his life in his village, where he is considered a ridiculous eccentric. Several novellas are really "sportsman's sketches," on various minor adventures of the narrator (who is not necessarily identical with Turgenev).

Almost all the pieces in *A Sportsman's Sketches* are directed against serfdom, the greatest evil in Russia at the time. One reads of landowners who are by no means superior but who can command their serfs as they wish. The occupations that the serfs take up are decided by their masters; in *L'gov,* Sučok has been in turn a coachman, a fisherman, a cook, a waiter, an actor, and so on. Serfs can be sent by their masters to do military service, and for whimsical reasons. Women serfs also lead tragic lives; their husbands are chosen by their masters, or, sometimes, good maid-servants are forbidden to marry. Even names can be changed; for instance, Sučok was christened Kuz'ma but must call himself "Anton" when working as a waiter. Often, these decisions are

made not only by the landowners but also by their mistresses
(as in *Malinovaja Voda,* the name of a spring) or by peasants
or employees to whom the master has turned over the management
of his estate (as in *Kontora* [The Office]). Without mentioning
acts of cruelty, Turgenev is able to present an impressive picture
of the inhumanity of serfdom. His portrayal of the peasants and
their life is at times idyllic (he was reproached for this), but he
does note that there are different classes of peasants. Besides
the influential peasant administrators, there is a new group of
rich peasants, later to be called *kulaki,* who attempt to exploit
their neighbors (see *Burmistr,* about a peasant administrator).
In several stories, Slavophile landowners are dealt with ironically;
their efforts to improve the lot of their peasants have proved
futile.

5. The style of *A Sportsman's Sketches* goes back partly to the
tradition of the Natural School. A list that has survived from
Turgenev's early period is entitled *Sjužety* ("themes" or "plots")
but contains no plots as such, only titles for physiological sketches.
Turgenev was indebted to the Natural School for information
about peasants and for purely stylistic features. Among these
features are detailed accounts of unimportant things, often with
an emphasis on the ugly; for example, things are often "sour,"
kislyj; there is even a "sour piano." The clothing of secondary
characters is described in detail and is often dirty, ragged, or
old; but stylish colors are called by their fashionable names. People
are described in detail, especially their actions, which are often
not at all significant. The attractive story *Pevcy* [Singers] is about
simple people's love of art, but it ends in a wild drinking scene
in a tavern. There are even fights in *A Sportsman's Sketches*.

This is a typical passage, from *Singers*:

> There appeared a smallish fat man with a limp. On one arm, he
> was carrying a rather clean, long peasant coat. The tall, peaked cap
> resting on his eyebrows gave his round, puffy face a sly, mocking expres-
> sion. His small, yellow eyes shifted continually back and forth; and a
> tense, restrained smile never vanished from his lips; his nose, which
> was long and pointed, stood out as insolently as a rudder.

There are also descriptions of attractive characters.
Turgenev's language is interesting and contains a modest

number of unusual and dialectal expressions, which he explains in notes. Individual pronunciations are given, such as the amusing turns of speech of a voluntary fool in *Lebedjan'*; *"rakalion"* becomes *"rrrakalioon."* First names such as Niktopolionyč and many of Turgenev's nicknames are strange; the name *Xor'* means "polecat," Kas'jan is nicknamed "Bloxa" ("Flea"), *Sučok* means "twig," and so on.

Some features of *A Sportsman's Sketches* are not typical of the Natural School. Turgenev emphasizes individual traits of character rather than status and profession. And he describes not only the ugly, but the beautiful as well: his landscapes were later considered classic. The last of the *Sketches* is the novella *Les i step'* [Forest and Steppe], a hymn to nature. Although Turgenev strikes out at romantic, aesthetic, and moral ideals (and not just in his portrayal of the Byronic and demonic Čertopxanov), there are many vestiges of these ideals in his work.

Turgenev soon realized that this manner, which he himself called his "old manner" (*staraja manera*), was outdated. His later works, especially his novels, show clearly that he has taken leave of the Natural School and turned to a new style, which can be called realistic. In his novella *The District Doctor,* Turgenev is obviously attempting to imitate the style of the early Dostoevskij, as V. V. Vinogradov indicates.

6. Turgenev took his work on his novels very seriously, and it was his novels that particularly attracted the reading public. These novels, which were intended to reflect Russian intellectual life over a period of several decades, are *Rudin* (1856), *Dvorjanskoe gnezdo* [A Nest of Gentlefolk] (1859), *Nakanune* [On the Eve] (1860), *Otcy i deti* [Fathers and Sons] (1862), *Dym* [Smoke] (1867), and *Nov'* [Virgin Soil] (1877). A short novel, *Vešnie vody* [The Torrents of Spring] (1872), which Turgenev called a *provest'*, may also be included in the list.

With the exception of *A Nest of Gentlefolk* and *The Torrents of Spring,* all Turgenev's novels follow the same pattern; they present typical educated progressives who represent an era in Russian life. The background and intellectual currents of the period are depicted. In addition to the intellectual, political, and social aspects of the works, there is in each a love story; the relations of the principal male and female characters are the focus of the story, and Turgenev pays particular attention to the lovers' first meeting and to the women's feelings as they fall in love. Because of the men's weaknesses, the love story ends unhappily. As a witty critic (V. Bazarov) has noted, Turgenev's men resemble the main character of Gogol's *Marriage,* who jumps out a window and escapes from his wedding. Turgenev's men shape the intellectual aspect of his novels and are mostly of the type that he calls the "superfluous man" (*lišnij čelovek*) in an early novella, *The Diary of a Superfluous Man* (1850). Perhaps for political reasons, the superfluous man finds himself unable to take part in public life in a way befitting his capabilities. This type has played an important part in Russian literature, although perhaps not such an exclusive role as literary historians once thought.

7. In *A Nest of Gentlefolk* and *The Torrents of Spring,* the love story is the plot of the novel. The central male character in *A Nest of Gentlefolk* is a gentleman landowner, Fedor Lavreckij, whose wife is unfaithful to him. Lavreckij returns from Paris to his estate, where he reads in the newspaper that his wife has died. He and the young Liza Kalitina fall in love and plan to marry. But Lavreckij's wife is not dead, and she reappears on the scene. Liza has had a strict upbringing, considers her life ruined and herself a sinner, and enters a convent. The atmosphere of provincial life is presented for the most part idyllically, though at times satirically, and it is one of Turgenev's most successful artistic achievements.

The Torrents of Spring deals with the love of a traveling Russian nobleman for a simple Italian girl. In the end, he leaves her for an empty Russian noblewoman. The work is set around Frankfurt am Main and is distinguished from Turgenev's other novels by an absence of motifs on Russian intellectual life and by its many allusions to art history and literature.

Turgenev's other novels give an account of the intellectual life of young Russians over a period of forty years. These novels should not be thought of as *romans à clef.* Although some characters resemble actual persons, whom Turgenev mentions in his letters, his characters are not, strictly speaking, portraits. The best example is in his first novel, *Rudin.* The model for Rudin was Turgenev's friend Mixail Bakunin; but Rudin's poetic speech is not at all like Bakunin's dry, philosophical pathos; and Bakunin's philosophy could hardly have attracted a visionary girl. Rudin's life and his death on the barricades of Paris in 1848 are inventions by Turgenev. The philosophical circle of the poor student Pokorskij is based on Stankevič's Hegelian circle in Moscow but bears only a typological resemblance to reality, all the more so since Stankevič was from a rich family, and there was not the same moralizing tone in his circle as in Pokorskij's.

Let us review the plots of Turgenev's novels.

Rudin, a man of the 1840s, visits an estate and meets a group of typical persons of the period. The daughter of the house falls in love with him. Rudin is a fascinating speaker and strikes almost everyone as charming, but he is unable to take the decisive step and marry the girl against her mother's will. Subsequently, we are told about Rudin's past, his college days, and his later life; because of the censorship, allusions to Rudin's political activity are vague. He is killed on a barricade in Paris in 1848. But this last scene was not added until 1860.

On the Eve deals with contemporary events. The principal male characters are three young men, an artist, a scholar, and a revolutionary. Since the censor would not have passed a novel about a Russian revolutionary, Turgenev introduces a Bulgarian, Insarov, who is studying in Moscow but is chiefly concerned with the Bulgarian struggle for independence. The heroine is a young noblewoman, Elena, who follows Insarov to his homeland; he soon dies, but she carries on his work.

Fathers and Sons is the most admired of Turgenev's novels, and the most controversial. The two principal characters belong to the generation of the 1860s. They are a young nobleman, Arkadij Kirsanov, who is a student, and his intellectual guiding light, another student, Evgenij Bazarov, son of a doctor. Bazarov is a nihilist—that is, a critical thinker who is, in reality, a materialistic skeptic. (The use of the word in this sense was introduced by Turgenev.) The two young men are contrasted with their fathers (or forebears), the older Kirsanov, reared in the tradition of the 1840s; his brother, who has moved in fashionable circles and returned to his estate after an unhappy love affair; and Bazarov's parents, simple small landowners. Bazarov is also contrasted with some pseudonihilists. The characters of the novel are fully developed, and Turgenev evidently intends to show that Bazarov is the most important personality in the work. Bazarov is so skeptical that he considers any action, particularly any political action, pointless, although he understands what is the matter with Russia. Social and political radicals attacked the work, mainly because Turgenev had ignored the political aims of the nihilists. The next novel in Turgenev's series on the Russian intelligentsia, *Smoke,* provoked more criticism. The novel satirizes the Russian political émigrés in Heidelberg, but it also presents the Russian aristocrats summering in Baden-Baden in an unattractive light. These two groups form the background for the love affair of the central character, Litvinov, who almost falls victim to a prominent society woman; but, when the woman proves indecisive, Litvinov returns to the woman he has been engaged to and to a life that promises quiet happiness.

Virgin Soil, the last novel in Turgenev's series, deals with a political movement that stirred young Russians in the 1870s: the attempt to enlighten the masses, politically and in other ways, by going to the people (*xoždenie v narod*). As in *Fathers and Sons,* there are various groups in the novel: young revolutionaries; landowners and officials, liberal and reactionary; and individuals who despair of going to the people and disseminating propaganda that will not be understood and who prefer instead to attain certain social goals—this last group is represented by Solomin, a factory manager. The principal character, Neždanov, takes part unsuccessfully in the activities of the young revolutionaries. Neždanov is in love with the niece of an aristocratic family, Marianna, who shares his political views; but the weak Neždanov commits suicide and Marianna marries Solomin.

8. Turgenev devoted himself with a passion to the construction and style of his novels. He attempted to discard his old manner altogether, but his satire is sometimes close to that of the Natural School. Otherwise, his artistic prose is one of the best examples of the realistic style. The metonymic style described in chapter I is more evident in Turgenev than in any other writer besides Ivan Gončarov.

The impact of Turgenev's novels on his contemporaries demonstrates that he was able to portray areas of Russian life with great verisimilitude. The most important of his metonymic devices

that make for this verisimilitude is his extension of the narrative
plane, in time (family history) and space (milieu).

In recounting family history, Turgenev emphasizes intellectual
relationships. Family history is presented more extensively in
A Nest of Gentlefolk than it is in any other of Turgenev's works,
and Lavreckij's habit of mind is largely attributed to his family
background. Elsewhere, Turgenev limits family history to the
surroundings and development of his principal character in the
antecedent action of the story. An example is the account of the
Moscow Hegelian circle that Rudin belonged to. Many of Turgenev's characters are landowners, and his descriptions of their
way of life are also a kind of family history. The personalities
and intellectual interests of characters are often clarified through
contrasts in their family backgrounds. Heroines, such as Natal'ja
in *Rudin* and Elena in *On the Eve,* usually take issue with the
older generation. Male characters also become embroiled; the
problem of *Fathers and Sons* is one that occupies Turgenev in
other works, as well.

Descriptions of milieu are as thorough as those of family history.
The intellectual atmosphere of the characters is emphasized
through contrast, such as the parody on the pseudonihilists in
Fathers and Sons and the portrayal of two groups of Russians
abroad, the gentry in Baden-Baden and the radical students in
Heidelberg, in *Smoke.* In *Virgin Soil,* there are young socialists,
more moderate liberals of the older generation, and the pa-
triarchial couple, "Fomuška i Fimuška."

In describing environment in detail, Turgenev suggests the
material situation of a character, his interests, and his personality. The dress of a character tells what sort of person he
is. When Rudin visits Ležnev, Turgenev notes: "Before him stood
a man ... almost entirely gray and bent; he was wearing an
old velveteen frock coat with brass buttons." When Rudin falls
on a barricade in 1848, he has on "an old frock coat girded with
a red sash." In *A Nest of Gentlefolk,* Liza Kalitina's dress is
described and adds to her charm. But Turgenev seldom describes
clothing in the manner of the Natural School.

Details that Turgenev mentions matter-of-factly are often of
great importance, such as the dress, gloves, and the perfume of
Mrs. Lavreckij and the simple clothing and furnishings of

Bazarov's father; his information is out of date (the picture of Hufeland on the wall); he is poor (a broken galvanic battery); he started out as a military doctor (Turkish guns, whip, and saber on the walls of the study). In *Fathers and Sons,* Turgenev describes in detail the Kirsanovs' manor house and the mode of life of the genteel Pavel Petrovič Kirsanov. Turgenev is a master of detail and is expert in using apparent trifles to add to his characterizations.

Turgenev's method of working on his novels shows that he first clearly imagined his characters in their surroundings. He knew their ages, their relationships with one another, their material means. In planning a novel, he made careful notes on his main characters and considered that the most important part of his work, an attitude typical of the realists' desire for verisimilitude. In these notes, Turgenev mentions acquaintances who have the features he wishes to give his characters—a practice that shows that his characters are synthetic creations and not copies of particular persons. Rudin combines features of Bakunin with those of other, more poetically inclined contemporaries. Turgenev's novels are not *romans à clef.* It was unfair to charge, for instance, that Gubarev, the unpleasant leader of the radical Heidelberg students, was based on Nikolaj Ogarev, a friend of Herzen and an acquaintance of Turgenev. Apart from the similarity of their names, Gubarev and Ogarev have nothing in common.

9. One of Turgenev's most important advances from the tradition of the Natural School is his method of psychological portrayal. Psychology is of interest to him in *A Sportsman's Sketches* and in his early novellas. In his novels, he devotes more attention to psychology, especially in his love stories. Turgenev keeps his distance from the psychological art of Dostoevskij and L. N. Tolstoj; he finds Dostoevskij's use of psychology too pathological and Tolstoj's use, which depends to a large extent on bagatelles, too impressionistic (although he does not call it that).

In his preliminary notes for the novels, Turgenev goes into the psychology of his characters; and sometimes these sketches are strikingly vivid. We still have drawings that Turgenev made of his characters, as a game, along with descriptions of the characters' personalities. Turgenev attached great importance to describing characters. They are not always depicted when they first come on the scene; sometimes the reader must put together a portrait from features mentioned in different places, but it is seldom that a portrait is missing. In *On the Eve*, Elena is described this way:

She was tall and had a pale, swarthy face, large gray eyes, and round eyebrows surrounded by small freckles, a straight forehead and nose, a pursed mouth, and a rather pointed chin. Her dark-blond, braided hair fell over her slender neck. . . . Her hands were narrow and pink, with long fingers; her feet were also narrow; she walked quickly, almost precipitantly, and bent somewhat forward.

In *A Nest of Gentlefolk*, Lavreckij has a "red-cheeked, genuine Russian face with the broad, pale forehead, the rather thick nose and the wide, regular (*pravil'nymi*) lips"; this face gives off an air of "health and enduring strength." In *On the Eve*, the young scholar Bersenev "appeared to be about twenty-three years of age and was swarthy (*černomazyj*) with a sharp, somewhat crooked nose, a high forehead, and a restrained smile on his broad lips; he lay on his back and looked thoughtfully into the distance, squinting his small, gray eyes." Turgenev does not always picture his principal characters as attractive or especially likable.

The gestures of the characters are also described, gestures that are sometimes unimportant and may be a carry-over from the Natural School. Gestures and facial expressions make character portraits more dynamic and telling. At times, Turgenev uses the method he finds fault with in Tolstoj, the repetition of small details, among them gestures, such as those of Uvar Ivanovič, a minor character in *On the Eve*, who moves his fingers in a certain way.

Facial expressions are given more attention. In *Fathers and Sons*, Bazarov's mother looks continually at her son. Her eyes "expressed not only devotion and tenderness; one saw in them also a certain sadness (*grust'*), mixed with curiosity and fear and humble reproach." A character's expression changes from scene to scene.

Turgenev describes the psychology of almost all his characters, if only in a few words. In *Fathers and Sons*, Anna Odincova is characterized this way: she

had no prejudices and no strong faith, did not shy away from anything, and was not moving in any particular direction. She understood many things clearly; many things interested her; but nothing satisfied her entirely, and she hardly wished to be entirely satisfied. Her mind was at once desirous of knowledge and indifferent. She never completely forgot her doubts but was never really troubled by them either.

At other times, Turgenev merely refers to something that has affected a character deeply: marriage to a man whom a woman does not love and who is unfaithful to her; loneliness; a profession that one has followed against one's will.

Naturally, Turgenev's treatment of psychology is deeper when he deals with events bearing directly on the story, although these descriptions may not at first appear important. Incidental characters are often handled in this way, characters such as the Russian roulette player in Baden-Baden, who, "with incomprehensible, convulsive haste, his eyes wide open and his chest on the roulette table, scattered the golden circles of louis d'or in all four corners of the table." There are many such passages that remind one of the Natural School.

. The most typical thing in Turgenev's novels is his treatment of love, especially the awakening of love, as in his description of Elena's sensations, in *On the Eve,* from her first vague feelings to her entry in her diary: "I have found the word; it has dawned on me. Oh, God! Be merciful. I am in love!" The first meeting between Rudin and Natal'ja is preceded by a gust of wind. This symbol for the climax of the story is more emphatic in *The Torrents of Spring.* Gemma is interrupted: "Suddenly, amid the great calm, under the cloudless sky, such a gust of wind came up that the earth seemed to shake. . . . For a minute there was a noisy roar. . . . The storm passed over like a flock of birds. . . A great calm set in again." In Turgenev's treatment of love, there are only fateful turns of fortune such as these; and it is no wonder that a crisis in love (as in this passage from *Smoke*) can provoke frenzy: "Suddenly he sobbed convulsively, furiously and venomously, fell face-down, and, swallowing hard and choking, with impetuous bliss, as though he wanted to rend himself and everything around him, buried his burning face in the pillow."

Although Turgenev was opposed to portraying the depths of the soul as Dostoevskij and Tolstoj did, he could not overlook the unconscious when he was dealing with love. He writes things such as: "The silence (*bezmolvnoe*) that arose between the two grew and strengthened" (*Smoke*) and "that which remained for both of them a half-suspected secret" (*Virgin Soil*).[1]

Descriptions of landscapes are important in Turgenev's work; but landscapes are usually the background for events. Nature is apparently indifferent, and descriptions of nature are mostly brief and full of striking, sensuous impressions—colors, odors, the freshness of the air, bird songs, and so on.

In Turgenev's last novels, *Smoke* and *Virgin Soil,* descriptions of psychology are shorter; and he returns to the practice of presenting confessions in letters, which form a kind of diary. An example is Neždanov's letters to his friend Silin, who is introduced into *Virgin Soil* to receive the letters.

10. In addition to his novels, Turgenev published frequent stories. From 1863 until his death, there was only one year when a story of his did not come out. His approximately twenty stories are of different kinds. Only a few of them are similar to his early novellas in *A Sportsman's Sketches. Poezdka v Poles'e* [A Trip to Poles'e] (1857) and *Stepnoj korol' Lir* [A King Lear of the Steppe] (1870), which, as the title suggests, concerns disloyal daughters, may be thought to resemble Turgenev's early stories. But *King Lear* was too long to be included in *A Sportsman's Sketches.* In *King Lear* and in several other novellas (the memories of childhood in *Punin and Baburin,* 1874; *Otryvki iz vospominanij* [Fragments of Recollections], 1881), Turgenev may have drawn on his own memories and combined *Dichtung* with *Wahrheit.* In all his other works, *Dichtung* prevails.

In contrast to the transparent plots of Turgenev's novels, his novellas are fairly complex. One of his best love novellas is *Pervaja ljubov'* [First Love] (1860), which is reminiscent of his love novel *The Torrents of Spring* and makes some use of autobiographical material; *Asja* (1857) also deals with love, and in it the hero again escapes from the heroine. *Faust* (1855) is in the same vein; a woman who has had a strict upbringing (her psychological background is rather complicated) experiences her first real love while reading *Faust,* and the affair ends tragically. The fateful aspect of love is more pronounced in these novellas than it is in Tur-

---

1. Turgenev's letters and essays contain important observations on literature and psychology and deserve more scholarly attention. (A. G. Cejtlin has done work on the subject.)

genev's novels. Even a simple man is subject to all the dangers of love (*Brigadir,* 1867).

The plots of Turgenev's "realistic" novellas are especially complex; in these works, he refrains from portraying typical characters, such as most of those in his novels; and the lives of his novella characters are even less typical (as in *Jakov Pasynkov,* 1855; *Nesčastnaja* [The Unfortunate One], 1868; and *Časy* [The Watch], 1876). Other novellas include the tragic story of a militant atheist who goes mad (*Rasskaz otca Alekseja* [Tale of the Priest Aleksej], 1877) and a delightful detective story (*Istorija lejtenanta Ergunova* [The Story of Lieutenant Ergunov], 1857).

Finally, Turgenev wrote several stories that are completely surprising and may be called, rather inexactly, occult. The many dreams in his novels (A. M. Remizov counts thirty of them) are a link with the romantic tradition. Several of Turgenev's novellas that are realistic in style are related in content to the magic or numinous novellas of romanticism. *Prizraki: Fantazija* [Phantoms: A Fantasy] (1863) is a first-person narrative of nocturnal flights with a vampire to distant deserts, ancient Rome, the Volga of Sten'ka Razin, Paris, and St. Petersburg. In 1866, Turgenev published his second fantastic story, *Sobaka* [The Dog], in which the apparition of a dog causes the hero to keep a real dog, who later saves him. *Strannaja istorija* [A Strange Story] (1869) tells of a magnetic man who, as a *jurodivyj,* or fool in Christ, leads an intelligent young girl to share his vagabond life. The two late stories *Pesn' toržestvujuščej ljubvi* [The Song of Triumphant Love] (1881) and *Klara Milič,* written the same year, are especially curious. Both of them hinge on a kind of love charm. The first is a stylization based on Renaissance novellas: Mucij, who has learned magic in the Orient, lures the wife of his friend Fabij with a song; murdered by Fabij, Mucij is brought back to life by his Oriental servant (possibly an imitation of E. G. Bulwer, according to M. A. Geršenzon). The second story takes place in Turgenev's time: Ardatov, a virtuous young man, falls in love with a singer; the singer soon dies and comes back to fetch him. Ardatov dies too, but not of a disease or through his own will; he is summoned and conjured by the dead woman. Even apart from the stylization in *The Song of Triumphant Love,* this group of novellas contains stylistic elements that go back beyond "the old manner" to romanticism, as S. I. Rodzevič and M. A. Geršenzon indicate.

11. In his early years (1843–1851), Turgenev also wrote for the stage. In his plays, he is a staunch opponent of the romantic tradition. After writing a parody on romantic tragedies and a "physiological sketch," *Bezdenež'e* [Short of Money], Turgenev struck out in a new direction. His plays are on a variety of subjects, and the landowners he portrays differ considerably from one another. There is the dense, obstinate woman who cannot live in peace even with her brother (*Breakfast at the Marshal's*, 1849) as well as the tragic figure of a man who must play the role of the buffoon and pretend he is not the father of his daughter (*Naxlebnik* [The Family Charge], 1848). Typical of Turgenev's theater are the idyllic scenes of life in the country and the tender and tragic turns of love in *Mesjac v derevne* [A Month in the Country] (1850). In addition to excellent dialogue, almost all Turgenev's plays are distinguished by the absence of obtrusively traditional tragic situations. Turgenev prefers to allow moods to develop gradually and often to end tragically. Some of his plays were produced in the forties and fifties but were, for the most part, not well received and were dropped from the repertoire. His plays were not rediscovered until the Moscow Art Theater, with its experience in Čexov's impressionistic drama, popularized them—*A Month in the Country* was produced in 1909; the success of the Art Theater with Turgenev and Čexov emphasizes the similarities in their plays.

12. Turgenev first wrote in verse and produced several short verse novellas. After the age of Puškin and his contemporaries, it was not difficult to write good poetry. Turgenev's novellas in verse on the life of the Russian landowner (*Paraša*, 1843; *Pomeščik* [The Landowner] and *Andrej*, both 1845) are studies in contemporary mores. Actually, all these works have the same theme: the decline into everyday life of young people who long for something better. These poems are written in various stanzaic forms (*Andrej* is in octaves) and go back to the tradition of Puškin's *The Little House in Kolomna*. In style, they are closer to the narrative poems of Lermontov. The confessions of the hero in *Razgovor* [Conversation] (1844) are very much reminiscent of the tone of Lermontov's *Mcyri*.

Some of Turgenev's lyric poems are more unusual. The most interesting are the ballads, told in conversation (*Ballad,* 1841; *The Abduction,* 1842; and *Fedja,* 1843), and the descriptions of scenery, without metaphor or pathos (cf. Nekrasov) but with an occasional allusion to the mood of the poet (as in *Utro tumannoe,* 1845, which Blok liked; see the cycle *Derevnja* [The Village], 1847, and the poem [1848] that furnished the motto for the concluding story in *A Sportsman's Sketches.)*

Turgenev's *Poems in Prose* were taken from his literary remains, which only recently have been printed in correct, complete form. Turgenev's title for the *Poems in Prose* was *Senilia;* they are short (although some run to three pages) lyric miniatures in rhythmical prose. The language contains few poetic features. Apparently, Turgenev deliberately used various levels of vocabulary. He portrays scenes from nature and everyday life and reflects on the transcience of existence and the futility and vanity of most human involvements; or he points to heroism and great virtue in some place where it has been overlooked. That is the pessimistic conclusion of Turgenev's life and work.

13. To Turgenev, language was one of the most important elements in writing, and he was particularly attentive to it. He fits into the "Puškin line" in Russian literature. A comparison of his drafts with the printed versions of his works shows that he attempted to lighten his language, to weed out everything he considered unnecessary. Like Gogol', who also cut his manuscripts mercilessly but with whom Turgenev had little else in common, he often sacrificed picturesque, subtle details and replaced them with more solid matter. In particular, Turgenev varied his style, although there are similar sentences and turns of speech and even similar scenes in different works. Turgenev wrote mainly in short sentences and almost always achieved the clarity of language that he sought.

Turgenev's "light" language differs in many respects from Puškin's. Turgenev is fond of adjectives and uses them freely. He does not observe Puškin's economy of language and often applies several adjectives to an object. In keeping with the realistic style, he avoids metaphors. Although there are comparisons in his writing, he uses them for concrete, psychological characteriza-

tions, as when he likens a governess to a bird, another governess
to a hunting dog, and the young Kirsanov to an officer hastening
to battle.

Turgenev's language is the normal literary language of his
day. He coined no neologisms, although he does seem to have
introduced the word *nihilism* and the term *oproščenie* (in the sense
of drawing outwardly close to the masses). Turgenev's few neologisms occur in the speech of his characters, such as *"sočuvstvennik,"*
"one who sympathizes," in *On the Eve.* He individualizes the language of his characters and introduces popular elements into peasant speech and showy French phrases into the speech of educated
people; sometimes his semieducated characters use incorrect turns
of speech or French mixed with Russian. Unusual words also
occur in the language of the narrator; some of these words Turgenev acquired in his native region; others are peculiar to groups
or individuals. But neologisms are exceptional in Turgenev; he
had probably heard most of his unusual words in conversation.

14. Turgenev's literary works and letters[2] show that he took
a rather negative view of the Russia of his day. Beginning with
A Sportsman's Sketches, his works contain many pages of satire.
But Turgenev's wit is not keen; it runs to caricature or broad
invective. It was just these satirical features that foreign critics
objected to. Julian Schmidt, a German journalist and literary
historian, thought highly of Turgenev but found that this satire
made his work "insufficiently poetic."

Turgenev was a Westernizer and rejected Slavophilism. But
the Westernizing tirades of his fictional character Potugin, in
Smoke, should not be taken to represent Turgenev's views: these
speeches parody primitive Westernization and amount perhaps
to self-parody.

In his early years, Turgenev's philosophical views were
influenced by the Hegelians, and he was familiar with the leftist
Hegelians of the period before 1848; but in time, he turned away
from philosophy. Even so, he was haunted by the thought that
a merciless fate controlled the lives of men. That is particularly

2. His letters are an excellent source for his opinions on Russian life and on
literary language.

evident in his treatment of love (see sec. 8 above); in *Senilia,* he implies that these blind forces affect individuals, whole races, and nature. Perhaps this force is nature itself—several passages give this impression. It is not clear whether Turgenev's study of Schopenhauer contributed to his pessimism, as M. A. Geršenzon points out.

IV

Gončarov

1. Among important writers of the second half of the nineteenth century, probably the most consistent Russian realist was Ivan Aleksandrovič Gončarov (1812–1891). Gončarov was born in Simbirsk (now called Ulyanovsk), a city on the Volga, and was therefore from the same region as N. M. Karamzin, I. I. Dmitriev, N. M. Jazykov, and D. V. Grigorovič. Although nobility had been conferred on Gončarov's grandfather for military service, Gončarov's father returned to the traditional merchant life of the family. Gončarov grew up in the landowners' world that he describes in *Oblomov*.

He received his early education in Simbirsk, partly at home and partly in a boarding school run by a priest. When he was ten, he was sent to Moscow, to a mediocre trade school. During vacations, he visited his mother in Simbirsk—his father had died in 1819. In Moscow, Gončarov became acquainted with modern Russian literature. In 1831, he passed the entrance examination at Moscow University, where he studied the humanities for the next three years. Although most of the members of the Stankevič circle (see vol. I, chap. VII, sec. 4) attended the same lectures, Gončarov did not share their political and philosophical interests and went his own way. Gončarov was influenced by the Moscow theater, as well as by the university.

In 1834, he returned home to a position as a minor official in the office of the governor. A year later, he obtained an appointment to the Office for Foreign Trade in the Finance Ministry in St. Petersburg, but he was not successful at the job.

Gončarov's literary connections enabled him to publish his first works. In 1835, some of his romantic poems came out in a handwritten magazine; in 1838 and in 1839, a novella by Gončarov was carried in the same magazine. There are romantic motifs in his novellas, although they are treated with light irony. In 1842, Gončarov wrote a novella, of which a later version, published in 1848, resembled the work of the Natural School and bore the subtitle *Očerki* [Sketches], typical of the school. The subject of this novella has been well characterized by a modern critic as a "portrayal of the life of Gogol's Xlestakov in St. Petersburg." Nothing has been preserved of a novel that Gončarov was working on at the time.

It was not until 1845 that Gončarov read to his friends chapters of his first novel to be published, *A Common Story,* which came out in 1848. At the time, he was already working on his second novel, *Oblomov,* from which he published the chapter "Oblomov's Dream" in 1849.

Apparently, Gončarov's literary talents were recognized in official circles; and in 1852 he received an offer to take a voyage on the frigate *Pallada.* The trip was interrupted in England and in South Africa when the ship developed trouble. In 1854, Gončarov was forced to return from Japan by way of Siberia because of the Crimean War. His description of his trip, the book *The Frigate "Pallada,"* appeared in 1858 and was well received.

At home, Gončarov resumed work on his second novel, *Oblomov,* but was often interrupted by his responsibilities as a censor and by trips abroad. When the novel appeared, in 1859, Gončarov was busy writing his third novel, *Obryv* [The Precipice], a book that he is supposed to have planned in the 1840s. "After twenty years' work," Gončarov said, the novel came out in 1869; and Gončarov is remembered as the author of three novels.

Gončarov left government service in 1867 and spent the last twenty-four years of his life alone in St. Petersburg, often sick, and attended by servants, many of them rather strange, whom he commemorated in the autobiographical sketches *Slugi starogo veka* [Servants of the Old Days]. His few published works from this period include his own interpretation of his last novel, his brilliant critical sketches on A. S. Griboedov's *Gore ot uma* (*Mil'on terzanij,* 1872), his sketch *Literary Evening* [Literaturnyj večer] (1877), and several novellas, which, like *Servants of the Old Days,* go back in many stylistic features to the Natural School (cf. *The Month of May in St. Petersburg,* 1891).

Gončarov was opposed to publishing writers' correspondence

and, in an auto-da-fé, destroyed most of the letters in his posses-
sion. Fortunately, the majority of the recipients of his letters
kept them, against his will. Gončarov's letters, especially those
published recently, are of literary as well as biographical interest
and show him to be a penetrating, well-informed critic of Russian
and foreign literature. He was apparently the only Russian writer
to take note of Charlotte Brontë.

2. Like the novels of Turgenev, Gončarov's A Common Story
deals with a theme typical of the period: the end of Russian romanticism and its ineffectual legacy.

In A Common Story, the romantic illusions of Aduev, a young
man from deep in the provinces, are destroyed by his uncle.
Although Gončarov presents only a decade in young Aduev's life,
the uncle's careful transformation of his nephew makes the work
a novel on development and education, an Erziehungsroman.
Young Aduev is full of romantic enthusiasm, especially in his
ideas on friendship and love. But he is only average; and his
uncle, a high official, has no difficulty in re-educating him and
turning him into a Philistine.

Young Aduev comes to St. Petersburg full of plans for reform,
which Gončarov does not go into. But his job turns out to consist
of copying the usual official papers. Aduev's fiancée in the country
has been reared in the spirit of romantic literature, and he
associates love with great passion. He soon experiences a number
of disappointments. He is frustrated in his attempt to become
a writer—he is not sufficiently talented, and his portraits of dis-
enchanted characters are perhaps dated. In his despair, young
Aduev returns to his home in the country, but finds that he is
no longer content there. His uncle succeeds in "analyzing" him,
predicting all the disappointments he endures and gradually
destroying his romantic dreams. By the end of the novel, Aduev
is a good official, has married well, and "is keeping pace with
the times."

Gončarov is no admirer of the "positive" uncle, although he
emphasizes positive features in him, such as diligence and con-
tempt for the idle Russian noblemen who carry on the cultural
life of their country. It is not at first clear whether Gončarov
approves of the calculation that Aduev's uncle considers essential
to all relationships, even to love. But in the end, the uncle is

a failure: his wife is grieved because he has based his marriage on calculation and cannot understand true feelings. The uncle has succeeded in re-educating Aduev, but has failed to educate his own wife (he attempted "cleverly to control her reason and her will and to subjugate her taste and character to his own.") The uncle's wife, Lizaveta Aleksandrovna Adueva, is a broken woman with "no vital play of thought or feelings" beside a man incapable of a happy marriage.

3. This first novel by Gončarov contains didactic features that displeased even readers indifferent to romantic ideals. It was soon overshadowed by his next two novels.

The name of the hero of Gončarov's second novel, *Oblomov,* soon became proverbial in Russia, although it often merely designated someone lazy. Gogol' mentions lazy people in *Dead Souls* and may have intended to portray Tentetnikov, in the second volume, as an elevated representative of this type (if one can assume that Gogol' plans for Tentetnikov to change; cf. Platonov in the same volume). But *Oblomov* is a tragedy of spiritual indolence, not merely of pleasant idleness. Oblomov's fall marks the end of a valuable life.

"Oblomov's Dream," the chapter published before the rest of the novel, tells of Oblomov's childhood on an estate that Gončarov considers typical of Russia at the time. In this chapter, Gončarov seeks the causes of Oblomov's physical and spiritual torpor, a question characteristic of realistic writers. Although Oblomov's education is dealt with only briefly, it is obvious that Moscow University, an important cultural center, awakened in him the qualities that Gončarov emphasizes, Oblomov's fine sensitivity and his moral purity, his belief in what is right. When Oblomov was a child, not even his "good genius," Stolz, the son of a German steward, could bring him to overcome the inability to work typical of "Oblomovka" estate, the inability to help himself in even the simplest situations (*"neumenie nadevat' čulki"* [the inability to put on his own stockings]). The estate had plenty of serfs and servants; Oblomov was reared in an atmosphere of "perpetual holiday" and developed an "inability to live." At college in Moscow, he learned passively and accumulated "complex archives of dead facts."

When the novel begins, Oblomov is living in St. Petersburg,

his formative years behind him. Government service has been as disappointing to him as it was to young Aduev; but Oblomov has had no "clever" uncle to turn him into a Philistine. He leads a strange, idle life that seems to the casual reader a dormant existence in a coffinlike bed. Oblomov is dominated by boredom (*skuka*—"boredom in an intensified form," according to the German scholar Walther Rehm), and he is troubled by his understanding of the contrast between the destiny for which he was created and his manner of living. But this realization does not tear him away from his vague yearning (*toska*) and spur him on to action. A detailed, epic portrayal of a single day in Oblomov's life gives a searching characterization of his soul. Some features of his life and mind are clarified aphoristically in later chapters of the novel. Oblomov is aware that he has no will power, but he does not understand how he came to be as he is (*"otčego ja takoj?"*) and cannot explain it (*"tak i ne dodumalsja do pričiny"*).

Foreign readers and critics, and some Russian ones, have sought the explanation for Oblomov in the "Russian national character" or "national psyche." Gončarov seems to have considered Oblomov a special case, although one shaped somewhat by conditions of the times, such as serfdom. Gončarov suggests that the German Stolz could perhaps save the Russian Oblomov.

Oblomov realizes that he might have followed a man who inspired will power and reason: "I shall never be able to make any progress alone." But, he says, "Lead me where you will," because he cannot set a goal for himself.

Oblomov's lethargy comes through in various situations, not just when Stolz pleads with him to act; that device would be too easy. Not even love can awaken Oblomov. His love for Ol'ga Il'inskaja might have helped, but nothing comes of it. Ol'ga Il'inskaja is one of Gončarov's greatest creations. She recognizes Oblomov's purity and tenderness and his genuine love for her, but she doubts whether he has any objectives that could satisfy her, for she is perpetually busy seeking "experience and life." Oblomov's tragedy is that he breaks off with Ol'ga, not because indolence has won out over love, but because he sees that he is not the spiritual equal of the girl.

Without Ol'ga, Oblomov's life is even sadder. He does not turn into a Philistine, but he does find solace with a simple woman who cares for him faithfully. There is an obvious strain of the author's caste prejudice in his portrayal of their marriage. Gončarov does not approve of marriage between an intellectual nobleman and a simple *meščanka*, or petit-bourgeois woman; it is a misalliance. Oblomov's decline, presented in great detail, consists not only in his marriage, but also in his vegetable existence, which differs from his life at Oblomovka in that he no longer experiences the joys of childhood.

Stolz's advice to Oblomov to work for work's sake does not necessarily ring true. Although his suggestions go further and have to do with the economic development of Russia, a life in business was not considered attractive by Russian intellectuals.

Stolz marries Ol'ga. He is not a dry businessman like Aduev's uncle; Gončarov implies that he is educated and sensitive. But marriage to him leads Ol'ga to a crisis similar to Adueva's. Stolz is horrified at the thought of the life she would have led with Oblomov. She takes a brave attitude toward her life with Stolz, but she senses that her equilibrium is threatened by his narrow aims. "Her soul entreats and seeks ... and is melancholy (*toskuet*)." Gončarov raises doubts about Stolz's humanity, although he emerges from the novel as the personal and historical victor over Oblomov and Oblomovka. In keeping with Gončarov's "objective realism," all the main characters in *Oblomov* ultimately fail in some respect, as they do in *A Common Story*.

4. Gončarov's third and last novel, *Obryv* [The Precipice], ends the same way. In rough drafts, it was called *Xudožnik* [An Artist]; it is the story of a creative man, a character of a different type and soul from Aduev or Oblomov. But the hero, Rajskij, is not a type that Gončarov likes; he is treated ironically; he is a "monster" of a hero (*"vo vsej svoej urodlivosti*," as Gončarov wrote in 1866). Gončarov carried his novel around with him too long, and Rajskij became "merely a wire to which puppets are attached" (Gončarov, 1869), a *ficelle* for the other characters in the novel. The novel also portrays three types of women and deals with the problem of a girl's "fall," a situation suggested to Gončarov, as he explains, by foreign novels, especially those of George Sand. The man who seduces the girl, the "nihilist" Mark Voloxov, becomes an important character in the work, if not the central character. Such complex composition and heterogeneous design

are by no means an exception in Russian realism, as can be seen in the novels of L. N. Tolstoj.

Rajskij is the same age as Gončarov. His artistic enthusiasm remains superficial; he is somewhat similar to Oblomov: incapable of hard, systematic work. He prefers to rely exclusively on his supposed talent, and he is doomed to remain a dilettante. Like Oblomov, Rajskij lacks the ability to live as well as to work. His two love affairs are carried on in St. Petersburg and on his grandmother's estate on the Volga. Rajskij's love for a society beauty, the widow Belovodova, is not reciprocated; either she does not feel and has never felt anything, in contrast to the agitated Rajskij, or she has learned to conceal her feelings. Rajskij does no more than attempt to "awaken" her. The second part of the novel takes place on the estate of Rajskij's grandmother, Tat'jana Markovna Berežkova. Here Rajskij meets Vera, with whom he falls in love, and her sister, the kind, naive Marfin'ka. These three women are Gončarov's most successful characters.

Rajskij makes no headway with Vera, since she is in love with the nihilist Mark Voloxov and gives herself to him as they are about to take leave of each other. Gončarov's contemporaries considered Mark Voloxov a malicious caricature of the "new man" rather than a skillful portrait; Gončarov was less familiar with the "new men" than were other authors of antinihilist novels. He calls Voloxov a "radical" and a "candidate for a demagogue," but shows him only as one contemptuous of conventions.

The grandmother is Gončarov's best representative of the older generation. She is intelligent, able to solve her problems (like Vera, she experienced a "fall" in her youth), and able to create around her an essentially healthy, if narrow and patriarchal, atmosphere. She is in a position to help Vera after her affair. The well-drawn, simple, happy Marfin'ka is a foil to the serious grandmother and to Vera. Gončarov had originally intended that Vera follow Mark to Siberia just as Ulin'ka was to have followed Tentetnikov, according to Gogol's plans for *Dead Souls,* and as the "Russian women" do in Nekrasov (see volume I, chap. IV, sec. 11, and chap. VIII, sec. 6). In the final version of the novel, Vera is stable and seeks independence from all views, including those of the older generation. After talking with her, even Rajskij admires her "daring and independent ideas and desires."

Evidently, she understands the hopelessness of following Mark before she gives herself to him. She loves Mark's courage and independence but does not agree with his views.

There are a number of secondary characters in *The Precipice,* some of them well portrayed, some of them not. Vera and other characters long for "serious work," a motif in *Oblomov.* But in *The Precipice,* those characters of the same mind as Stolz are paler than he (such as Tušin). Vera marries Tušin and can look forward to a quiet family life. In contrast to *A Common Story* and *Oblomov,* there are only suggestions in *The Precipice* of the disappointment Vera will experience with Tušin.

5. All Gončarov's novels have much the same typical features, which have not yet been sufficiently studied by scholars and cannot yet be adequately characterized. Gončarov's novels are similar in that he attempts to work devices of the Natural School into his plot. This tendency is obvious in his treatment of a day in Oblomov's life at the beginning of that novel and in the entire first part of *The Precipice.* Other passages in these novels remind one of the physiological sketches of the Natural School. There are similarities between characters—Oblomov's visitors, the grandmother's servant and acquaintances in the descripton of Rajskij's first day on the estate. Other passages in the novel, such as "Oblomov's Dream" and sections on Rajskij's youth and the grandmother's past, offer the genetic explanations for characters required by the realistic theory of the novel (see chapter I).

In realistic novels, but not in novellas, subplots are developed along with the main plot, as in part IV of *Oblomov.* Often these subplots clarify the main plot through parallelism or antithesis, as in the case of Marfin'ka and the grandmother.

Gončarov may be the most "objective" of all Russian realists. He believed that he had described life as it was. He realized, however, that the essence of writing was selecting "from nature (*iz natury*) certain features to create verisimilitude (*pravdopodobie*), that is, to achieve artistic truth," since "there is by and large little artistic truth in reality" (letter to Dostoevskij, 1874). Gončarov doubts that he has portrayed correctly things he has not really observed, such as the society world of Belovodova. He is wrong in saying that he sought mainly to draw life as it is and that the tendentious portrayal of the nihilist Mark

Voloxov was accidental (1869). In all Gončarov's novels, there is didacticism, although it is less obvious than that of Dostoevskij. When Gončarov moralizes, he usually allows his characters to speak for him or cleverly works his views into the plot, as in his remarks on the causes of Oblomov's intellectual laziness and on Rajskij's failures. In Gončarov's rough drafts, there is considerably more sententious material. Perhaps he intended it for his own use and therefore deleted it mercilessly. Many of Gončarov's later comments on his work clarify his novels, though he writes tendentiously to justify himself.

6. It is more difficult to analyze Gončarov's style than to describe the main compositional features of his novels. He recognized the problems involved in portraying types, as can be seen in his letter to Dostoevskij. For good reasons, critics of Gončarov's novels have been unable to decide whether his characters are types or individuals. He certainly intended that Audev, Oblomov, the grandmother in *The Precipice,* Rajskij and Stolz be types. In other instances, he emphasizes features that he considers typical, such as Vera's vague longing for freedom. But his types have so many well-described individual characteristics that they hardly seem typical. Even the characters most like types, such as Oblomov and the grandmother, have such exaggerated typical features that it is clear that, behind a mask of objective realism, Gončarov is a satirist (Oblomov's indolence) or a panegyrist (the great moral stature of the grandmother). Objections to Gončarov's method—for instance, to his treatment of Mark Voloxov—also apply to his efforts to mask himself as an "objective realist." He is not convincing when he says that Mark is not a type but an individual.

Gončarov's presentation of characters and their surroundings shows that he is a great epic writer. His narratives flow slowly, more slowly and smoothly than those of any other Russian realist. He is perhaps better able than any other Russian writer to retard his narratives, a skill that the Formalists considered especially important for literary prose.[1] The delayed action of Gončarov's narratives is filled with material that amplifies the story and

---

1. On the other hand, Gončarov later avoided more than any of his Russian contemporaries the devices of estrangement,"making it strange," which are present in his early work.

characters. In part, these details merely contribute to the effect of verisimilitude, an aspect of Gončarov's writing that escaped those of his readers who thought that most of *The Precipice* was superfluous, since Rajskij was a finished character from the outset and did not develop. M. M. Stasjulevič, publisher of the magazine *Vestnik Evropy,* in which *The Precipice* appeared, did not agree and said that Rajskij emerged as a complete type as well as an individual only because of the accumulation of small details and incidents.

In developing characters, Gončarov relies largely on the opinions of other characters (as in their reaction to Vera's affair) and on character's analyses of themselves. As a result, the orchestration of individual motifs is less obvious in his work than it is in Dostoevskij's; and the impression of objective reality is greater.

This impression is not wrong; but naive admirers of realism (or, rather, of a realism they misunderstand) are indignant at Gončarov's deviations from their kind of realism and at his devices for achieving verisimilitude. Their displeasure with Gončarov has continued to the present. Other admirers of realism have chosen not to recognize the realism in Gončarov and have ignored everything in him that they dislike.

7. Gončarov's works presented a special problem to Russian critics and readers, who were used to seeking answers to the problems of life in works of literature, answers that ranged from solutions to moral questions to plans for improving the world. In contrast to Dostoevskij, L. N. Tolstoj, and many·other Russian writers, Gončarov has nothing to say about these questions—at least, not directly, His sententious remarks and allusions could go unnoticed. His plea for work ("work for work's sake") and for moral purity is not very much his own view. Gončarov was politically conservative. He recognized the efforts, energy, and desires of the younger generation but did not agree with them on the issues of the day. The inadequacy of his views does not diminish his importance as a literary realist.

V

The Radicals of the 1860s

1. I shall group together several prose writers as radicals of
the 1860s because their political and social views are similar
and because their literary aims, styles, and methods of composition are related.

Some writers in this group were popular in their time but were
almost forgotten by the end of the 1870s, and they have only
recently been rediscovered and considered by some to be predecessors of socialist realism. The subject matter of their work makes
them seem more dated than their contemporaries. The main radical writers of the 1860s are Nikolaj Gerasimovič Pomjalovskij
(1835–1863), Aleksandr Ivanovič Levitov (1835–1877), Vasilij
Alekseevič Slepcov (1836–1878), Nikolaj Vasil'evič Uspenskij
(1837–1889), and Fedor Mixajlovič Rešetnikov (1841–1871). Other
writers in the group were less talented. The emphasis placed
on the insignificant I. A. Kuščevskij (1847–1876) by some literary
historians—in particular, D. S. Mirsky and Vsevolod
Setschkareff—appears to me completely unfounded.

2. The ideological kinship of these writers consists in their political radicalism and their social populism (*narodničestvo*). Because
of the strict censorship of the 1860s, they could not express their
social opinions freely. They agreed that they were almost all
indebted to the important ideological leader Nikolaj Gavrilovič
Černyševskij (1828–1889), who was also a writer. Whether or
not they understood all Černyševskij's ideas is another question.

Not all the literary works of this group are didactic. In some
novels, novellas, and journalistic sketches, the writers express
their own ideas, directly or through characters. Usually, the
manner of narration is intended to lead the reader to some conclusion. There is a strong connection between most of the works
of these writers and the physiological, semijournalistic sketches

57

of the Natural School revived by the radicals of the 1860s, although features such as hyperbole and grotesquery are less evident in the radicals. The radical writers thought that they were continuing the stylistic tradition of Gogol'. They deceived themselves. In almost all their writings, there are passages that remind one of Gogol'; but these men do not have Gogol's fine humor or his qualities of language, such as rhythm and euphony. Like Černyševskij, they thought of Gogol' as a negative satirist. Significantly, not a single word or expression from the works of the radical realists, with the possible exception of *podlipovcy* and *kisejnaja devuška,* has come to be used by educated Russians.

3. Historically, the greatest contribution of radical literature was that it introduced a new kind of character. Grigorovič and Turgenev had attempted to portray the common people (*narod*) down to the lowest levels. But in the radicals, there is neither Turgenev's idealization of the peasant nor the sentimentality of Grigorovič. After the radicals, the treatment of villages in Čexov and Bunin is nothing new.

The tendency of Russian realism to present a wide variety of characters was carried further by the radicals, who were interested in the new class, the proletariat, as well as in the peasants. The radicals show factory workers who are not protected by the authorities and have not organized resistance of their own. Vagabonds cast off by society and *Lumpenproletarier* are described long before Gor'kij's first stories.

Another new group dealt with were nonnoble intellectuals, the *raznočincy,* from the petty bourgeoisie and from families of clergymen and minor officials. Occasionally, *raznočincy*—among whom were such men as V. A. Slepcov—turned to revolutionary activities. Otherwise, almost the only profession open to them was the civil service. In the literature of the period, as in that of the Natural School (for instance, the early novels of N. A. Nekrasov), one reads of students and others from modest circumstances who are distressed and in search of work.

At this time, the concept of the "superfluous man" became current. Superfluous men were those who could not find a place in Russian society or a reasonable occupation. Later, this idea was extended to characters in romantic literature, such as Onegin, Pečorin, Tentetnikov, Čackij, and Bel'tov. There was an important difference between these superfluous romantic noblemen and the *raznočincy* of the 1860s: the *raznočincy* felt rejected by society and had great difficulty finding work; the superfluous men had a comfortable if aimless life (see Tentetnikov in *Dead Souls*). The men of the 1860s felt driven to revolutionary activities,[1] whereas the superfluous men of the 1830s and 1840s, as presented in literature, were capable only of vague protest; for instance, Čackij flees Moscow to find a "place for his wounded feelings." Gogol' planned for Tentetnikov to be arrested by the police, but that is only hinted at in the surviving part of *Dead Souls*.

4. The radical writers of the sixties sympathized with the revolutionaries mainly because they did not think that reforms such as the emancipation of the serfs had gone far enough. They were partly right in what they said about these belated reforms. The radicals were not content to work toward goals within reach[2] but made demands that were out of reach at the time. Instead of social reform, the radicals favored revolution and expected to be supported by an uprising of the dissatisfied masses. They thought that this uprising would come soon and give rise to a new society, but they had only a vague idea of what the new society would be like. Some radicals of the sixties believed that socialist communes would bring forth a new socialist order as advocated by Charles Fourier and his followers, who believed that socialism could take root in the bourgeois or capitalist world.

Consequently, the radicals felt that they should vigorously oppose moderate liberals and their "illusions" of gradual, cooperative reform. Flaws in reforms, for which the bureaucracy and landowners were responsible, and the shortcomings of liberal reformers were attacked zealously in radical literature. Little distinction was made between adherents of the old order and opponents of it who were not socialistic. The radicals even broke with such stalwart older socialists as Herzen.

Since socialistic ideals could not be discussed openly, writers were limited to negative criticism. This criticism was directed

---

1. See Dmitrij Čiževskij, *Russische Geistesgeschichte*, II (Hamburg, 1961), 88 ff.
2. *Ibid.*

at shortcomings in the social and political systems and at the family, church, science, and philosophy. This critical mood is evident in Turgenev's nihilist character, Bazarov.[3]

Negative types are often portrayed primitively and tendentiously. They are blatantly bad in what they do and say. Such obviously wicked characters occur perhaps only in classicist tragedies and in Gor'kij. It is not difficult for the positive heroes to stand up to these villains, who are generally liberals or spokesmen for the authorities. Neutral characters, not predestined to be condemned or exalted, are portrayed by Pomjalovskij.

5. The radical writers emphasized the content of their works, which was seldom openly didactic but tended to be instructive and propagandistic. Several stylistic features of their works are connected with these aims, in particular the use of the colloquial language of various social levels. There is dialect, jargon—such as that of divinity students, university students, and workers of different trades and professions—and the language of the petty bourgeoisie. Although there is little real folklore in the radical writers, most of them were interested in folklore.

The style of the radicals is particularly characterized by the absence of metaphoric language. Descriptions of landscapes are short and consist mostly of stock phrases. Little attention is paid to beauty of language. Characters are described briefly. The radical writers are indebted to the Natural School in their portrayal of unattractive people and in their treatment of landscapes, cities, and the details of everyday life.

Great emphasis is placed on clever dialogue. There is a general tendency to approach life satirically and ironically, but writers are limited by their inadequate talent and their concern with ideology, which deprives them of the detachment needed for good irony. By and large, these writers are too angry and too bitter.

Nevertheless, in all the radical writers under discussion there are positive features of style and composition, features carried further in later literature. This impression is confirmed by the drafts and notes these writers left behind, although unfortunately not all their remains are available.

---

3. Evgenij Bazarov, central character of Turgenev's novel *Fathers and Sons.*

6. As mentioned above, all the works of the radical school go back in a sense to Nikolaj Gavrilovič Černyševskij. Although Černyševskij was primarily an economist, sociologist, and politician, he tried his hand from the late 1840s on at literature. His only work to attract attention was his novel *Čto delat'?* [What to Do?], which he wrote in 1862 and 1863 while under arrest in the Peter-Paul Fortress and which he published in 1863.

The novel has a certain art, that of an experienced journalist, and it was thought by many readers to be of interest as social and socialistic propaganda although of little literary value. In the novel, Černyševskij meant to show the new men in contemporary society, men who, he felt, were a phenomenon of the 1860s and would soon make a contribution: "A few years will pass and people will call to them, 'Save us!,' and people will do as they say." The future will be "bright and beautiful." In the novel, the medical student Lopuxov converts a petit-bourgeois girl to the ideal of enlightened egoism and marries her. A friend of Lopuxov, the young scholar Kirsanov, comes between him and his wife. Lopuxov decides to give his wife her freedom by pretending to commit suicide. The last part of the novel contains a description of the milliners' co-operative that she founds. Both of the principal male characters are typical intelligent *raznočincy,* and the parents of Lopuxov's wife are egoistic materialists. The opinions and conversations of Lopuxov and Kirsanov are undoubtedly the best parts of the novel; but their absence of feeling and the primitively adventurous plot of the story make poor literature indeed. Although the revolutionary Raxmetov is not directly involved in the action of the story, he is a strict ascetic, a leader (*komandir*), and the most interesting person in the book; Černyševskij considers such men the "salt of the earth."

All in all, the novel was most effective in what it did not say. As Černyševskij wrote, "The penetrating reader may guess that I know much more about Raxmetov than I tell." Černyševskij's heavy language did not diminish the popularity of the work, but later editions of it had to be printed abroad.

7. Nikolaj Gerasimovič Pomjalovskij was the son of a St. Petersburg deacon. He studied at a seminary, where he contributed to a hand-written student magazine. Later, he taught at a school for workers in St. Petersburg, briefly attended St. Petersburg

University, and published in rapid succession (from 1859 to the fall of 1863, when he died) several novellas and two novels, *Meščanskoe sčast'e* [Bourgeois Happiness], which he called a *povest'*, and *Molotov*. In his last year, he wrote *Seminary Sketches*.

The hero of both of Pomjalovskij's novels is Molotov, a *raznočinec* who comes into conflict with the aristocratic, or "good," society of the day. Pomjalovskij only suggests how Molotov gradually realizes his situation. Typically, Pomjalovskij does not step up the conflict but allows Molotov to find solace in a Philistine happiness that the author considers inadequate for a vital man. The other principal character of the novel is the nihilist Čerevanin, who only criticizes existing conditions. These two main characters are hardly positive heroes. The women seem to give more promise, but they are capable only of vague longing to escape from family life. Here Pomjalovskij was forced to fall back on stock phrases about the "insurmountable moral forces." His readers understood what he was driving at.

In his novels, Pomjalovskij attempts to get away from Turgenev's kind of realism and go in the direction of the Natural School, although not so far as other radical writers. His *Očerki bursy* [Seminary Sketches] is written entirely in the style of the Natural School. The dark picture of life in the seminary (disputed by some critics) and of the cruel methods of instruction that allow no intellectual freedom is gloomier than anything Dickens wrote about the old English private schools. Pomjalovskij's opinion that the entire curriculum of the school is "dead scholasticism" is further evidence that he was a materialist and atheist.

In the last months of his life, Pomjalovskij was at work on plans for at least two novels that were to deal with Russian slums (*truščoby*).

8. Fedor Mixajlovič Rešetnikov came from Ekaterinburg (now Sverdlovsk) and was the son of a minor post office official. He received little education, worked for the government, and, in 1861, began publishing narratives, poems, and plays that are awkward in content and composition and are often mere imitations. In 1863, he went to St. Petersburg and became acquainted with modern literature. He wrote sketches (*očerki*) on Russian regions and social classes. Among these is the story *Three Brothers* (1863), about miners from the Urals.

In St. Petersburg, Rešetnikov lived in great poverty but worked on longer narratives, some of which attracted general interest. Among these works is the short novel *Podlipovcy,* on peasant life in northeastern European Russia. The peasants' economic poverty is shown to be connected with their intellectual poverty and their complete lack of education; they are almost savages. Rešetnikov's peasants are quite different from those of Turgenev or Grigorovič. Their language is primitive, often barely intelligible (in keeping with the tradition of the Natural School). The main characters leave their village in search of work and perish miserably. Their children become workers and attain some culture; they begin "to understand something" and ask questions about society.

Rešetnikov's visit to the Urals in 1865 provided him with material for two novels about miners, *Gornorabočie* and *Glumovy,* 1865 and 1867, neither originally published in its entirety. These loosely constructed novels deal with workers and with intellectuals, such as a schoolteacher. Rešetnikov's sympathies are obviously with the workers, who agitate for their rights but achieve no more than the intellectuals, who protest as much and usually find consolation in drink. Rešetnikov's peasant women are energetic and moral. His novel *Gde lučše?* [Where Is It Better?] (1868) was not completed; in it, characters look for work, go to different regions—Nizhni Novgorod, St. Petersburg, and others—and take up various professions. Eventually, even drink fails to console them; they commit suicide or at least agree that they would be better off in the grave.

Rešetnikov's first novels about workers are close to the physiological sketches of the Natural School, but in *Where Is It Better?* he presents detailed scenes of cities and landscapes. Here the tradition of the Natural School is too confining. His novel on minor officials, *Svoj xleb* [One's Own Bread] (1870) is mainly about women and their vocations and is equally pessimistic.

Rešetnikov's works have a social and political significance far greater than their literary value. They have received less attention than the works of radicals who wrote mainly about intellectuals and appealed more to educated readers.

9. The most talented and best-read of the radical writers was Vasilij Alekseevič Slepcov (1836–1878), the son of a nobleman and officer. After attending exclusive schools in Moscow and the provinces, Slepcov briefly studied medicine at Moscow University. His acquaintance with V. I. Dal' prompted him to write sketches on his travels (1861). He associated with Černyševskij's circle, collaborated on the *Sovremennik,* undertook a longer series of sketches, on the town of Ostashkov (1862–1863). At the same time, he published several novellas and brought out the novel *Trudnoe vremja* [Hard Times] (1865). He planned other novels but did not complete them.

Slepcov was also known for organizing a commune of young intellectuals in 1863 and was imprisoned briefly. Leskov describes this commune tendentiously in his novel *No Way Out* (see chapter VII, section 3). In his later years, Slepcov wrote little.

Slepcov's sketches vary in quality, as can be seen from his lesser known, recently published pieces. Sometimes he writes clearly and concretely; sometimes he resorts to flat jokes—he has no real feeling for humor—and to unfounded, fantastic assertions that only the densest reader could accept.

In his novellas and novels too, Slepcov is tendentious. Most characters in his novellas are peasants; others are urban poor, landowners, and intellectuals. His novellas seldom have plots; they consist of dialogue and broad sketches of reality. He approached the impressionistic style. In his dialogues, characters reveal themselves incapable of thought; the tragi-comic predicaments in which they find themselves suggest that they are not merely uneducated, but stupid as well.

Slepcov's best work by far is his novel *Hard Times.* Some characters in the novel are well portrayed, others merely caricatured; there are liberals, optimists, and unthinking intellectuals and landowners who believe that conditions in Russia are normal and who extol reforms that Slepcov considers inadequate. Their world is bleak. There is despair in Slepcov's occasional comments and in the thoughts of the principal character, Rezanov, a populist, arrested often in the early sixties, who now leads a solitary life. Ideologically, *Hard Times* can be compared with Černyševskij's *What To Do?* But Slepcov's novel is a work of art; his characters do not make speeches. In side remarks, he criticizes the reforms of the day and the philanthropy of the liberals. His narrative method is related to that of impressionism. *Hard Times* makes light of the peasant reforms; Slepcov seems to think that lack of progress will make it easier to put through his program of sweeping change. "The worse things are, the better."

10. Another writer who should be grouped with the radicals is Nikolaj Vasil'evič Uspenskij, a popular author in his time. Born in 1837, he was the son of a village priest. He entered a seminary, went to the medical academy in St. Petersburg, and enrolled at St. Petersburg University. In 1858, he began to write for Nekrasov's *Sovremennik*. Nekrasov expected him to develop into a major writer. He sent Uspenskij abroad, where the young man spent his time in pursuit of cheap pleasures. Visiting him, Turgenev was astonished by his lack of culture. Uspenskij returned to Russia and continued to decline morally. He broke off with his patrons and neglected literature. In 1889, he committed suicide.

Uspenskij's early short novellas are full of brief social and political references that agree with the views of the *Sovremennik*. He is at his best in writing dialogue, the most striking feature of which is the stupidity of speakers of all social classes. His portrayal of the masses was controversial because the failures of his peasants seemed due to their denseness, not to their poverty and lack of education.

Uspenskij's novellas are often plotless and employ the same impressionistic devices as Slepcov's. The use of language, especially simple popular language, is the forte of this luckless pretender to a prominent place in Russian literature. At this writing, in 1966, Uspenskij is still occasionally said to be great, though unrecognized, and he is compared with such truly great writers as Dostoevskij.

11. Aleksandr Ivanovič Levitov wrote plotless *očerki*. The son of a village clergyman, Levitov was born in 1835. He studied at a seminary and at the medical academy in St. Petersburg, and he was exiled to the North in 1856. After his release in 1859, he worked for various magazines, among them Dostoevskij's *Vremja,* and published his sketches and novellas in book form (1865–1874). Levitov lived and died in poverty. In contrast to many of his contemporaries, he wrote of the fate of man, of peas-

ants, *raznočincy,* and industrial workers. He often spoke his mind in a sort of journalistic lyricism. Unlike most writers who shared his views, he dealt with the emotional experiences of his characters.

12. Other, less important writers sympathized with the common people—that is, they were of the populist school—but they imitated the idealized, good-natured, sentimental works of Grigorovič and Turgenev, without their talent. Among these writers are N. N. Zlatovratskij (1845-1911), P. V. Zasodimskij (1843–1912), and A. Osipovič, the pen name of A. O. Novodvorskij (1853–1882). It was not until the end of the century that such writers as V. G. Korolenko and D. N. Mamin-Sibirjak got away from these two styles, the naturalistic and sentimental, which were sympathetic to the masses but out of date.

VI

Dostoevskij

1. There is still too little known about Fedor Mixajlovič Dostoevskij's life. The personality of his father, Mixail Dostoevskij, is disputed. A Ukrainian, the elder Dostoevskij attended a Greek Catholic seminary and ran away from it to study medicine in Moscow, where he later practiced at a hospital. He sent his two sons, Mixail (1820–1864) and Fedor (1821–1881) to military school, out of avarice or because he could not afford anything better. Fedor Mixajlovič attended a French boarding school in Moscow and the engineering school in St. Petersburg, where he met students with a literary bent, such as D. V. Grigorovič. Dostoevskij's interest in literature is evident in his correspondence with his brother; they mention Homer, Shakespeare, Schiller, E. T. A. Hoffmann, Victor Hugo, Goethe, and others, most of whom they have read in French. Dostoevskij's works of this period have not survived.

Dostoevskij served briefly in the army, resigned his commission, and devoted himself to writing. In 1845, he published his first novella, *Bednye ljudi* [Poor Folk], and became instantly famous. He was hailed by Nekrasov and the critic Vissarion Belinskij. After the appearance of Dostoevskij's longer novellas, *Dvojnik* [The Double] (1846) and *Xozjajka* [The Landlady] (1847), this initial enthusiasm waned. In 1846, Dostoevskij met the socialist M. V. Butaševič-Petraševskij (1821–1866) and joined his circle and another group frequented by writers. The revolution of 1848 frightened Tsar Nicholas, who believed in absolute monarchy and the status quo. When the Petraševskij circle was denounced by one member, the other participants were arrested in the spring of 1849. It is uncertain how active Dostoevskij had been; it is possible that he was one of the more radical members. In any case, he was among those sentenced to death and pardoned only at the site of execution. His sentence was commuted to four years' imprisonment in Siberia. His novel *Netočka Nezvanova* was being published at this time and was left unfinished.

On his release from prison, in 1854, Dostoevskij was forced to serve as a private in the army in southern Siberia. In 1855, he became an officer and married the widow of a minor official. Little is known about his wife. In 1859, he was allowed to leave the service and return to European Russia. He went first to Tver and was then admitted to the capitals. He and his wife separated, and she soon died. Dostoevskij and his brother published the magazines *Vremja* [Time] and *Èpoxa* [The Epoch]. Mixail was known as a writer of the Natural School and was officially the publisher of the magazines. *Vremja* was closed by the government in 1863 over a petty misunderstanding, and *Èpoxa* failed for lack of subscribers. Mixail died in 1864.

Dostoevskij's political views in these troubled times (1855–1865) are unclear. He invited former members of the Petraševskij circle to work on his magazines, but he also turned to such ideological mavericks as the philosopher N. N. Straxov and the critic A. A. Grigor'ev, who are best thought of as conservatives. Dostoevskij's two women friends, A. Korvin-Krukovskaja and Apollinaria (or, as she called herself, Polina) Suslova, associated with radicals. A trip to Western Europe, on which he visited Aleksandr Herzen in London, made an unfavorable impression on Dostoevskij. He thought of himself and his colleagues as being close to the soil (*počvenniki*); although they were not Slavophiles, they wanted Russia to go its own way.

The debts incurred when the *Èpoxa* closed and debts left by his brother almost drove Dostoevskij to prison. To escape, he went abroad for several years, after marrying for a second time in 1867, and lived wretchedly in Switzerland, Italy, Bohemia, and Dresden until 1871. He was forced to write constantly and hastily.

After his return to European Russia, in 1859, Dostoevskij published a number of works, including *Zapiski iz mertvogo doma* [Memoirs from the House of the Dead] (1861–62), the reminiscences of a convict, who is not identical with the author; two long stories, *Djadjuškin son* [Uncle's Dream] and *Selo Stepančikovo* [The Village Stepančikovo]; and two novels, *Unižennye i oskorblennye* [The Humiliated and Insulted] (1861) and *Prestup-*

lenie i nakazanie [Crime and Punishment] (1866). In Dresden, he wrote two more novels, *Idiot* [The Idiot] (1868) and *Besy* [The Demons] (1871); in English and in Camus's dramatization, this work is entitled *The Possessed,* which is perhaps the best translation of the title.

Dostoevskij's second wife, Anna Grigor'evna Snitkin (1846-1918) was practical and able and helped to improve his situation. When he returned to St. Petersburg in 1871, he was able to work in peace. In 1875, he published *Podrostok* [A Raw Youth]; and, five years later, the novel *The Brothers Karamazov* began to come out; the last installment did not appear until early 1881. In late 1880, Dostoevskij delivered a speech at the Puškin celebration in Moscow and made a profound impression on everyone. In early 1881, Dostoevskij died of a lung disease, which he is said to have contracted in prison. Apart from his literary works, he published a monthly magazine, *Zapiski pisatelja* [A Writer's Diary], filled mainly with his own articles. This magazine, the ideas in Dostoevskij's novels—especially in *The Possessed*—and the appearance of his novels in a "reactionary" magazine added to his unpopularity among radicals, who had rejected him since his first two magazines in the early 1860s. In Dostoevskij's lifetime, most critics viewed him unfavorably. At his funeral, it turned out that he had a number of admirers, if not followers, among young Russians. But the metropolitan of St. Petersburg denied him burial at a monastery. He found that Dostoevskij was a mere novelist who had written "nothing special." And so, at his death, Dostoevskij was considered a second-rate writer.

2. There is not space here for an analysis of all Dostoevskij's works or of his ideology. The essential thing is the stylistic development of his works.

Dostoevskij's three most important early novellas form an ascending line. They reflect the influence of various writers, mainly Gogol'. The famous saying, "We all come from under Gogol's 'greatcoat'" does not occur in Dostoevskij's work or in any reminiscences of him. Apparently, it goes back to a French diplomat, Melchior de Vogüé, who wrote frequently about Russia but visited Russia only after Dostoevskij's death. The saying may actually have been handed down from Dostoevskij, since he was interested in Gogol'.

Like Gogol's *The Greatcoat,* Dostoevskij's *Poor Folk* is a novella about a minor official. Gogol's character is emotionally shaken at having to buy an overcoat. Dostoevskij is concerned mainly with the feelings of the elderly Makar Devuškin, who meets a needy girl, Varen'ka Dobroselova, in the city. Makar attempts to take care of her, although he makes a miserable salary. To avoid gossip, they do not see each other but write letters. In his letters, Makar uses clumsy everyday language; Varen'ka writes in good literary Russian and in a longish letter describes her childhood and youth. The correspondence is carried on from early April to late September, takes about one hundred pages, and gives Makar an opportunity to tell of his wretched situation at work, the cramped quarters in which he lives, and his poverty. He does not complain much and assumes that his position is natural. His intellectual views are narrow. Makar's letters show with great sensitivity how his concern for Varen'ka develops into genuine and hopeless love; his last letter closes with a cry of despair, for Varen'ka is marrying a man whom she does not and cannot love and is to leave St. Petersburg.

The improbability of the form (the "poor folk" could hardly have carried on such an extensive correspondence) and the frequent sentimentality are more than outweighed by the concise, even narration of the story.

Dostoevskij took another step forward in *The Double,* a novella with echoes of Gogol'. The story treats the insanity of a minor official and is reminiscent of Gogol's *The Memoirs of a Madman* and *The Nose.* When *The Double* begins, Jakov Petrovič Goljadkin has lost the favor of his former chief and benefactor and must give up all hope of marrying the man's daughter, Klara. The narrator is fictitious and is almost on a level with Goljadkin, but sometimes rises above an awkward narrative manner. His habit of repeating himself contributes to a fine psychological portrayal. The crisis comes when a double, a namesake of Goljadkin, appears, scorns him, and forces him out of "all his relations in life" and out of his job (some scenes are reminiscent of Hoffmann's *Klein Zaches*). It is not clear whether the second Goljadkin is real or is a figment of Goljadkin's imagination (the artist A. Kubin considered him a figment in his very adequate illustrations for a 1922 edition of the work). It is vaguely suggested that Goljadkin's madness may have been brought on by pangs of conscience, perhaps over a broken promise of marriage.

Dostoevskij liked this novella and, after his return from exile, revised it but did not point up the principal theme, which is Gogol's theme that everyone must have his place in life. Goljadkin learns what it is like to be replaceable, and the discovery destroys him.

That is a social problem that Dostoevskij transforms into a psychological one, just as he does with poverty in *Poor Folk*. In his next novella, *The Landlady,* there is no social problem at all, and that angered the critic Vissarion Belinskij, who had favored Dostoevskij.

The central character in *The Landlady* is from a different walk of life: Ordynov is a young scholar, a church historian. The influence of Gogol' and E. T. A. Hoffmann show up in only a few passages. This is perhaps Dostoevskij's first *fully* original work. The novella has little plot—not that it resembles a physiological sketch of the Natural School, but rather, reality, fantasy, and dream tend to merge. Ordynov is a new type in Russian literature, a dreamer. Gogol' foreshadows the type in his artists, Piskarev in *Nevskij Prospekt* and Čartkov in *The Portrait.* Ordynov lives only for scholarship, for a creative grasp of ideas that is closely related to art. He rents a room in the apartment of a strange couple, both of them obviously simple; the husband is old, but his wife, Katerina, is young and pretty. During an illness, Ordynov falls in love with Katerina, carries on real or imaginary conversations with her, and listens to her strange confessions. According to her, the old man has killed her parents and abducted her; her story sounds as though taken from a folk tale or folk song. If Katerina does tell all this and it is not a dream, it is still uncertain whether it is a real confession or a poetic fantasy. The old man appears willing to give Katerina her freedom, but she stays with him and does not go away with Ordynov. The old man explains her decision psychologically: "If we give a weak person his freedom, he will take it only to give it back to us." That is the first suggestion of Dostoevskij's later ideas. When Ordynov recovers from his illness, he finds that the strange pair has gone. In the brief conclusion to the novella, the couple is made to appear even more mysterious. Was the old man Katerina's husband, or her father? Was he an Old

Believer—that is only alluded to—or was he one of the band of thieves and smugglers discovered in the same house?

3. It is as though Dostoevskij has tried to rid these novellas of the "burden" of a story and of external events in order to concentrate on psychological experiences (he goes further in this direction in the unfinished novel *Netočka Nezvanova*). In this respect, he expands the physiological sketches typical of the Natural School and makes them psychological. Perhaps the only feature of the Natural School in Dostoevskij's writing is the somber picture of St. Petersburg and its officials. Dostoevskij cannot have been fully aware that he was creating the psychological novel, but he made great progress in his novellas. He learned from the writers to whom he looked, from Gogol', E. T. A. Hoffmann, Balzac (he had already published a translation of *Eugénie Grandet*), Hugo, and perhaps Dickens. But mostly his novellas are his own "discovery," though still a rather modest one. The young Dostoevskij anticipates the "philosophical" Dostoevskij in his interest in the problem of freedom (*The Landlady* treats the questions of freedom and weak persons) and in the problem of human existence, which, he feels, is not based on passion, reason, or will power. The external world is deceptive, as Dostoevskij emphasizes in his treatment of St. Petersburg, which seems always like an apparition about to dissolve (see the novella *A Faint Heart*). This image of the city goes back to the romantics, to Gogol', and partly to Puškin.

4. Dostoevskij returned to the theme of the deceptive world in two other novellas. While in exile, he had been put in touch with philosophy by a German official, Baron Ferdinand Petrovič von Wrangel, and he intended at that time to write a philosophical work. That he did not is perhaps just as well; but, in all his later works, philosophical motifs are evident. The two novellas in question are *Uncle's Dream* and *The Village Stepančikovo,* published in 1859 but planned earlier.

Uncle's Dream tells of the conflict between a vivacious girl in love and "uncle," an old prince whose body is made up of prostheses and who can hardly tell dream from reality. The girl's mother plans to marry her to this living wreck, but this plan is thwarted. In a brief epilogue, the girl appears happily married to a governor general. She has made her way in society, but she is actually as unhappy as she was with her mother or would have been with the old prince.

The ending of *The Village Stepančikovo* (actually, it is an estate) is more pleasant. A group of vivacious, rather likable people are as full of illusions as is the prince in *Uncle's Dream* (or as are many of Gogol's characters). The landowner is kind and good-natured and, like his mother, he believes completely in a Russian Tartuffe, Foma Opiskin, who dominates the family and, in a typically Russian fashion, impresses everyone with his seeming piety, learning, and wisdom. The other characters pursue various goals, all of them illusory. Finally, Foma Opiskin is put down, though not turned out. Here, Dostoevskij again follows Gogol', who often deals with the pursuit of illusions.

It has been suggested, incorrectly, that Foma Opiskin was intended to be a parody on Gogol', as Ju. N. Tynjanov notes. Actually, Opiskin's speeches are a parody on edifying literature in general. There is nothing about his remarks that associates them particularly with Gogol's edifying works and letters.

5. Beginning with *Crime and Punishment*, Dostoevskij's great novels are ultimately didactic. The oldest Slavic didactic novels are translations from Byzantine literature, such as *Stefanit and Ixnilat, Barlaam and Josafat, Axikar the Wise,* and *The Story of the Seven Wise Men.* In the seventeenth and eighteenth centuries, didactic literature was developed by such Western writers as Swift and Rousseau; but the didactic element in their work was usually contained in dialogue and did not especially interfere with the story. Russian translators of the Scot John Barclay's allegory *Argenis* and of François Fénelon's *Télémaque* and imitators of these translations, such as the classicist M. M. Xeraskov and the romanticist V. F. Odoevski, did not carry on the literature of Swift and Rousseau; but it was available and the critic Vissarion Belinskij refers to it on occasion. Dostoevskij revived and altered the didactic novel and created the "polyphonic novel," as M. M. Baxtin indicates. In Dostoevskij, the didactic element is closely related to the action of the work. Edifying matter is contained in the conclusions to be drawn from the novel, in dialogue, and in interpolations, such as Raskol'nikov's brief essay, Father Zosima's reminiscences, and Ivan Karamazov's *Legend of the Grand Inquisitor.* Dostoevskij offers no ultimate

answers to the questions raised in his novels, which differ particularly from the tendentious novels of L. N. Tolstoj—a view also expressed by the scholar F. A. Stepun.

There are other typical features in Dostoevskij's didactic novels. To an unusual extent, his characters are identical with the ideas they stand for. They could be called personified ideas if Dostoevskij were not so skillful at presenting them as human beings, even when they are obsessed with their ideas—a further step in the method of type portrayal that goes back to Gogol'. The most essential characteristic of Dostoevskij's didactic novels is that all his spokesmen, even those of views that he rejects, are given a fair hearing; Dostoevskij makes their arguments as strong as possible. As a result, his didactic novels are as capable of developing philosophical conversations and ideological conflicts as are dialogues. In some cases, Dostoevskij had to invent his philosophical opponents; at the time, there was no Russian spokesman of philosophical "enlightenment" so profound as Ivan Karamazov and no atheist like Kirillov. Of course, there are ideological caricatures in Dostoevskij, such as Smerdjakov and several of the revolutionaries in *The Possessed;* but by and large, his didactic novels give the impression of dealing with problems that he has not resolved. They contain a philosophical and religious search that seldom yields ultimate answers.

Dostoevskij can hardly be thought to have had a coherent religious view of the world as he was writing *Crime and Punishment.* The arguments of his characters are reminiscent of the controversies in classical tragedies and surely reflect processes going on in his own soul. His letters shed less light on these problems than do the drafts of his novels that have become available in recent decades. These drafts contain many references to further unresolved problems and allusions to paths that Dostoevskij saw but chose not to take.

6. *Crime and Punishment* (1866) has a simple, transparent plot like those of the detective stories later to become so popular but differs from detective stories in that it concentrates on the soul of the criminal. Raskol'nikov does not kill the old pawnbroker for her money, but to prove that a strong man can act as he pleases. The investigator, Porfirij Petrovič, is, like many of Dostoevskij's characters, a greater master of psychological analysis

than could have been found at the time, and he solves the crime through the use of psychology. He brings about Raskol'nikov's confession by fanning his smouldering doubts in himself and his power.

Raskol'nikov's ideas of the strong man are often associated with Nietzsche's superman, but that is not entirely correct. (The theme is suggested in Puškin, in his allusion to Napoleon in *Evgenij Onegin*, chapter II, section 14; there are similar thoughts in the works of other romanticists).

Raskol'nikov is not a true representative of the Napoleonic type. But Dostoevskij does not ascribe his fall to facile pangs of conscience. The environment he meets—the Marmeladov family, especially Sonja, who has been forced into prostitution through poverty and the cruelty of her stepmother—shows Raskol'nikov the way to salvation. Two outcasts from society, a murderer and a prostitute, read the Gospels together; but this act does not solve the problems confronting Raskol'nikov and Dostoevskij. In the epilogue, Raskol'nikov's conversion is said to be incomplete. Dostoevskij does not suggest how he will develop.

7. Dostoevskij's next novel, *The Idiot* (1868), was the product of much reflection. In several of the drafts, the main character, an epileptic,[1] was to have become a criminal. In the final version, he is a figure who served as a model for Christ in Nietzsche's *The Antichrist*. Dostoevskij thought of the "idiot," Prince Myškin, as a synthesis of Christ and Don Quixote. The feature of the idiot that Nietzsche considered characteristic of Christ was his inability to bear the suffering of others, as Ernst Benz points out. That is the basis of Myškin's kindness and willingness to help: he is almost completely altruistic. But, like Don Quixote, he is naive; he inadvertently brings about tragic complications and suffers a relapse into his incurable illness.

The first part of the novel is a masterpiece of composition, perhaps better in that respect than anything Dostoevskij wrote afterward. In describing the events of one day, he skillfully reveals the personalities of the principal characters and develops Prince

---

1. Dostoevskij suffered from epilepsy. Whether he had his first attack of the "divine illness" in his youth or while he was in Siberia is one of the many obscure points of his life.

Myškin. In particular, Myškin shows his ability to win people over. His moral character is explored, and he displays his excellent mind, especially in a scene at a reception at General Epančin's, where he discusses questions that were troubling Slavophiles, Westernizers, and Dostoevskij (not all Myškin's opinions are necessarily Dostoevskij's). Behind the tragic developments of the novel is the psychological instability of a man who has no will or whose will has been broken and paralyzed through altruism.

This problem gives rise to all the complications of the work, especially Myškin's two loves, which are only superficially romantic. He feels a genuine spontaneous love for Aglaja Epančina and a love mixed with sympathy for the courtesan Nastas'ja Filippovna, and these two loves tear at him. Nastas'ja is ultimately murdered by Myškin's adversary, the merchant Rogožin.

The ideal of the "absolutely good man" (*položitel'no prekrasnyj čelovek*) that Dostoevskij wished to portray in Myškin can evidently not stand up to reality. The reality of the novel is often phantasmagoric, as when Natas'ja throws Rogožin's 100,000 rubles into the fire; as in the scene at Myškin's dacha; and as Natas'ja flees with Rogožin from the church where she is to marry Myškin. Dostoevskij conceded that, among the motley human types, there were a number of "fantastic characters," from the cynical nihilist Ippolit and his companions to General Ivolgin, whose incredible lies are hardly equaled in literature. All that, along with the psychopathological aspect of the work, such as Myškin's sensations before his epileptic attack (the aura), and the human types that are not new in Dostoevskij but are important, such as the primitively emotional merchant Rogožin and the "terrible woman" (*xiščnaja ženščina*) Nastas'ja Filippovna, produces an atmosphere scarcely found in any other novel of Dostoevskij.

8. *The Possessed* deals with contemporary questions and general problems of morality; it was controversial for decades. It is enough to recall that, during the Russian Revolution, Gor'kij spoke repeatedly of its "harmfulness." *The Possessed* is a reactionary or antirevolutionary novel, of which there have been many and of which not one has outlived its own time, not even those of such an important writer as Nikolaj Leskov.

The eternal problem that Dostoevskij takes up in *The Possessed* is the role of will power in the "existential economy" of the soul, a problem touched on in *Crime and Punishment*. The criminal plot of *The Possessed* is based on a unique episode in the revolutionary movement, an episode that caused Dostoevskij to re-examine the basic assumptions of the movement. He explores these assumptions of Russian rationalistic enlightenment in his usual fashion, by analyzing and criticizing them in a polyphony of human voices.

In 1871, after Dostoevskij had started work on *The Possessed*, he read reports of the trial of S. G. Nečaev, who had gathered a small group of revolutionaries, deceived them about the size and strength of their organization and his position in it, and sought to bring the members closer by murdering the suspected police agent Ivanov and giving the revolutionaries a sense of common guilt. Dostoevskij borrowed from the trial these and other details, such as Nečaev's issuing proclamations in the name of a nonexistent organization. Nečaev and his activities are the basis for the part of *The Possessed* that Dostoevskij called a pamphlet.

Dostoevskij had drawn up plans for his "pamphlet" before reading of Nečaev's trial. His notes make clear that the basic idea of the novel was to be that the enlighteners and revolutionaries of the 1860s, as represented by Petr Verxovenskij, were the intellectual descendants of the generation of the 1840s; in Dostoevskij's plans for the novel, Verxovenskij's father bears the name of the most typical representative of the forties, Granovskij. There are many references, mostly veiled, to specific persons of the forties and sixties. Turgenev is caricatured as the writer Karmazinov.

It is not just the revolutionaries who are portrayed unfavorably. The educated members of the older generation fare no better, especially the inept authorities, from Governor Lemke to minor officials and officers. They have no values with which to counter the revolution and are intellectually inferior to the revolutionaries. A Slavophile, Šatov, is morally better; but his ideas and his religious faith originate in a sense of national feeling and amount only to a wish to believe, to force himself to believe. The only truly good people in the novel are a not very intelligent officer and a woman who sells religious literature from door to door. The only believer is the somewhat abnormal Mar'ja Timofeevna. Never before had Russia been portrayed so somberly and hopelessly.

The Possessed is by no means a *roman à clef* as has been maintained. It combines literary caricature and a doubtful genealogy of the men of the sixties with the two important ideas mentioned above.

The strong-willed central character, Nikolaj Stavrogin, is refined, handsome, rich, and intelligent. All the other characters are partly dependent on him. His mother lives for him alone; three other women, Daša, the aristocratic Liza, and Mar'ja Timofeevna Lebjadkina, to whom Stavrogin is secretly married, are in love with him and devoted to him. Even more important is the fact that the male characters are intellectually dependent on him and are reflections of his excellent mind. Among them are the theoretician of atheism, Kirillov; the Slavophile, Šatov, who is murdered, as was Ivanov in the Nečaev affair;[2] the Nečaev of the novel, Petr Verxovenskij; and, to some extent, as a parallel to Stavrogin's mother, his intellectual father and tutor, Stepan Verxovenskij, a man of the 1840s and the father of Petr.

Petr Verxovenskij sees in Stavrogin a strong man who could make a contribution to the revolution as a usurper. The escaped convict Fed'ka murders Mar'ja Timofeevna and her brother, believing that he has carried out an assignment given by Stavrogin.

Stavrogin dominates many people but is at the nadir of existence. At the end of the novel, he commits suicide, not because he is threatened by the authorities, as are the other revolutionaries (Petr Verxovenskij has escaped in time), but because he is spiritually empty. The examples of his strong will are not always convincing. They give evidence of mental illness and can be explained by the absence of an intellectual pole for his inner life. In the first version of the novel, published in a magazine, Stavrogin is said to have had a vision of the devil; but, when the novel came out in book form, this passage had been deleted. Dostoevskij does not say that the spiritual pole lacking in Stavrogin is religion. All in all, the religious motif in *The Possessed* is weaker than in any other novel of Dostoevskij.[3]

2. In the published version of the novel, Dostoevskij omitted a number of interesting observations he had planned to attribute to Šatov; they would have emphasized the productive power of Stavrogin's mind, for they go back to his thoughts.

3. At the request of the editors of the magazine, Dostoevskij omitted an important episode, one that Camus worked into his version of *The Possessed*: Stavrogin's

Provincial life in *The Possessed* is pictured as a fantastic masquerade, full of ghostly figures. Some scenes are as incredible as those in *The Idiot;* some, such as the ball, are more so, because many people are involved. These scenes are particularly characteristic of Dostoevskij, since they take place in a society conscious of enlightenment and rational principles. Dostoevskij criticizes these principles by presenting the psychology and ideology of the revolutionaries, their rejection of every tradition not justified by their primitive logic. They reject religion and philosophy, or "metaphysics," and the bases of human society, the family and the state. Allusions to the works of Russian "enlighteners" such as Černyševskij, Pisarev, and V. A. Zajcev and slightly altered quotations from their works made Dostoevskij's objections clear for readers of his time. To a large extent, he identifies the "enlighteners" of the sixties with the men of the forties; and there are allusions to Herzen, Belinskij, T. N. Granovskij, and their contemporaries. The rejection of all nonrational tradition, he says, leads to political utopianism, to the expectation of a social upheaval in the near future, and to the unattainable and intolerable task of attempting to make everyone equal and of dictating public and private life. The rejection of "irrational" tradition leads to a fantastic cultural philosophy, to the denial of aesthetics, morality, and religion, which are said to be worthless or are explained as products of man's egoistic drive. Older liberals are helpless when confronted with these views and have nothing better to offer.

This gloomy picture is relieved only by a vague belief in the spirit of the Russian people. Dostoevskij has no positive views to offer in *The Possessed*; he is negatively didactic.

9. In 1875, Dostoevskij published a novel, *Podrostok* [A Raw Youth], with which he had been able to take his time and which is also strongly didactic.[4] From 1879 to 1881, he published his

confession to the retired Bishop Tixon, who is living in a monastery. This episode is intended to show Stavrogin's spiritual power: he is not afraid to confess a terrible crime. Tixon points out to Stavrogin that he has confessed, not out of repentance, but out of pride. Although this episode is important to the novel, Dostoevskij did not reintroduce it into later versions.

4. This novel has been wrongly called unsuccessful. See H. J. Gerigk's book *Versuch über Dostoevskijs "Jüngling,"* Forum Slavicum, volume IV, Munich, 1965.

longest and most ideologically involved novel, *The Brothers Karamazov,* a didactic criminal novel with long philosophical digressions.

The three young Karamazov brothers are sons of the old debauchee Fedor Pavlovič, and they represent three types of men. The oldest brother, Dmitrij, a former officer, is wild and unrestrained and ruled by his passions. The second, Ivan, is an educated thinker whose rationalism goes far beyond primitive enlightenment. The youngest of the brothers, Aleša, is a Christian and lives as a novice in a monastery with a starets, the monk Zosima. Dmitrij believes that he is entitled to a sizable sum from his father. Dmitrij and his father also compete for the favors of the same provincial courtesan, who is another example of the "cruel woman." When the elder Karamazov is murdered, all the evidence points to Dmitrij, although in reality the father has been killed and robbed by his illegitimate son, the servant Smerdjakov. The jury finds Dmitrij guilty of the murder. Although complex, the novel is well constructed and contains many different levels of meaning. There are important secondary characters, particularly female.

One of the principal themes of the novel is that of psychological types. The three types of men embodied in the brothers Karamazov are, as Dostoevskij emphasizes, directly connected with the types of the "Christian poet" Schiller in his *Letters on the Aesthetic Education of Man* (with which Dostoevskij also associates the typology of *The Robbers*). The question of the higher type of man is not resolved. The monk Zosima and his follower Aleša Karamazov appear closest to this type. Dostoevskij demonstrates that in every man there are higher spiritual powers and potential dangers. The men in the novel have various relationships with women, all of whom are quite different in their personalities. The variety of types shows up mainly in the moral actions of the characters. Of particular interest to Dostoevskij are the rationalists, especially Ivan Karamazov, who coldly judges and condemns the other characters, including his own father. When his father is murdered, Ivan senses his moral responsibility for Smerdjakov, whom he may unconsciously have influenced. Ivan's rejection (*neprijatie*) of the meaningless world is expressed in his "Legend of the Grand Inquisitor" and in his thoughts of the devil, who appears to him in a vision and confirms the senselessness of existence with his theory of the "eternal return," which anticipates Nietzsche's views. The basest rationalist (enlightener sui generis) is the murderer Smerdjakov. But contemporary society, as presented, for instance, in the courtroom proceedings, also subscribes to the views of primitive enlightenment.

There are a number of secondary motifs in the novel. Dostoevskij tells the history of the Karamazov family and of other characters; and, in these digressions, he is a typical realist ("metonymic" composition). Fedor and Dmitrij compete for Grušen'ka; Dmitrij has a fiancée, Katerina, whom he has won with his magnanimity. Psychologically, Katerina is more like Ivan, to whom she is attracted. Aleša talks with a sick girl, Liza Xoxlakova, and with boys from the high school. Besides an actual father, Aleša has a spiritual father, the monk Zosima, whose death comes as a religious disappointment. The courtroom scenes are masterful. One case appears to characterize the whole of Russian society. On the basis of the evidence, Dmitrij is sentenced to a long term in prison. Smerdjakov confesses his guilt to Ivan, gives him the money he has stolen, and commits suicide. The jury does not believe Ivan's testimony about Smerdjakov, especially since Ivan is in a neurotic state—the devil has appeared to him the night before and carried on philosophical discussions.

Dostoevskij meant to continue the story of these characters in another novel. Dmitrij was probably to have escaped from prison. Aleša was to have become a revolutionary, a turn that shows that *The Brothers Karamazov* does not resolve the problem of the higher man, not even in Dostoevskij's view.

10. Dostoevskij's style and composition contain a number of interesting features. His novels have basically simple plots, which are sometimes complicated by abrupt turning points and parallel plots. As criminal novels, they are hardly suspenseful. It is only in *The Brothers Karamazov* that Dostoevskij leaves the mystery to be cleared up at the end. In content, his novels are purely psychological. There are always conflicts between different kinds of men and, in particular, between men with different views of the world; and the clash of ideas is connected with the personal conflicts of the characters. This "polyphonous" nature (in M. M. Baxtin's phrase), this polyphonous "orchestration" (my own

term—D. Čiževskij) contradicts the writer Vjačeslav Ivanov's opinion that Dostoevskij's works are "novel-tragedies." Dostoevskij's novels resemble plays in the predominance of dialogue, in the occasional theatrical monologues, and in the tense crowd scenes, which have led to theatrical adaptations of these novels by writers such as Camus and Adamov. Dostoevskij's novels also resemble plays in their tendency to concentrate action into short spans of time, during which plot lines cross, characters approach crises in their lives, and characters meet for the first time, as at the end of the first part of *The Idiot* or in the encounter of all the Karamazovs in Father Zosima's cell. But these similarities with plays are not sufficient for Dostoevskij's novels to be called tragic drama.

The didactic nature of his novels comes in theoretical interpolations, sometimes in the speeches of characters, sometimes in their writings, confessions, and treatises: Stavrogin's and Ippolit's confessions in *The Idiot*; Zosima's confession; Zosima's biography by Aleša Karamazov; Raskol'nikov's treatise in *Crime and Punishment* and Šigalev's in *The Possessed*; the works of Ivan Karamazov—*Poèm, Geological Upheaval,* and *The Legend of the Grand Inquisitor*; the novella by Karmazinov-Turgenev; and a number of letters by characters. There are many references to writers, philosophers, and painters, often in the form of allusions to their works or in easily recognizable quotations. In the original drafts, there are more of these references. There is much to learn about Dostoevskij's sources from a thorough analysis of his texts, a task far from complete. Dostoevskij does not merely borrow; he is stimulated by other writers but usually remains independent (see sec. 12 below).

The didactic aspect of Dostoevskij's novels is often temporarily set aside. The final catastrophe frequently leaves corpses, rejected convicts, and madmen in its wake.

In his novels, Dostoevskij uses a fictitious narrator; sometimes the line between the narrator and Dostoevskij is unclear, as in *The Possessed*. Dostoevskij borrows from the contemporary press, oral reports, and historical works. His language is extremely diverse, and this goes back partly to his notes, made in prison and elsewhere. He works on a number of linguistic levels, from colorless bureaucratic language to pathetic language reminiscent of the enthusiastic romanticism of Gogol' and Marlinskij, and didactic language, which is at times unctuous and hypocritically pious. Dostoevskij is partial to dialogue on all levels of speech, smooth or faltering. His dialogue is individualized, as in Kirillov's language in *The Possessed*.

11. Dostoevskij is drawn to epithets, which range from those that merely intensify ("greatest," "extraordinary"—*črezvyčajnyj*—"strongly," "principally") to original ones, such as "crooked-mouth-German" (*"germano-kosorotyj"*). He is fond of denigrating and contemptuous adjectives ("lazy," "dirty," "ugly," "stinking," "miserable," "malicious"). His neologisms are rare, but those that occur are usually striking (*"vtorostpennost'"* [insignificance], *"nakidčivost',"* *"odnoidejnost',"* *"kumirnij"* [idolatrous], *"rasstanovočno";* and the verbs: *"kaprizit'sja,"* *"na-provorit',"* *"vyzlit'sja,"* *"bezlesit'"* [to destroy forests], *"razženit'sja,"* *"namečtat' ").* Many peculiar expressions, such as *"on menja derz-nul"* instead of *"udaril,"* go back to Dostoevskij's notes on the speech of the common people. His metaphors are infrequent; his symbolic images are more important.

12. Beginning with his early novellas, Dostoevskij develops a system of effective symbols. Among them is St. Petersburg dissolving in the evening fog (an influence of Puškin and of the Natural School) and on a rainy night (*The Faint Heart, The Double,* and so on). Another symbol is satanic nature as an evil insect, such as a louse or a spider, a symbol that goes back to Schiller, as Ralph E. Matlaw indicates. Changes in men, often for the better, are associated with the rare images of nature in Dostoevskij, in particular with the sunset and slanting rays, sometimes simply with a sunbeam, as in the case of Raskol'nikov and Myškin. The anthill is a symbol for collectivization, for communal living that suppresses or neglects individuality; the "Crystal Palace," taken from the London World Exhibition, is a symbol for socialism; a corner (*ugol*), for man's self-isolation; Napoleon, for a really or supposedly strong man, and so on.

There is symbolic meaning in the parallels between types of people, the fates of people, and individual acts; examples are Sonja and Dunja in *Crime and Punishment,* the youth and Lambert in *A Raw Youth,* and Ivan and Smerdjakov in *The Brothers Karamazov.* This parallelism leads occasionally to counterparts, as in the case of *The Double,* Stavrogin and the characters in *The Possessed* who are innerly dependent on him, and Ivan and Smerdjakov in *The Brothers Karamazov;* the motif of doubles may be borrowed from E. T. A. Hoffmann. Individual features of characters may take on symbolic meaning, as the color blue in connection with Katerina in *The Landlady.* This symbolism opened new avenues for literary realism, and later writers consciously or unconsciously followed Dostoevskij.

13. Descriptions of nature play an unimportant part in Dostoevskij and are usually reserved for conveying symbolic meaning (see sec. 12). The appearance of characters is seldom described in detail. By and large, only their psychological qualities are presented. There are a number of problems in Dostoevskij's style that have not been adequately dealt with. An example is the extensive humor in his works, humor that is often cruel in a distinctive way.

14. Dostoevskij has a particular instrumentation (see sec. 5 above) for philosophical motifs. Comments on important subjects are made in dialogue. Since problems are discussed by different kinds of characters, different aspects and solutions are considered. The problem of "higher man" is mentioned by several characters in *The Brothers Karamazov.* Since Dostoevskij associates the higher man with an angelic life, and this type is best represented by Aleša, he is called "angel" and "cherub," seriously and jokingly, by his brothers, his father, Mrs. Xoxlakov, and her daughter Liza. Schiller's theory of types is of great importance in the work of Dostoevskij. Even Fedor Karamazov, who has read little, mentions Schiller, as do all three brothers, the public prosecutor, and the defense attorney. There is a similar treatment of the problem of the higher man, which is differently interpreted (Napoleon) in *Crime and Punishment,* and of the thesis that everyone shares everyone else's guilt. Dostoevskij emphasizes the significance of beauty, especially in *The Brothers Karamazov* ("beauty will save the world"), and the ambivalent, ambiguous nature of beauty (see sec. 5 above).

Thus ideas are shown to be independent of men and disseminated by them, and Dostoevskij's novels exist on two levels. Everything that happens to the characters has a higher meaning. Dostoevskij succeeds in asking eternal questions that affect all men, although he does not necessarily consider his answers final and valid for all men.

In a literary history, one can only enumerate Dostoevskij's questions and answers and wait for another occasion to analyze them. Central problems in Dostoevskij are the dual nature of man (in man's heart, God contends with the devil), and the suppositions of his existence (religious faith, without which every man would sink to the "nadir of existence") and the sources of man's creative power (the seeds of ideas come to us "from other worlds"). Another important problem is beauty, which undoubtedly exists but is ambiguous. Freedom is of greater value but is also problematical and, if misused, can lead to satanic willfulness. The problem of freedom is closely connected with the problem of theodicy. How is it possible that in the world created by God there is unmerited suffering and human cruelty? God faced the choice of creating a world in which there would be no friction and all men would be happy, but in which there would be no freedom, or of giving man freedom as his greatest treasure, but a treasure that man, as a finite, limited creature, could misuse for malicious and selfish purposes. God could only pick the second alternative (this thought of Dostoevskij was taken up by N. A. Berdjaev). A final important problem in Dostoevskij is whether everyone is guilty for everyone else. In no case should the views of Dostoevskij's characters be thought of as the edifying opinions of Dostoevskij (as Berdjaev and V. V. Rozanov do).[5]

I have had space only to mention these questions and answers of Dostoevskij and have had to pass over his most characteristic theoretical work, *Zapiski iz podpol'ja* [Notes from the Underground] (1864), and other important writings. *Notes from the Underground* deals with the problem of freedom reduced to arbitrariness and is an example of Dostoevskij's dialectic, which, like that of Plato, primarily criticizes ideas. *Notes from the Underground* is of particular importance in understanding Dostoevskij's intellectual development. In 1864, he was still far from his relatively harmonious, if not final, view of the world expressed in *The Brothers Karamazov.* Just as the opinions of Dostoevskij's

---

5. Nietzsche made a similar mistake in taking Prince Myškin to be his model for the image of Christ in *The Antichrist* (Ernst Benz; see sec. 7).

characters should not be considered his own, so his works should not be assumed to form a whole and contain a coherent system of thought (as R. Lauth and other German critics have indicated). This warning is especially important, since Dostoevskij is often regarded as a philosopher and prophet, even though his "prophecies" have proven false in many respects. He had the benefit of various philosophical advisers. In Siberia, he came under the influence of Baron Ferdinand Petrovič von Wrangel; in the 1860s, that of N. N. Straxov, whose mark can be seen on *The Brothers Karamazov*; and in his later years, that of young Vladimir Solov'ev, some of whose personality is said to have gone into Aleša Karamazov. It was from these men and not from his own reading that Dostoevskij learned the ideas of Kant.[6]

Dostoevskij contrasted his idealism with realism, but declined to call himself a psychologist. He wished to be a "realist in the higher sense." As we have seen, he shares many features with other Russian realists. It would be interesting to examine his views on literary theory and his literary criticism. He is not a writer or thinker in a single vein.

6. See the recent brochure by Ja. Golosovker, *Dostoevskij i Kant; razmyšlenie čitatelja nad romanom "Brat'ja Karamazovy" i traktatom Kanta "Kritika čistogo razuma,"* Moskva, Izdatel'stvo Akademii nauk, SSSR, 1963.

VII

Leskov

1. Nikolaj Semenovič Leskov was from the South of Great Russia, a region from which many writers have come. His father, the son of a priest, was educated in a seminary. When Nikolaj was born, in 1831, his father was a government official in Orel province. In 1832, the father took a position at the law court in Orel; in 1839, he bought a small estate near Orel.

In 1841, Nikolaj began attending high school in Orel, where he read widely. After the death of his father, in 1848, Leskov was forced to leave high school and start work in a records office. There he met a number of interesting people, among them the Ukrainian ethnographer A. V. Markovič and his wife; she published Russian and Ukrainian novellas under the name of Marko Vovčok (see chapter XI, sec. 9).

In 1849, Leskov moved to Kiev, where he lived with his uncle, a professor of medicine. He met students and professors and supplemented his education through conversation and reading. At the time, he seems to have been interested mainly in philosophy; later, he refers to Kant, Hegel, D. F. Strauss, Feuerbach, and Ludwig Büchner. He learned Polish and Ukrainian and read Polish and Ukrainian literature, to which his own works are related. In Kiev, he worked as an official in the department of military conscription. In 1857, he went to work for Alexander Scott (in Russia, he was called "Škott"), the English husband of his mother's sister. Like Leskov's father, Scott was a steward. Since Scott managed estates in different parts of Russia, Leskov was required to take long trips, just at the time of the liberation of the serfs.

Leskov did not begin to write until 1860, when he was twenty-nine. His first works were essays, which he published, among other places, in medical and technical magazines and newspapers. In 1860, he again took a job as an official but quit after two months and went to St. Petersburg to devote himself to journalism.

In St. Petersburg, Leskov contributed at first to various newspapers and magazines but was soon engaged to work for serious periodicals such as the *Otečestvennye zapiski* and those of the Dostoevskij brothers. He wrote on the national economy in the magazine of I. V. Vernadskij, an economics professor. He also delivered lectures to the Russian Geographic Society, mostly on economics. He met a number of writers and journalists; and V. I. Dal' (see Volume I, chapter IV, sec. 6) and P. I. Mel'nikov-Pečerskij (chapter XI) were important to his development. He also frequented the Moscow circle of Countess E. Salias-de-Tournemir, the publisher of the magazine *Russkaja reč'*.

In 1862, Leskov's promising career received a setback of a kind not unusual in Russia. He acquired the reputation of being a reactionary and all but an agent of the police. As a result, for more than twenty years he had great difficulty in publishing his works. The liberal press turned them down, and they were ignored if they appeared elsewhere. For a time, he wrote under the pseudonym Stebnickij. The source of Leskov's trouble was a misunderstanding. In May 1862, large fires broke out in St. Petersburg. There was a popular rumor that students, or revolutionaries, had set them (one has only to remember the rumors in Russia that doctors spread cholera). Leskov mentioned these rumors in an essay and expressed surprise that the police had done nothing to refute them. Incredibly, his article was interpreted as an accusation of the students; and this slander against Leskov was taken seriously by all the press. No one who had mentioned in conversation that the revolutionaries might have set the fires (among those who thought so were Turgenev, Annenkov, and Kavelin, all of them liberals) took up publicly for Leskov. After this blow to his reputation, Leskov took a trip abroad, during which he acquired a better knowledge of the Slavic world, in the Ukraine, Poland, and Galicia; and he then went on to Paris.

While in Paris, he wrote several sketches on life there and his first important novellas. His experience in the Baltic region and in Pskov enabled him to write a notable account of the Old Believers after his return to Russia. He was forced to rely on second-and third-rate magazines, since he was branded a reactionary. He seemed to confirm his "negative" reputation in his two novels *Nekuda* [No Way Out] (1864), which deals with contemporary young socialists and a St. Petersburg commune, and *Na nožax* [At Daggers Drawn] (1870-71). His forte was the novella, as he seemed to realize.

In the 1870s, Leskov took a second trip abroad and visited Paris, Vienna, Prague, and Warsaw. At about this time, he experienced an ideological crisis and drew close to L. N. Tolstoj. In the 1880s, Leskov became a follower of Tolstoj, although he disagreed with him on some questions.[1] Through Tolstoj, Leskov met the radical art critic V. V. Stasov, the religious philosopher Vladimir Solov'ev and his friends, the painter N. N. Gè (Gay), and others. During Leskov's last years, his work was evaluated more objectively, particularly in a series of articles (later published as a book) by A. L. Volynskij in the *Severnyj vestnik* (1892), the magazine in which the first Russian symbolists were to appear. Leskov spent the last decades of his life in St. Petersburg and died there in 1895.

Late in life, Leskov still did not enjoy great popularity. In 1902 and 1903, his selected works, with almost all his total works, were published in thirty-six slender volumes as a supplement to an illustrated weekly. These selected works served at least to make him better known. He received little recognition; and that which came was often from unexpected sources, such as Gor'kij, who defended even his "reactionary" novels. Since the 1920s, Leskov has been appreciated more, and valuable studies of his work have been written. Abroad, he is one of the most popular Russian writers, along with Gogol', Dostoevskij, and Čexov; and there the editions of his works are more numerous than in Russia.

2. Abroad, Leskov is valued largely as a portrayer of "exotic" Russian subjects and as a supposedly typical Orthodox writer. The first point is correct; more than any other Russian writer, Leskov turns to the remote and curious regions of Russia, often in those novels that may be thought romans à clef. The notion that he is a typical writer of the Orthodox Church is erroneous.

---

1. The caricature of Tolstoj's followers in *Zimnij den'* [A Winter Day] (1895) is hardly an attack on the principles of Tolstoj's teachings.

Not only was he close to Tolstoj, who can hardly be considered an Orthodox thinker, but in his early years as a writer, Leskov sympathized with Protestant ideas and Anglo-Saxon tendencies. Later, German Protestantism, Hussitism, and Russian "Protestant" sects seemed to him as genuinely Christian as did the Orthodox Church. As a young man, he was skeptical of official Church circles; later, he had an aversion to them.

Leskov's remarks on his political views, on life in Russia, on the Slavophiles, and on the Baltic Germans (in his last years he spent his vacations in the Baltic provinces) are ambivalent. His ideology is the most disorderly of any nineteenth-century Russian writer, not because he was indifferent or neutral, but because he represented both sides of an issue with equal passion. This tendency leads to exaggerated conflicts in his works.

Leskov's style is hardly even; but he is perhaps the truest continuator of the tradition of Gogol'; like Gogol', Leskov was opposed to even, uniform literary language and, like Gogol', he was given to playing with the stylistic levels of language.

3. Leskov wrote several novels, of which *No Way Out, At Daggers Drawn*, and *Soborjane* [Cathedral Folk] deserve consideration, the first two not because of their literary value but because of their type. Other "reactionary" novels of the time include those of Viktor Kljušnikov (1841–1892) (not to be confused with Ivan Kljušnikov), those of V. Krestovskij and Aleksej Pisemskij, and Dostoevskij's *The Possessed*.

No Way Out and *At Daggers Drawn* treat different periods in the radical and revolutionary movement. The first deals with the utopian plans of the early 1860s. In the foreground of the novel is a St. Petersburg commune, a society of young socialists under the direction of the poet V. A. Slepcov (see chapter V, sec. 9). The title of the novel and Leskov's tendency to deal in caricatures reveal his bias; and the way of the young socialists proves to be a blind alley. The revolutionaries are not portrayed uniformly well; some of the marginal characters are excellent. The action is less even than in the works of the great Russian novelists. The "little people," who in Leskov's view are morally often the best, are not clearly contrasted in this novel with the supposed heroes.

At Daggers Drawn is better constructed, primarily owing to the plot, which consists of a number of crimes. Leskov portrays men who have overcome their "nihilistic" past and now exploit those who are still blindly dedicated to revolutionary ideals. In addition to naively devout revolutionaries and criminal "pseudonihilists," there are well-rendered "little people" in the effective atmosphere of the small town. Nevertheless, this second antinihilistic novel seems an incohesive mosaic of types and scenes. Even so, an important feature of Leskov's portrayal of types is evident; he presents positive characters well, an ability that neither Turgenev nor Gončarov possesses. Leskov shows positive characters among the sincere revolutionaries as well as among the "little people."

When *At Daggers Drawn* came out, Leskov had almost finished his most important novel, *Soborjane* [Cathedral Folk], which appeared in 1872; chapters of the work had been published in 1867–68. Because of the role of clergymen in the novel, it occupies a special place in nineteenth-century literature. The central characters are the clerics in a cathedral town: the archpriest Savelij Tuberozov, the deacon Axilla Desnicyn, and the priest Zaxarija Benefaktov, who plays a lesser part. The story has to do with happenings in Stargorod, where there are nihilists as well as clergymen, and with Tuberozov's relations with the church authorities in the district capital. Tuberozov is one of Leskov's positive heroes but is in no way exaggerated. Tuberozov's inner life and spiritual searching are revealed through his diary, where his own thoughts are interspersed with thoughts derived from his reading. He is distinguished by spiritual warmth, sincerity, and peaceableness and by a quality that seems to contradict these, a courageous stubbornness in dealing with people. Minor conflicts lead to a dispute with civil officials, who are supported by the church authorities. Only Tuberozov's death saves him from possible disciplinary action. The deacon Axilla is naive and sometimes superficial, large and strong. He is loyal to Tuberozov and is held in check and ennobled by him. These characters are a pair of types in the manner of Don Quixote and Sancho Panza and are, in Leskov's opinion, a symbolic representation of Russian life. Structurally, *Cathedral Folk* is as uneven as Leskov's other novels. The principal character, Tuberozov, is the only real pivot for the many scenes and episodes; the action of the novel is grotesque, serious, and moving. Stylistically, the novel is also uneven; character portrayals alternate with Tuberozov's observations, with conversations, and with pretty descriptions of landscapes, such as the well-known depiction of a storm. Leskov calls attention to the chronicle form of the novel, which accounts for its motley character, and to the absence of a love story.

Leskov published other novels and several long novellas, different in form from his novels. He also attempted to write other "chronicles," including one on the Plodomasov family (there is a woman named Plodomasov in *Cathedral Folk*). Leskov called most of his works novellas (*rasskazy* or *povesti*).

4. Despite the diversity of Leskov's novellas, they fall into three major types: "key" novellas, that is, novellas in which actual persons or places are presented in fictional guise; novellas that portray human passions; and novellas that deal mainly with "good people."

He wrote many key novellas. The real persons and events portrayed are not always generally known, and some can no longer be made out. Many of these novellas are in the form of reminiscences and use the real names of characters. Among these stories are *Meloči arxierejskoj žizni* [Trifles from the Life of a Bishop], *Inženery-bessrebreniki* [Disinterested Engineers], *Kadetskij monastyr'* [Cadet Monastery], and *Pečerskie antiki* [Eccentrics from Pečersk]. (Pečersk is the section of Kiev where the Crypt Monastery is located.) The long novella *Čortovy kukly* [Devil's Dolls] (1890), which Leskov calls a "chapter from an unfinished novel," is set in an obscure country and involves characters with strange names. It is based on an episode in the life of the Russian painter K. P. Brjullov, whose wife is said to have been the mistress of Tsar Nicholas I. In other novellas, real persons appear, but often with fictitious backgrounds and circumstances. In his last years, Leskov treated a number of small, typical episodes in Russian history on the basis of documents that he also published, partly or wholly, often in the *Istoričeskij vestnik*.

5. Leskov deals with passion in his early novella *Ledi Makbet Mcenskogo uezda* [Lady Macbeth of the Mcensk District] (1865). The only feature that the main character, a merchant's wife, has in common with Lady Macbeth is her strong will. She prompts her lover to kill several people, including her husband, whom

she does not love. She and her lover are arrested; but on their way to prison in Siberia, her lover is attracted to another woman. As they are all crossing the Volga, "Lady Macbeth" drowns her rival and herself. Like Axilla Desnicyn in *Cathedral Folk,* the main character in *Očarovannyj strannik* [The Enchanted Wanderer] (1873) is a passionate, but "sincere, good Russian warrior." When the story begins, he is an elderly monk. He knows horses and has been a coachman and rider; he is at a loss to explain the restlessness that has caused him to wander so much. He was taken prisoner by the nomads east of the Volga but escaped and traveled around Russia. He has been a performer at fairs, a children's nurse, a novice in a monastery, and a soldier and officer in the Caucasus. He has often been about to commit acts that would have been considered crimes in the "civilized" world. All his life, Ivan Sever'janovič has been moved by his love for animals, people, and nature, even for forms of life quite foreign to him. He possesses an aesthetic feeling of sympathy. He is still torn between life in a monastery and dying a "death for his people" in a war that looms ahead.

Leskov presents a gallery of people and landscapes, all of them seen through Ivan's eyes. Looking through the eyes of others is a characteristic technique of Leskov. For example, in the early novella *Voitel'nica* [The Amazon] (1867), the experiences of an intelligent young woman are told from the point of view and in the vulgar language of a procuress. It is typical of Leskov to take on various literary and ideological tasks in the same work.

6. The most important group of Leskov's novellas is undoubtedly that about good and just men. For this reason, he is often thought of as a religious writer, especially in Germany. An analysis of these novellas reveals that Leskov is primarily a moralist, though with religious tendencies, and that his religion and morality have been strongly influenced by the views of Tolstoj and by Protestantism. He is fond of writing novels about pious people and clerics and is a specialist on the life of the Russian clergy.

The best-known novella of this group is *Zapečatlennyj angel* [The Sealed Angel] (1873), which treats many aspects of Russian religious life, such as icon-painting and the Old Believers and the senseless persecution they are subjected to: an icon of an angel is taken from them and barbarically sealed up with wax.

The innocent suffering of the Old Believers arouses the sympathies of an Englishman living in Russia. Leskov puts a great deal of color into the work; he studied the Old Believers and icon-painting and wrote several essays on these subjects. The novella *Na kraju sveta* [On The Edge of the World] (1875) shows that Leskov had doubts about the Orthodox Church. A bishop visiting a diocese in winter is caught in a snowstorm and is saved by a "half-savage" Siberian nomad. The emphasis of the story is on this incident and not on the exotic North with its polar night. Missionary work cannot and does not need to be carried on among these primitive "heathen" nomads; although they have not been taught Christian doctrine, they live more morally than Christians do. Later, Leskov portrays the popular preacher Ioann Sergiev (Ivan Kronštadskij) in *Polunoščniki* [At Midnight] (1891). He treats the priest satirically and attempts to show how Tolstoj's teachings or related ideas are taken over by a poorly educated merchant family. These stories are told by an uneducated female narrator and are among the best examples of Leskov's use of grotesque language.

Leskov's adaptation of saints' lives and stories from the old Patericon makes up a special group of novellas and shows how far removed he was from Church tradition (as do his *Notes of an Unknown*, 1884). *Gora* [The Mountain] (1890) is based on Christian legend but could as well have been written by an atheist. The details of the story come from a study of Egyptological literature. In other novellas of this kind, Leskov places so much emphasis on moral questions that the religious aspect of the legend is hardly touched on.

Not all Leskov's novellas about "good people" have to do with devout people and clerics. A number of them deal with righteous men (*pravedniki*), men who attempt to realize their moral ideals in everyday life and, as a result, undergo trying experiences. One of Leskov's first works deals with such a man, nicknamed "Sheep-ox" ("*Ovcebyk*," the Russian name for the musk-ox and the title of the story, 1863). "Sheep-ox" intends to lead a rigorous life in keeping with his high moral principals. He fails and commits suicide. Other stories in this group are more typical and less tragic. *Odnodum* (which means "a man with one thought") [1879] is about a police official in the provinces who takes no bribes, must live on his salary, and therefore cannot afford to live in a style "appropriate to his position." *Pugalo* [The Scarecrow] (1885) is the story of a lonely peasant who takes in the orphaned daughter of an executioner and saves her from distress. *Figura* [The Figure] (1889) tells of how an officer leaves the army rather than ruin a private who, while drunk, has insulted him. *Pavlin* (a man's name) [1874] and *Nesmertel'nyj Golovan* [The Immortal Golovan] (1880) are variations on the same theme, one treated later in L. N. Tolstoj's *The Living Corpse*: the theme of a man who disappears in order to give his wife her "freedom." All these novellas deal with the good "little people" of Russia, with the "righteous," although Leskov grouped only a few of the novellas under this classification. His "positive types" are not saccharine or unctuous, but are vivid human beings, sometimes with great weaknesses. He portrays these people artfully and, in most cases, cannot have imitated foreign or Russian models or even saints' lives; his characters are too different from saints in Church legends.

7. Leskov wrote a number of stories about strange events, real and imaginary, and about Russian customs and habits. Among these are descriptions of blatant despotism on the part of sometimes cruel Russian landowners, as in *Tupejnyj xudožnik* [The Hairdressing Artist] (1885); there are depictions of the boisterous feats of Russian merchants, as in *Čertogon* [Exorcising the Devil] (1879), and of corrupt officials; and there are such improbable cases as *Nekreščenyj pop* [The Unbaptized Priest] (1877). Leskov's many anecdotes, light and profound, can be included in this group.

8. Leskov's only play, *Rastočitel'* [The Spendthrift] (1867), should not be passed over, for it has real theatrical qualities. It has to do with the struggle of a young merchant against an old man who dominates the merchants in his city. The old man has no scruples, is supported by the merchant organization, and easily puts down the young progressive merchant, who is declared a prodigal and committed to an insane asylum. He escapes from the asylum and sets fire to his factory, which is now in the hands of his enemies; his girl friend commits suicide. These melodramatic effects do not weaken the force of the play; but the poor reception given the piece prevented Leskov from doing further work for the theater.

9. Leskov's novellas are constructed similarly. The action is presented in short chapters, each with a complete episode. Some chapters are devoted to brief conversations or encounters; some are only a commentary. Leskov often feels called on to explain unusual characters and plots, sometimes in the newspaper language he uses in his journalistic works.

The peculiarities of Leskov's stories are often suggested in the title, some of which are rare proper names. *"Pavlin"* is a given name; *"Golovan"* and *"Sheep-ox,"* nicknames. The name *"Kotin"* is not only unusual, but is used with the nickname *"Doilec"* ["Milker"]. Titles such as *Čertogon* are also uncommon; others can hardly be translated, such as *Zajačij remiz* (the term for a decisive defeat at cards), a novella first published in 1917.

Leskov aims at surprise. Suspense is often created at the end of a chapter: "And then something unexpected happened"; "The following episodes included something really terrible"; "That was by no means the end of the affair" (after an episode that seemed to be the end of the affair); "We shall see what happens next." Or Leskov writes "What good could come of it?" and "And people asked, 'What happened to him next?'" As he narrates, he asks himself similar questions: "Where did he run?", "What did he plan to do?" These monologues are familiar from "Byronic poems" (volume I, chapter III, secs. 12 and 14) and occur frequently in Leskov's work. The beginnings of his chapters also create suspense: "I waited for the solution"; "Scarcely had he" (done something); "The presentiment was not good"; and, again, questions, such as "How did he run?" This narrative technique calls for a new turn in the action in every chapter and is not unusual. Victor Hugo employs it often, as in *Quatrevingt-treize,* in *Notre Dame de Paris,* and especially in his early works. But the readers of the 1860s and 1870s turned to literature for instruction and a clear point of view, which Turgenev, Dostoevskij, and Tolstoj gave them. They were cool to Leskov's narrative art; his novellas seemed strained and affected. It was not until the twentieth century—and then it happened gradually—that Leskov's devices were found attractive and interesting.

Ideologically, Leskov was not indifferent. He had thoughts that he wished to pass on, but he was almost always as interested in some artistic, compositional, or linguistic task as he was in the idea of the work. His contemporaries did not see the veiled point of his works and did not care for his formalistic "games." There is plenty of evidence of this in the critical remarks of his time and in books that appeared after his death. One of Leskov's most popular novellas, *Levša* [The Left-handed Smith and the Steel Flea] (1881) was criticized for its plays on words and its folk etymologies. Actually, it is a substantial and perhaps profound anecdote and comments satirically and symbolically on Russia's "cultureless culture." But, as noted, all Leskov's works were condemned before they appeared; and this one was no exception.

10. The most important aspect of Leskov's works is language. Like most realistic writers, he is disinclined to use neologisms, especially since he is writing in prose (there are mild neologisms, such as *"birjuzit," "očudačel," "oevropeilsja"*). But he was able to enrich the Russian language as none of his contemporaries did. There are at least three thousand rare words in the 1902 f. or 1956 ff. editions of his selected works. He did not coin all these words, but borrowed freely from many sources. His primary source, like Turgenev's, was the dialect of Orel province. And, like Turgenev, he explains dialectal words in his stories. Before he began to write, Leskov had learned other languages and dialects. He retained them and had such a sure feeling for them that years later, in *Zajačij remiz,* he was able to write entire conversations in almost perfect Ukrainian, a language he had learned in 1849. It is interesting to compare his Ukrainian with Gor'kij's awkward attempt at it, for example, in his *Jarmarka v Goltve.* Leskov also learned Polish and quotes Polish poets, even in his letters. It was in Poland that he heard the Yiddish that he sometimes uses. Later, in Moscow and St. Petersburg, he learned Russian dialects. He uses foreign languages less often but tries to work at least isolated German and French words into his stories (*"ambassada," "mon aman"* in Russian orthography, even *"pomersikat'"*). He emphasizes the poor command of foreign languages of uneducated Russians. There are unintentional Ukrainianisms in Leskov's own language and Ukrainian proverbs and expressions deliberately taken from linguistic literature and put into his works (examples are *"s odnogo boku," "nedovolen na odnogo grafa," "xvoroba,"* and *"sxopilsja so stula,"* in the sense of "got up quickly").

More important is Leskov's use of argot. By and large, he employs the jargon of the little man and the bureaucratic and business jargon remembered from his youth. Church Slavonic, with its many compound words and archaisms, plays an important part in his work. He improved his Church Slavonic through reading and through associating with clergymen.

In his last years, Leskov read saints' lives and theological writings. Here he was helped by his familiarity with the literature of the Old Believers. Late in life, he began to read historical documents and write historical articles; and additional archaisms and historical expressions found their way into his work. He was also interested in medicine and botany, but the many plant names in his works could go back to popular sources. He draws on the language of political radicals and the technical language of economics. Occasionally, he uses words from the argot of rogues and thieves and explains the words.

All this shows[2] that Leskov's language should be characterized not only according to stylistic level (for instance, with the signs $0, +1, +2$ or $-1, -2, -3$ and so on for elevated high style, colloquial words, and vulgarisms) but also according to the origins of words, the particular region or walk of life from which they come.

Besides argot, there are many words in Leskov that he must have heard in conversation. These invididual coinages are mostly corrupted foreign and literary Russian words—corrupted forms had occurred frequently before Leskov, especially in the works of the Natural School. Some of these coinages are products of folk etymology; that is, they have been altered according to their supposed "inner form"; the speaker has incorrectly associated them with familiar words. Leskov collected these words and added others of his own, which were generally humorous. Such words play an important part in two stories already mentioned, *The Left-handed Smith and the Steel Flea* and *At Midnight*. Here Leskov follows the example of Gogol', Vel'tman, and Dal' but goes further and uses many more of these words than do his predecessors. He employs simple corruptions, such as *"plakon"* for *flakon*, *"surop"* for *sirop*, and *"sterlinovaja sveča"* for *stearinovaja*; but

2. As suggested in Dmitrij Čiževskij, *Über die Eigenart der russischen Sprache* (Halle/Saale. Max Niemeyer, 1948).

he is even fonder of folk etymologies with secondary meanings. For *fel'eton,* he writes "*kleveton*" (from *kleveta,* "slander"); for *barometr,* "*buremer*" (from *burja,* "storm," and *merit',* "to measure"); for *mikroskop,* "*melkoskop*" (from *melkij,* "small"). He also changes Russian words: for *poščada,* he uses "*proščada*" (from *proščat',* "to forgive"); for *dvuxmestnyj,* "*dvuxsestnyj*" (through association with *sest',* "to sit down").

Leskov's vocabulary has had little influence on literary Russian. The language of this neglected and maligned writer should be treated primarily as a historical phenomenon. In the early twentieth century, Leskov's stylistics had a considerable influence on Russian modernistic ornamental prose.

VIII
Poetry

1. During the age of realism, poetry was much neglected. A number of talented writers chose not to write at all in verse. I. S. Turgenev used poems to add to characterizations in his novels, ascribing them to various persons portrayed, such as Neždanov in *Virgin Soil*. In magazines, poems were used only as fillers, a custom that has continued to the present. The Dostoevskij brothers published poetry only occasionally in their magazines; in several issues there was none at all. Smerdjakov's observations on the futility of verse, in *The Brothers Karamazov* (part II, book V, chapter II) are a parody on the views of the enlighteners of the 1860s. Russian and foreign classical writers, among them many poets, were still valued; but no one wished to condescend to write verse. Poets were translated, but mainly for the content of their work. Extremists, such as D. I. Pisarev, the popular critic, and V. A. Zajcev, one of the most radical proponents of enlightenment, attacked Puškin and Lermontov.

There were certain areas in which poetry was thought appropriate. For ideological propaganda and satire, it was preferable to allude to certain thoughts in verse; and that accounts for the popularity of the translations of Pierre Jean de Béranger's songs. Parody usually amounted to making fun of poetry in general or of particular poets. Nevertheless, there were a few epigones of poetry and a number of individualists who stood apart from the mainstream of literature. The most popular poets were those who were ideologically "modern," and among them some were quite talented.

2. The first of these poets is Nikolaj Alekseevič Nekrasov (1821–1878).[1] Nekrasov was born in the Ukraine but grew up

1. [Sometimes the date of Nekrasov's death may be seen as December 27, 1877. This is according to reckoning by the Old Style (Julian) calendar used in Russia until 1918. According to the New Style (Gregorian) calendar, he died January 8, 1878.—EDITOR]

in northeastern central Russia, on the Volga. His father was an uneducated, crude, cruel landowner. His mother was apparently Polish; it has also been said that she was from a Ukrainian family living in Poland. Nekrasov is almost the only Russian poet who dedicated poems to his mother, and to mothers in general. After attending high school in Yaroslavl, he went in 1838 to St. Petersburg where he began taking the entrance examination for the university. Since he did not follow his father's wish and join a fashionable regiment, his father withdrew all support from him, and Nekrasov spent several indigent years in the slums of St. Petersburg. Although he had not passed the university examinations, he had published his first poem in 1838 and in 1839 had put out a volume of romantic poems under the title *Mečty i zvuki* [Dreams and Sounds].

In 1840–41, he published a number of theatrical reviews, essays, adaptations of French vaudevilles, and several novellas, some of them long, on the life of the poor in St. Petersburg, works stylistically similar to those of the Natural School. In 1842, Nekrasov met Belinskij and the writers of the Natural School. From 1843 to 1846, Nekrasov published three almanacs of works by the Natural School. For the first of these almanacs, he wrote a feuilleton in the new style, in light verse, on everyday life in St. Petersburg.

From then on, Nekrasov devoted much attention to poetry. In 1847, he went to work on the editorial staff of the *Sovremennik,* the magazine founded in 1836 by Puškin and managed since his death by P. A. Pletnev.[2] In 1848, Pletnev leased the magazine to a professional journalist. Nekrasov was director of the *Sovremennik* until 1866 and, after it was closed by the government, he was publisher of the equally influential *Otečestvennye zapiski* from 1868 to 1877. He was an excellent publisher. In the most difficult years of political reaction, he obtained good literary material and, to some extent, got around the censorship. He also saw to it that his magazines prospered. After the death of Nicholas I, a new collection of seventy-four poems by Nekrasov appeared,

2. Professor Pletnev was a friend of Puškin and took over the magazine to support Puškin's widow and family. Since it was almost impossible, in the last years of Nicholas I, to obtain permission for a new magazine, the radicals were eager to lease existing magazines; and the *Sovremenik* fell into their hands.

in 1856. The 1,400 copies of it sold out in two weeks. Until 1861, he published many poems in the *Sovremennik*. The success of the magazine was due partly to the efforts of the radical critic Dobroljubov and the scholar-journalist Černyševskij. Dobroljubov died in 1861, at twenty-five. Černyševskij (1828–1889) was exiled to Siberia in 1862. After censorship became stricter and the *Sovremennik* was closed in 1866, Nekrasov published in the *Otečestvennye zapiski*, which he put out together with Saltykov-Ščedrin (chapter X). Despite difficulties with censorship, Nekrasov directed both magazines largely in the spirit of radical political populism.[3] He was extremely popular and financially secure. While a publisher, Nekrasov continued to write prose works, some of which portray actual persons (in the character Glažievskij, one recognizes Dostoevskij). But Nekrasov was known as a poet and has been thought of as a poet by succeeding generations. In most editions of his work, his prose is neglected. After a long and difficult illness, he died of cancer early in 1878. His funeral was an impressive tribute, in which many young Russians took part.

　3. There was for a long time disagreement about Nekrasov's work. Among those who sympathized with him politically were moderates and supporters of populism. Some who opposed him politically thought well of his verse, among them Dostoevskij and Grigor'ev. Turgenev praised individual poems of Nekrasov but could find "no poetry" in his verse; and Fet and the able critic A. V. Družinin commented ironically on it. There was also criticism of Nekrasov's work based on political objections.

　In the late nineteenth century, Nekrasov was rediscovered by the symbolists, and his close connections with Puškin and Lermontov were shown. The symbolists stressed the importance of Nekrasov in the history of Russian poetry; and some of them, in particular Andrej Belyj, followed partly in his footsteps.

　4. One of Nekrasov's important contributions to Russian poetry was the expansion of its vocabulary. He used words that had

---

3. Populism was a radical socialist movement that arose in the 1860s and continued until the mid-1880s. Supporters of the movement sought mainly to build a socialist system on the supposed Russian socialistic tradition (*mir*) and addressed themselves to the Russian peasants.

seldom occurred in Russian verse, compound words, superlatives, participles, all of them long and rather prosaic. It is not unusual to find lines in Nekrasov with only one stress. For Example:

и в Великобритании   and in Great Britain

x x x x x x́ x x

Long lines in Nekrasov often lack two stresses. Nekrasov uses other kinds of words "too long" for his line, foreign words and bureaucratic expressions:

дома с оранжереями   houses with conservatories
его превосходительство   his excellency

x x́ x x x x́ x x

Nekrasov renewed the poetic language of his time with everyday colloquial words, prosaisms, and vulgarisms. With these apparently unpoetic words, he created genuinely lyrical moods, as in his long confessional poem *Rycar' na čas* [Hero for an Hour]. Technical expressions from the publishing business and from economics make their way into his poetry, words such as *èkonomíčeskij, melanxolíčeskij, metaforíčeskij, pedagogíčeskij, metodíčeskij,* and *praktíčeskij* (the first four words have six syllables, the last two words, five and four).

Nekrasov enriched his language with diminutives used by the common people: cow, *"koróvuška"*; nightingale, *"solóvuška"*. He uses diminutives of serious words: *"smértuška,"* "death"; *"zabótuška,"* "worry." He makes diminutives of proper names (*"Kalistrátuška," "Varváruška"*); of city argot, which often takes on a pejorative shading (*"delíšečki"* for *dela,* "deals"); and of adjectives and adverbs (lively, *"živëxon'kij"*; sick, *"bol'nëxon'kij,"*; quickly, *"skorëxon'ko"* from *skoro*; quietly, *"tixóxon'ko"* from *tixo*).

Iterative verbs and other verbs, such as *xážival,* "used to go," *ponapíxival,* "stuffed full," and the present gerunds ending in *"-či"* (*umirájuči,* "dying"; *razmyšljájuči,* "thinking") are another group of long, folksy-sounding words in Nekrasov's poetry.

5. These lexical elements often have dactylic endings, which are as important in Nekrasov's reform of rhyme as is his use of the reflexive ending *"-sja"* for the usual *"-s'."*

The kinds of words Nekrasov introduced into poetry or the kinds he emphasized tended to make poetic language more dactylic, as K. I. Čukovskij points out. It would probably be more correct to say that these words lend themselves to ternary meters (in traditional Russian prosody, one distinguishes dactylic, anapestic, and amphibrachic ternary meters). Ternary meters were seldom used before Nekrasov, but they occur frequently in his verse. His practice of beginning a line with the stress on the third syllable (x x x́) has caused scholars to speak of the anapestic character of his poetry. Dactylic rhymes (the line ending x́ x x) and dactylic endings in unrhymed verse had occurred before, but were considered features of folk poetry.

Anapests seem particularly suited to long lines of contemplation. The thoughts of the poet during a walk under an autumn moon are treated in the poem *A Hero for an Hour*:

> Покоришь—о ничтожное племя!
> неизбежной и горькой судьбе,
> захватило вас трудное время
> неготовыми к трудной борьбе . . .

> x x x́ x x x́ x x x́ x
> x x x́ x x x́ x x x́   etc.

Submit, O petty race, to your inevitable and bitter fate; hard times found you unprepared for the struggle. . .

Nekrasov often treats ballad themes in the same meter:

> по торговым селам, по большим городам
> я не даром живал, огородник лихой . . .

> x x x́ x x x́ x x x́ x x x́
> x x x́ x x x́ x x x́ x x x́

I, a skillful gardener, have not spent my time in vain in small market towns and large cities. . .

This example shows that ternary measures permit additional stresses on the "weak" syllables of the line.

Ternary measures sound different when the first syllable is stressed, that is, in one of Nekrasov's frequent dactylic lines:

Поздняя осень. Грачи улетели,
лес обнажился, поля опустели. . . .

x́ x x x́ x x x́ x x x́ x   etc.

It is late autumn. The rooks have flown away, the forest is bare, the
fields are empty.

Binary measures occur often in Nekrasov's satirical poems and
are by no means neglected in his other work.

Nekrasov's contemporaries paid little attention to the new form
of his poems, although they considered his rhymes strange. His
rhymes are conditioned by the forms he introduced. Actually,
these forms were not new, but it took a popular and talented
poet to make them literary. His main new form consisted of variations on satirical couplets, which had been mostly limited to vaudevilles. P. A. Vjazemskij had written poems of this kind, in imitation of Béranger. As Nekrasov was writing, L. A. Mej, M. L.
Mixajlov, and V. S. Kuročkin were making rather good translations of Béranger, whose couplets require vulgarisms and foreign
words and lend themselves to deliberately humorous rhymes. For
example, Nekrasov rhymes *biblióteki* with *živótiki* ("libraries" and
"bellies") and *restorácii* with *grácii* ("restaurants" and "graces").
He was not concerned about exact rhymes, since unstressed vowels
in Russian are considerably reduced and permit approximate
rhymes. A contemporary of Nekrasov, A. K. Tolstoj, advanced
a theoretical defense of approximate rhyme, which was later sanc-
tioned by Blok and by the Futurists, such as Majakovskij. A
number of Nekrasov's rhymes are only orthographically approximate (*tut—trud*; *nemeckij—mesteckoj*). Readers used to traditional poetry found these rhymes as bad as those that were phonet-
ically approximate, such as *žalkimi—palkimi* and *poslednij—
letnij*, and grotesque, such as *Ovidij—subsidij* ("Ovid,"
"subsidies") and *Antip—dagerotip* ("Antip," a peasant name,
"daguerreotype").

As mentioned, the symbolists and their contemporaries were
the first to appreciate the formal aspect of Nekrasov's poetry.
His contemporaries were much more interested in the content
than in the form of his verse.[4]

4. Nekrasov's poetry was distorted by censorship, and because his work fell
into the hands of a publisher who did not care for him, it was published in this
distorted form until the revolution of 1917—the copyright term had not run out.

6. Once the romanticists had broken with the old theory of genres, the realists did not return to these forms. Nekrasov is being ironic when he refers to some of his poems as "modern" ballads and odes. In most cases, these poems are parodies on genres. But one is justified in speaking of Nekrasov's "ballads."

Whether the narrator is the poet himself or a character, Nekrasov's narrative poems have their place in the development of the Russian ballad. Among them is *The Gardener* (1846), in which the main character allows himself to be arrested as a burglar rather than betray the landowner's daughter with whom he is having an affair. In *Vlas* (1854), a ballad that Dostoevskij valued for its poetic beauty, a rich peasant falls ill and realizes the wrongs he has done; he distributes his property among the poor and goes to raise money for a church. *Sekret* [The Secret] (1855), which Nekrasov called a ballad, tells of two brothers quarreling over their inheritance as they stand beside their dead father. Nekrasov also wrote narrative ballads about civil servants.

Another group of Nekrasov's poems at least close to a traditional genre includes his lyrics on personal experiences. These poems are elegies, of a sort, and contain reminiscences from his unhappy childhood, lines on frustrated love, and, in his last years, desperate cries brought on by cancer. Especially typical are his few observations on his duty to his country and people; he regrets that he is unable to stand with the revolutionaries fighting for their ideals (*On the Volga, A Hero for an Hour,* both written in 1860, and *Unynie* [Melancholy], 1874). He himself called some of these poems elegies (1853, 1873–74).

Nekrasov wrote a number of poems that can be called genre portraits. Here, he depicts drunks, dreamers, men dogged by bad luck, a rich courtesan and a poor prostitute (*Ubogaja i narjadnaja* [The Wretched and the Fancy]). Men on their way to exile in Siberia—apparently political prisoners—and men already in exile in Siberia are presented in *Nesčastnye* [The Unfortunate] (1856). One of the prisoners depicted is probably Dostoevskij. *Thoughts before a Splendid Front Door* tells of peasants who have come to the city with no hope of being heeded. Apart from these serious poems, there are humorous and satirical pieces, such as *Gazetnaja* [The Newspaper Reading Room], *O pogode* [On Weather], and *Sovremenniki* [Contemporaries]. In these verse feuilleton pieces,

Nekrasov uses caricature and grotesquery; for instance, a retired censor "censors" newspapers and magazines that have already been published.

In some of these poems, Nekrasov expresses his political, social, and moral views. For example, in a conversation on a train he tries to explain to a boy that it is not the government or engineers but poor, exploited workers who have actually built the railroad (*Železnaja doroga* [The Railroad], 1871).

A special group of Nekrasov's poems treats the Russian peasant. Many of these go back to his visits to his estates in the 1860s and deal with preparations for abolishing serfdom and with abolition, which he thinks has failed. In contrast to his descriptions of poverty and tragedy (a village that has burned, a poor mother who has lost her only son), Nekrasov also wrote idyllic scenes, about peasant children or episodes intelligible to a child (the speeches of "Uncle Jakov," a traveling salesman; a hunter who saves rabbits from a flood; a bear that is thought to be a general, in the ballad *General Toptygin*).

This group of poems is among the finest examples of the use of language in Nekrasov's work; his use of popular speech and poetic folklore is unsurpassed in nineteenth-century Russian literature. His imitations of folk songs make up another group of poems, some of which have become genuine folk songs.

Nekrasov wrote several long "epic" narratives. *Princess Trubeckoj* and *Princess Volkonskij* are about two women who follow their husbands to Siberia after the suppression of the Decembrist Revolt in 1825. *Saša* (named for the woman who is the central character) is an early (1855) novel in verse and bears a certain resemblance to the novels of Turgenev. *Korobejniki* [Traveling Merchants] (1861) is a later verse narrative. The younger of the two main characters leaves his fiancée, and the two men go off to a series of colorful adventures. On their return, they are robbed and murdered. In *Moroz* [Frost] (1863), Nekrasov tells the idyllic recollections of a widow who freezes in the woods while preparing to bury her husband.

Nekrasov worked a long time on his great epic *Komu na Rusi žit' xorošo?* [Who Is Happy in Russia?], which was probably begun in the early 1860s. The opening employs a fairy-tale motif. Several peasants want to find out who is happy in Russia, and they obtain a magic table that enables them to travel through the country. Nekrasov combined various plans with this beginning and sought to portray important types of peasants. The views and ideals of a young man from the country, the son of a psalm reader, were to have been the subject of a continuation of the epic.

Another group of Nekrasov's poems deals with the profession of the poet, a popular theme in Russia since the time of the romanticists. Service to the people, Nekrasov's poetic ideal, and the tragic fate of his muse are themes of these pieces, mostly short, which began to appear in 1850. Related to these poems are poems dedicated to the memory of political journalists, primarily Belinskij, Dobroljubov, Pisarev, and Černyševskij, and of the Ukrainian writer Taras Ševčenko, all of whom Nekrasov considered allies.

This brief survey passes over some important works of Nekrasov; but I have thought it more worthwhile to discuss the main elements of his poetry.

Nekrasov used a variety of sources, but he was an unusually independent writer. His prose and part of his poetry obviously go back through the Natural School to Gogol'. Nevertheless, scholars such as Boris Ėjxenbaum can rightly maintain that Nekrasov developed out of the high style of Puškin and Deržavin. Nekrasov's art goes far beyond the traditions that influenced him. Although the pathos of Deržavin and Puškin was not alien to him, he considered himself a follower of Gogol'. His variety of linguistic devices is perhaps no greater than Gogol's, but it is of a different kind. He uses Gogol's stylistic devices in his verse, as do the later poets Majakovskij and Belyj.

7. Since Nekrasov's finished work has an easy fluency, the effort he expended on his poetry is often overlooked. He was forced to express himself in allusions (for no very satisfactory reason, the art of allusion was referred to in Russia as "Aesopic language"), and he could hardly write about his positive, or socialistic, ideals. Perhaps, like many of his contemporaries, he had only a vague idea of the socialistic future. But he certainly believed in the spiritual and creative powers of the Russian people and thought that, once the people were free, they would make a better life for themselves.

Nekrasov thought that a writer should be primarily a citizen (a *graždanin*). He calls his own muse one of "vengeance and grief"

(*Muza mesti i pečali*); that is, he believes that it is the aim of literature to make the reader aware and strengthen his will to resist. Thinking back to his own early prose, he recognizes already, in 1850, that a peasant woman who has been publicly whipped is a sister of his muse. This muse is a "sad companion of the sad, poor people" "who are born for work, torment, and chains" and who have led the poet through "the dark abysses of violence and evil, of work and hunger." Nekrasov thinks that he can reform the "passions and errors of the masses" (*tolpa*), since the poet

> питая ненавистью грудь,
> уста вооружив сатирой,
> проходит он тернистый путь
> с своей карающею лирой

goes along his path of thorns punishing with his lyre, nurturing his breast with hate; his mouth is armed with satire.

But the poet recognizes that a word of rejection can be a word of love, that "the heart that has grown tired of hating can no longer love." The double motif of love and hate runs through Nekrasov's poetry; he sees his verse as evidence of his sympathy:

> стихи мои—свидетели живые
> за мир пролитых слез

My verses are living witnesses of the tears shed for the world

and thinks of them as a song of sorrow rather than of revenge:

> Мой стих уныл, как ропот на несчастье,
> как плеск волный в осеннее ненастье
> на северном пустынном берегу. (1874)

My verse is as sad as the murmur against misfortune, as the splashing of the waves in an autumn storm on a lonely northern shore.

In 1874 and in the last years of Nekrasov's life, prospects for the future appeared in a different light from that of the belligerent 1850s and 1860s. Sadness played an important part in his verse. The words *ugrjumyj, unylyj,* and *surovyj* are increasingly typical of his late poetry, as K. I. Čukovskij indicates. Evidently, malice (*zloba*; cf. also "angry," *ozloblennyj* and the like) prevails in part of the world, if only in the form of *pošlot'* (a difficult word to translate; it signifies a dull-witted, unconscious baseness. Gogol' also spoke of *pošlost'*, but the new sense that Nekrasov attributed to it is the one that has come down to us). Nekrasov portrays a gallery of characters who are evil incarnate. These exploiters range from serf-owners, who have not yet died out, to modern business men, some of whom are from the lower classes. Opposed to these exploiters are men with patience (*terpenie*) enough to break down any resistance, a patience that Nekrasov sometimes calls *tupoe,* "dull-witted." In individual relationships, such as marriage, Nekrasov often explores this same contrast, between a frequently unconscious malice and loving, forgiving patience.

Nekrasov does not lose sight of moral purity and beauty in this dark world. He finds these qualities in women and children and in all those opposed to evil, though he can often only allude to the struggle. In *Who Is Happy in Russia?*, his portraits of positive types such as peasants, a peasant's wife, and an educated young man from the country, are unfinished (see sec. 6 above).

9. Nekrasov's portraiture is realistic; that is, it is almost always concrete, although his recurrent types (the heartless official, the censor, the policeman, and, on the other side, the peasant and worker, who have no rights, the prisoner, the peasant's wife, and the child exposed to injustice) sometimes acquire a symbolic meaning and universality. The *people* is Nekrasov's holy of holies. Popular speech and folklore enable him to vary traditional poetic forms in many ways (by adding naive, playful, puzzling, or serious stories, edification, sermons, laments, dances) and to include vulgarisms in his chansons when he is dealing with the urban poor.

Nekrasov makes less use of metaphor than do the romanticists. He prefers similes to metaphors and often introduces his similes by popular turns of speech, such as *"slovno, čto."* His similes are generally concrete and have no sentimental coloring, as S. V. Šuvalov indicates.

Among the typical motifs in Nekrasov's work is the lament for the Russian peasants, for example, for those who come to the capital to seek justice but are sent away from a high official without being heard.

и застонут . . . Родная земля!
Назови мне такую обитель,
я такого угла не видал,
где бы сеятель твой и хранитель,
где бы русский мужик не стонал?
стонет он по полям, по дорогам,
стонет он по тюрьмам по острогам,
в рудниках на железной цепи.   (1858)

And they will groan. . . . O homeland! Name me a place—I've never seen it—where your sower and protector, the Russian peasant, has not groaned. He groans in the fields, on the roads, in the prisons, and in iron chains in the mines.

Nekrasov's contemporaries and political allies thought that he was not by and large ready to take up the people's struggle for their rights:

Покоришь—о ничтожное племя!
неизбежной и горькой судьбе,
захватило вас трудное время
неготовыми к трудной борьбе.
Вы еще не в могиле, вы живы,
но для дела вы мертвы давно,
суждены вам благие порывы,
но свершить ничего не дано.

Submit, O petty race, to your inevitable and bitter fate; hard times found you unprepared for the struggle. You are alive; but for this cause you have long been dead. You were given noble instincts but were destined to accomplish nothing.

Nekrasov finds words of sympathy for the common people, especially for women and children. In his last, unfinished epic he introduces a young man with a song of hope:

Ты и убогая,
ты и обильная,
ты и могучая,
ты и бессильная,

Матушка-Русь! . . .
Сила народная,
сила могучая,
совесть спокойная,
правда живучая. . . .
Рать подымается—
неисчислимая,
сила в ней скажется
несокрушимая.

You are poor and rich, powerful and weak, Little-Mother Russia! . . .
The strength of the people, the powerful strength, the easy conscience,
the enduring justice. . . A vast army will arise, its force will be inde-
structible.

Many of Nekrasov's pungent turns of speech have become
popular sayings in Russian.

10. None of Nekrasov's contemporaries defended the same views
in similar verse. Oddly enough, they generally adhered to the
older poetic tradition.

The most important of his contemporaries was Nikolaj
Platonovič Ogarev (1813–1877), who is remembered almost exclusively as a political ally of Herzen. Ogarev was from a family
of wealthy landowners. He grew up in the country and went to
Moscow University. Herzen was a fellow student, and the two
of them became lifelong friends. Like Herzen, Ogarev was arrested
in 1834 and exiled to the provinces. In 1839, he was permitted
to return to Moscow, and he began publishing his poems, which
were well received. From 1842 to 1844, Ogarev traveled abroad
and wrote a number of poems, including a group on Italy. After
a sad life in Russia, he emigrated in 1856 and collaborated with
Herzen in putting out the revolutionary newspaper *Kolokol* [The
Bell]. He continued to write after Herzen's death and published,
among other things, his poetry, both old and new. Many of his
poems, some of them impressive, were not published until the
1880s and later.

The dominant mood in Ogarev's poetry is melancholy, which
is evident even in his "belligerent" poems, for he could not overlook
the failure of the revolutionary movement since 1848. In most

of his lyric poems, he proceeds from reminiscences (*vospominanija*). Of the approximately three hundred poems in the latest editions of his works, about one fourth are devoted to reminiscences; and remembrance plays a part in many of his other poems. As early as 1839, at twenty-six, Ogarev believed that he was "living in memories." Memory "carries the soul away with it," "torments" the poet, or "shows him the way." He writes of the "sacred distance (or 'sacred calm') of memories" and uses a number of circumlocutions for "memory" and "memories": "images of bygone days," "distant place of bygone days." He hears "sounds chosen from his past life," "shadows of the past appear before him," and so on.

While still young, Ogarev already lived in a world of memories of childhood. At twenty-eight, he thought of himself as old; several times he says that he is dead. In his later poems, the word *memory* appears less often; but he says that one must live only in the "vernal freshness of memories." He frequently writes about the dead; he often depicts scenes of leave-taking and funerals and dwells on the time that will transform everything. Sometimes his memories are joined with dreams (*mečty, grezy*) of the future. Since he often writes without regard for censorship, he portrays his dreams openly; and his poems contain, more so than do those of other poets, prophetic visions of a future revolution and of the destruction of Russia. Typically, Ogarev's few pretty descriptions of the Russian countryside were written abroad and are presented as memories. His love poems are filled with reminiscences.

The dominant mood in Ogarev's early poetry is the same disappointment that is found in the romanticists, a mood to which he gives the old-fashioned-sounding name *razuverenie*.

Besides melancholy, Ogarev treats night and autumn in his lyrics, and writes about an abandoned house, a wanderer, a night watchman. Unattractive portraits of provincials he has known are themes of his lyrics, as are reminiscences of friends with whom he has lost touch (only Herzen was a lifelong friend) and memories of his first love. A series of Ogarev's poems on his unhappy love has only recently been made known; written in 1841, most of these poems did not come out until 1888 and from 1953 to 1956. His few narrative poems on peasants cannot be compared with Nekrasov's. His poems are formally excellent and show great sincerity, but they lack strength and individuality of expression. Perhaps critics are correct in speaking of Ogarev's "pale melancholy."

11. It is different with Ogarev's long epic narratives, some of which have only recently been published. A large, original fragment is his confessional lyric poem *Jumor* [Humor], begun in 1840–1841 and published abroad in 1857. Twenty-seven years later, Ogarev wrote another fragment, intended to be a continuation of this poem, and it appeared partly in 1869, partly in 1953. These two fragments are among the best examples of octaves in Russian; only a few stanzas are constructed differently. As in the work of Puškin, of the Polish poet Juliusz Słowacki, and of Byron, octaves lend themselves in Ogarev to a free play of thought. His observations on his own time, with their many allusions to persons and events, his reflections on himself, his life, and his friends, the scenes he draws of St. Petersburg and Moscow, and his hope for a better future make his poetic confession one of the most impressive written by a man of the 1840s, a man who has taken leave of the idealistic philosophy of this "remarkable decade." In the second part, Ogarev tells of his visit to Poland, which came under harsh rule after the uprising of 1831 and for which he felt great sympathy. In the third part, Ogarev is an emigrant and has broken off with friends who have "betrayed" their revolutionary ideals. He expresses hope for a better future and asks who will be the hero of the future. In this work, Ogarev writes in clearer, stronger language than that used in his lyrics.

Ogarev's verse narratives are interesting. *Derevnja* [In the Country], written in 1847, published later, is reminiscent of some of Turgenev's early verse and prose tales. The central character is a wealthy landowner, "the master of his freedom," educated and well-traveled. He returns from abroad to live on his estate and becomes mired in a drab life devoid of intellectual interest. Ogarev thinks that that is the typical fate of a Russian and curses "this country":

Да будет проклят этот край. . . .
Уйду, чтоб каждое мгновение
в чужой стране я мог казнить
мою страну, где больно жить,
все высказав, что душу гложет,
всю ненависть или любовь быть может.

Cursed be this land. I shall go away so that, abroad, I shall be able
every moment to punish my country, where living is so wretched. I shall
tell everything that is gnawing at my soul—all the hate, and, perhaps,
all the love.

These contradictory feelings of hate and love for Russia
dominate Ogarev's political poetry.

Gospodin [The Gentleman] (published in 1857), another novella
in verse, depicts a young man's spiritual decline. The autobiographical novella in verse *Matvej Rataev,* begun in 1856, published
in 1886, leaves the fate of the central character unresolved—he
too has moved to the country after living in St. Petersburg and
Moscow.

Two of Ogarev's best works written abroad are *The Trip,* notable
for its colorful scenes of Russia, and *The Tale of a Police Officer*
(1859), about two convicts similar to Dostoevskij's convicts in
Memoirs from the House of the Dead. Long verse narratives, such
as *Jumor,* seem to bring out Ogarev's power of expression better
than do his lyrics.

Most of his short prose narratives remained unfinished. He
did not carry out his plans to write his memoirs.

12. Little needs to be said of the other radical poets. They were
formally quite traditional and, in their subject matter, went no
further than Nekrasov. Only a few of their poems were widely
circulated.

Mixail Larionovič Mixajlov (1829–1865) wrote political poems
and verse in the elegiac style of the late romanticists. He was
an important translator of Goethe, Schiller, Heine, and Béranger,
and he wrote novels, novellas, and a play. In 1861, he was arrested
and sent to Siberia for six years. There he continued to write
poetry, but he was not equal to the hard life and died in 1865.

Like L. A. Mej (see chapter IX, sec. 5), Mixajlov was concerned
with translating Béranger exactly; but Vasilij Stapanovič

Kuročkin (1831–1875) wrote free renderings of the French poet and won greater popularity. Kuročkin was one of the most successful satirical writers for the popular magazine *Iskra* [The Spark].

The critic, journalist, and collaborator of Nekrasov, Nikolaj Aleksandrovič Dobroljubov (1836–1861) was a gifted poet. It is typical of his time that he devoted his talent mainly to parodies, which appeared in the *Iskra*.

Aleksej Nikolaevič Pleščeev (1825-1893) was a political radical and, like Dostoevskij, a member of the Petraševskij circle. In 1846, he published a volume of poems that his contemporaries took to be expressions of protest. He was arrested at the same time as Dostoevskij and forced to serve in a regiment stationed first on the Asiatic border and later in Asia. When he was allowed to go back to European Russia six years later, Pleščeev turned again to literature. He was highly regarded as a translator of Heine and of Slavic and English writers. His own poems, with their occasional echoes of Nekrasov, were better known than were those of Ogarev, since they were published in Russia.

Of poets "of the people," the peasant Ivan Zaxarovič Surikov (1841–1880) enjoyed a certain popularity with his vague populism. But he was outside the mainstream of literature. Of interest are his attempts to imitate folk songs and the poetic manner of Aleksej Kol'cov.

IX

Poetry (Continued)

1. Russian poets who avoided political issues were not very popular. Sociopolitical literary critics called them adherents of "l'art pour l'art," although few of them were indifferent to current issues, and then only in their poetry. They were accused of writing "pure art" merely because they did not share the views of the sociopolitical radicals or because they had remained "idealists" or had retained their religion.

Formally, these poets were epigones of the romanticists. All poets of this period were, to some extent, with the possible exception of Nekrasov; and, interestingly, even poets close to his views could not follow his poetic and linguistic innovations or, more likely, did not notice them. The only influence Nekrasov seems to have had was, through his couplets, on satirical writers in the *Iskra*. In Russian versions, Béranger lost the popular quality of his songs. Russian translations of Heine were almost orthodoxly romantic, and his antiromantic barbs were lost. For that matter, Russian translations of Heine were generally weak.

2. The leading poet of "l'art pour l'art" was, of course, Afanasij Afanas'evič Fet-Šenšin (1820–1892). He was the son of a German woman, Karoline Foeth, whom a Russian landowner, A. Šenšin, had taken away from her husband in Hesse and brought back to Russia, and he did not know whether Šenšin or Foeth was his father. Fet attended a Baltic German school and Moscow University, where he was close to Apollon Grigor'ev and his friends. In 1840, he published a small volume of verse and began contributing to literary magazines of various leanings. For a time, he was an officer in a regiment in Kremenchug, in the Ukraine. When he married, he settled, in 1857, on his estate in Orel province and was a friend of L. N. Tolstoj and Turgenev. He also saw Tjutčev; and Tolstoj, Turgenev, and Tjutčev thought highly of

his work. His conservative essays incurred the wrath of liberals and radicals. His tales and his translations of Goethe's *Faust* and poems, Heine, Hafiz (from the German translation), and the Roman poets, are forgotten and are not part of his important work. Fet was an admirer of Schopenhauer and translated his principal work. He also left lengthy memoirs.

3. Fet's poetry reveals that, although he is akin to the Russian romanticists in spirit, he does not share their views on poetry and the profession of the poet. He does not think of himself or of any other lyric poet as a prophet, teacher, or leader. In this respect, Fet is truly a "pure" lyric poet. His lyrics touch only occasionally on his view of the world, and they tell almost nothing about his life, as Ja. P. Polonskij pointed out. By contrast, Tjutčev wrote many poems on his intimate life; but, in these poems, subjective experience takes the form of thoughts and concepts and tells much about his life and views.

Fet's typical poems describe an instant when he senses eternity in a personal way. These moments have to do with experiences of love and nature and signify a separation from time and a release from earthly life. In one poem, Fet says that the poet must melt the transient being of a moment and recast it in the gold of eternity.[1]

> этот листок, что иссох и свалился,
> золотом вечным горит в песнопение.

This leaf, withered and fallen, burns eternally gold in song.

Fet did not notice that hardly any other poets were still writing about withered, dying leaves.

Fet thinks that this elevation of the momentary into the eternal is possible, since all life that the poet celebrates lies on the boundary between two worlds. "Nature senses, as it were, this double life" and is "fanned" by the breath of the two worlds, one temporal and one eternal. Poetry is created in the instant when the poet

---

1. It is almost impossible to translate Fet's poetry, even into prose. Most of the translations here attempt to render the sense, which is often obscured by his personal vocabulary and constructions, and not the literal meaning of his poems. *Feci, quod potui.*

"shoves off" the "living skiff" of his life from the "shore" of the temporal world. He should

> Одной волной подняться в жизнь иную
> учуять ветр с цветущих берегов.
> Тоскливый сон прервать единым звуком,
> упиться вдруг неведомым, родным . . .
> чужое вмиг почувствовать своим,
> шепнуть о том, пред чем язык немеет.

Raise himself on a wave to another life, feel the wind from the flowering shore, interrupt with a single sound the melancholy dream [of life—D.Č], suddenly drink his fill of something unknown but familiar . . . feel at once that something belonging to another belongs to him, whisper of something about which the tongue cannot speak

and

> на волне ликующего звука
> умчаться вдаль, во мраке потонуть

On the wave of a triumphant sound, rush into the distance and sink in darkness.

One cannot speak precisely of this full moment that reveals a glimpse of eternity and effaces the rest of life. Consequently, Fet attempts to describe the feeling with unusual words, images, and metaphors, which sometimes sound clumsy. No other Russian poet speaks so often as does Fet of the impotence of language: "I can find no words for the song of the heart"; "man's words are so coarse that one is ashamed even to whisper them"; "words are ineffectual" (bessil'ny),

> Как беден наш язык: хочу и не могу . . .
> не передать того ни другу ни врагу,
> что буйствует в груди прозрачною волною.

How poor our language is: I want to but cannot tell friend or enemy what is raging in my breast like a transparent wave.

> О если б без слова
> сказаться душой было можно!

O, if one could only speak through the soul without words!

Neither the world nor men answer the poet:

> —никто не отвечает! . . .
> воскреснут звуки и замрут опять.

No one answers. . . . Sounds rise only to die out again.

The following lines should give an idea of Fet's many love poems:

> у ног твоих раскину я узорныії
>   живой ковер.
> Окрылены неведомым стремлением
>   над всем земным,
> в каком огне, с каким самозабвением
>   мы полетим!
> И, просияв в лазури сновидения,
>   предстанешь ты
> царить навек в дыхание песнопения
>   и красоты.

I shall spread at your feet a living patterned carpet. In what fire, with what oblivion of ourselves, shall we fly, borne by an unknown yearning, over everything earthly. You will appear radiant in the azure of a dream and will rule forever in the breath of song and beauty.

But happiness of the moment may be deceptive.

> Что это—жизнь или сон?
> счастлив ли я или только обманут?

What is this—life or a dream? Am I happy or merely deceived?

Fet's love poems, which he was still writing a year before his death, are by no means autobiographical pieces but, rather, lyric dreams addressed to an unknown, or eternal, lover (the girl who may have been his "eternal lover" died tragically in the 1850s).[2]

Fet's unusual images require unusual words, some of which

---

2. Literary criticism has nothing to do with the biography of a writer! It seems appropriate here to mention again that a writer's works are not identical with his biography.

are obscure or at least misleading. His favorite time is night.
In the night, he hears (or sees, or hears *and* sees—his poems
are full of synesthesia) the prayers of the stars and moon. Words
such as "prayer," "holy relic" (*svjatynja*), and "Godhead"
(*Noc'—put' do božestva*, "night is the way to the Godhead") are
not to be understood in a concrete religious sense. "Prayer" refers
rather to participation in genuine, eternal being, and "holiness"
and "Godhead" describe this being. In Fet's sense, the word
"freedom" (*svoboda*), so popular at the time, does not refer to
political freedom. He says that his contemporaries have never
understood "this proud word" "in their hearts." By freedom, Fet
means escape from the "greedy fortuitousness" of worldly being
into the "fresh darkness" (*svežejuščaja mgla*) of a moment sepa-
rable from time and chance. He uses the "proud" word "happiness"
the same way—differently from everyone else. He expects to find
happiness but does not know what it is. He says, "What kind
of (happiness)? I don't really know." He experiences moments
of happiness, in a dream, when a bell rings and "everything is
clear." There is happiness in this ringing. When he is awake
at night, he hears the "mysterious choir of the stars" and

> светлый ангел шепчет мне
> неизъяснимые глаголы

A bright angel whispers to me inexplicable words.

In Fet's view, poetry is the awakening of the soul at these
supernatural sounds; the soul "vibrates as resonantly as the string
of an instrument." Not words but the sounds of the soul are the
essence of poetry (as in Puškin). Or the sounds of une soul are
a "word of elemental life" (*stixijnyj*, "elemental"; see this word
and *stixija* in the discussion of Tjutčev in Volume I of this work).
The poet hears the word, and "the supernatural life (in the night)
carries on a conversation with the soul"; this conversation is the
"breath of its eternal current," an experience also subject to doubt:

> Заря, и счастье, и обман—
> как сладки вы душе моей! . . .
> Как к этим призракам прильнуть
> хочу мгновенною душой!

The glow of dawn, happiness, and deception—how sweet you are in my soul. . . . How I should like to nestle to these phantoms with my momentary soul.

As a poet, Fet could best be classified as a visionary (a name also applicable to Tjutčev).

4. Fet was very early a Platonist, in that vague, somewhat misleading sense that many romantic poets were. Later, he read Schopenhauer and found a number of images for his metaphysical visions. He saw that he might hit on words for the most subtle nuances of his vision and that these words could lead to the eternal. He had formerly liked to speak of the "mystery" ("*tajna*") of earthly existence, life, and eternity but had done so in "enigmatic words," since he was, in the 1840s, one of the first Russian masters of "dark" poetry. In the 1860s, he wrote an almost intelligible poem (with a motto from Schopenhauer) in which he speaks of being able to "see directly from time to eternity" at the "call of the beaming gold eyelashes of the stars":

> и пламя твое узнаю, солнце мира . . .
> И все, что мчится по безднам эфира,
> и каждый луч, плотской и безплотный—
> твой только отблеск, о солнце мира,
> и только сон, только сон мимолетный.

And I recognize your flame, sun of the world . . . And everything that rushes about the abysses of the ether, and every corporeal and incorporeal beam of light is only your reflection, O sun of the world, and is only a dream, only a fleeting dream.

He uses other images for this brief participation of man, this "earthen vessel," in the world of eternity. A swallow in flight touches a pond with its wing—is this act not a symbol of man's striving:

> не так ли я . . .
> дерзаю на запретный путь
> стихии чуждой запредельной
> стремясь хоть каплю зачерпнуть?

And do I not also venture onto the forbidden path as I strive to capture a drop of the distant, transcendent element?

Following Schopenhauer, Fet speaks of "unknown powers" or "secret forces" in love; and in a dialogue in his prose tale *Kaktus*, he presents Schopenhauer's concept of love. The image of the flight of the poet or lover, on the wings of enthusiasm, is another example of vague Platonism. Even late in life, Fet preferred to intimate his meaning.

Fet also wrote several balladlike narrative poems. In his unusual miniature poems on nature, he speaks clearly enough but only suggests his meaning. His description of the Russian countryside is well known:

> Чудная картина
> 	как ты мне родна:
> белая равнина,
> 	полная Луна,
> свет небес высоких,
> 	и блестящий снег,
> и саней далеких
> 	одинокий бег.

Lovely scene, how familiar you are: white plain, full moon, light of the high heavens and glistening snow, and the lonesome journey of the distant sleigh.

In his poetic tales, Fet writes more clearly and tells somewhat ironically of his college days.

Fet sought and achieved ultimate obscurity in his verse. Although he has much to say, his poems are almost always short, from eight to sixteen lines, and concise. He is a master of the impressionistic style. Sometimes he intensifies this style and writes sentences with no verb, sentences that convey a mood, but no image. He takes great care with the form of his poems: in some, there is anaphora in every line; some poems consist of a single sentence; others contain apparently pointless repetitions of sonorous words, such as "rhododendron, rhododendron." All that repelled his contemporaries, though they did not yet know the word *formalism* with which to condemn his poetry. Fet's use of synesthesia ("fragrant rhymes," "I hear trembling hands") and oxymoron and his occasionally bizarre turns of phrase, not always effective and at times purely rhetorical, were received with a smile by Fet's friends. Turgenev wrote sharp but good-natured parodies on his verse; and Fet's poetry was a welcome target for realistic parodists. He was not really recognized until he was discovered by the symbolists, in particular by Aleksandr Blok. Even the symbolists had little use for Fet's translations, as of *Faust* and the Roman elegists, because here his language is too often his own and not that of the poets translated. In his imitations of Heine and the Persian poet Hafiz (from the German translation of G. F. Daumer), Fet's concision prevents him from achieving the grace of the originals.

His own brief impressionistic poems are among the greatest lyrics in Russian.

5. In some respects, Lev Aleksandrovič Mej (1822–1862) was also an innovator. At eighteen, he published several poems and then vacillated for the rest of his life between the civil service, which he disliked, and journalism. He was a typical Bohemian, and, despite the help of his practical wife, was pursued by financial difficulties.

Mej's poetry is remarkably versatile. He knew a number of languages; and his literary remains contain translations of Slavic literary poetry, Slavic and Greek folk songs, and Ancient Greek, German, and French poets. He was particularly interested in Heine and Béranger. Unfortunately, his translations are not always correct, though he strove for accuracy. His original poems are more important, but contemporaries hardly noticed their individuality.

An important group of Mej's poems is his imitations and transcriptions of folk poetry. In unrhymed meters based on the byliny,[3] he dealt with several historical themes, the biography of Prince Aleksandr Nevskij in the Chronicles; the Old Russian tale of the destruction of Ryazan, with the principal hero, Evpatij Kolovrat; the tale of a magician in Novgorod, from Nestor's Chronicle of 1071; and a tragic fifteenth-century love story, also taken from the Chronicles. The model for these long poems was a bylina transcribed by Mej on the defeat of Old Russian warriors

---

3. *Byliny,* popularly *stariny,* are epic songs, which are still performed and are set in an indefinite time in the past, actually in the period before the Tartar conquest in the thirteenth century.

(*bogatyri*). His imitations of songs consist of ballads based on folklore (among them a long poem, *Oboroten'* [The Werewolf], 1858, which anticipates Nekrasov's vocabulary and style) and purely lyric songs. Besides the able use of popular language and Old Russian lexicon, these poems are distinguished by unusual metaphors and similes such as those Esenin later employed. These comparisons seem to have been taken from the peasants' world of fancy. For example:

Slezy devič'i—rosa ("a maiden's tears are the dew").

Mečetsja i plačet, kak ditja bol'noe . . . ozero lesnoe ("a lake in a forest ripples restlessly and cries like a sick child").

Veter . . . serym volkom ryščet ("the wind darts like a gray wolf").

Veter s list'ev vodu venikom smetaet ("the wind sweeps the water from the leaves with a broom").

Noč' okoško davno zanavesila ("the night had long since curtained the window").

Zor'ka . . . bez alogo povojnička ("the dawn without its crimson scarf").

[The bright night] *s mesjaca slovno rubaxu snjala* ("seemed to take the shirt off the moon").

In Mej's other poetry, such metaphors are less frequent.

Besides lyric poems, including the sort of album verse Puškin had made fun of, Mej wrote imitations of oriental poetry, descriptions of nature, songs and ballads, and many poems on classical themes, among them short anthological poems and poetic games, such as acrostics. He wrote in a variety of forms—for instance, in hexameters, octaves, and sestinas. A ballad on a folkloric subject (*Vixor'* [The Whirlwind]) is in anapests. His rhymes rely partly on Biblical, classical, and place names and are often unusual and bold. Scenes from everyday life are juxtaposed with memories. In form, most of Mej's poems go back to the romantic tradition. But his verse contains new elements, such as deliberate vagueness and boldness of expression and an expanded vocabulary. Archaisms still occur, but along with colloquialisms and vulgarisms. There are often conspicuous neologisms (compound words, such as *mnogočlennaja sem'ja gorodov*, "many-membered family of cities"; *trudnotesnyj put'*, "difficult and narrow way"; *gromozvučnyj*, "loud-sounding"; unusual neologisms, such as *bespredmetnaja tišina*, "aimless quiet"; *vozroždency*, "the resurrected ones";

verbs such as *okorallit'*, "to make level with the coral"; *oblistit'sja*, "to cover oneself with leaves"; *okornit'sja*, "to take root").

Mej's poetry does not give a clear idea of his view of the world. Like the romanticists, he assumed that there were two worlds, *here* and *there*, almost as in the work of Žukovskij. Mej believed in personal immortality and thought that nature was alive and in it was

вечныії строії любви и красоты

The eternal system of love and beauty.

Mej seems to have loved the Russian people, but his love may have been an aesthetic matter, and his knowledge of the common people may have been based on his study of folklore. He justifies himself as a poet through the intuitions of his spirit.

глядишь—и не видишь ты мир—но высоко
тогда созерцает духовное око. (1840)

You look—and do not see the world; but your spiritual eye ascends the heights.

He believes that all sins will be forgiven him:

за песни красоте свободного певца

For the free singer's songs to beauty.

In all his various themes and forms, Mej took pains to express himself well. He portrayed the ancient and Biblical world with the same care as he did Russia and the Russians. It is only his scenes of Russia that have kept him from being classified as a poet of art for art's sake. It was said, however, that his knowledge of conditions in Russia was based only on folklore. (See also chapter X, sec. 12.)

6. Count Aleksej Konstantinovič Tolstoj (1817–1875) was included quite unjustly among writers of "pure art," since he had clearly defined religious views and was politically a liberal, and these attitudes are plain in his poetry. He condemned Russian absolutism as it had existed in the past, particularly in the sixteenth century. But he referred to himself as "*dvux stanov ne*

boec, a tol'ko gost' slučajnyj" ["not a combatant, but merely a chance guest in two camps"] and called on those who shared his opinions to "swim against the current" (*"protiv tečenija"*). Tolstoj was not in the literary mainstream of his time. From an impoverished branch of the Tolstoj family, he was reared in the house of an uncle, the romantic writer Antonij Pogorel'skij[4] (see Volume I of this work, chapter IV, sec. 15), in the Ukraine. As a child, Aleksej accompanied his uncle on trips abroad and once met Goethe. Later, he lived at the court in St. Petersburg and was close to the crown prince, the future Tsar Aleksandr II. He led such an active social life that he had little time for literature. Nevertheless, in 1840 he published three fantastic romantic novellas, two of them in French. Two of the novellas are about vampires. Several of his poems also appeared at this time. His literary relationships with Puškin, Žukovskij, and others were superficial, but he got to know Gogol' well on an official trip to Kaluga in 1850. In 1851, along with the Žemčužnikov brothers, Aleksej, Vladimir, and Aleksandr, he produced a comedy that would today be considered theater of the absurd. Together with the Žemčužnikovs, he wrote a number of parodies that were published under the pseudonym "Koz'ma Prutkov" and are still popular. Tolstoj's relations with his later wife, who was at the time still married to a colonel, forced him to relinquish his ties with the court. He began to publish poetry, first in Nekrasov's magazine, later in that of the Slavophile Ivan Aksakov. But Tolstoj did not really agree with the Slavophiles. In 1859, he left his position and afterward lived mainly on his estate in the Ukraine and abroad. He was never active in literary circles. Besides poetry, he wrote a historical novel, *Prince Serebrjanyj,* in the 1860s, and several plays (see chapter X, sec. 13). After an extended illness, during which he lived mostly abroad, Aleksej Tolstoj died on his estate in 1875.

During his lifetime, Tolstoj was not admired by any group. He had attacked the radicals and enlighteners and was distinguished from the Slavophiles by his approval of Western Europe and the Europeanization of Russia under Peter I. Ideologically, he was closest to romanticism of any poet of his time. Later,

---

4. Pseudonym of Aleksej Alekseevič Perovskij.

the symbolists did not care for Tolstoj. Andrej Belyj called his verse weak, and no one took issue with that view.

7. By and large, Tolstoj concentrated on his poetry. His prose works are interesting but open no new directions, as can be seen in his novel on the period of Ivan the Terrible, a favorite work of young people.

Tolstoj's verse searches for new forms. Occasionally, he patterned works on Russian folklore; but more important are his efforts to reform rhyme. He was the first, and for a long time the only, proponent of approximate rhyme, which Vladimir Majakovskij later popularized. Tolstoj defends approximate rhyme in a letter to B. Markevič (February 4, 1859, in French, unfortunately not published at the time), in which he correctly observes that, in Russian, unstressed vowels are considerably reduced and that these "indefinite-sounding" vowels sound somewhat alike. Tolstoj gives examples from his poem *Ioann Damaskin*: *stremniny—dolinu*; *pustynja—otnyne*; *imja—imi*; and *syna—kručiny*. One could add to this list such examples as *vody—prirodu*; *vzore—gorja*; *vaše—Timašev*; and *Antipator—teator* (perhaps in imitation of Heine's humorous rhymes). Tolstoj uses a number of rhymes, some extreme, with French and German words (he wrote many poems in German). In some cases, only the spelling makes his rhymes seem approximate; but at the time, these rhymes were considered incorrect or poor. Russian poetic tradition permitted rhymes only with vowels and vowels plus *j*.[5] These innovations were hardly noticed at the time, but they placed a much larger stock of rhymes at the poet's disposal.

Tolstoj's genres and themes come, by and large, from the romantic tradition. He has a number of traditional themes: the poet's calling, the poet who reveals new worlds hidden in the soul, night, living nature, Slavic mythology, the double, the choice of one's way of life. His many love poems contain new motifs: love is not only a force that stirs men's souls but is also a cosmic force.

---

5. Not enough material is available to indicate to what extent Tolstoj followed the example of Ukrainian poets, especially T. Ševčenko.

Когда Глагола творческая сила
толпы миров воззвала из ночи,
любовь их все, как солнце, озарила,
и лишь на землю к нам ее светила
нисходят порознь редкие лучи.
И порознь их отыскивая жадно
мы ловим отблеск вечной красоты.

When the creative forces of the word [Logos] called forth the crowd of worlds from night, love, like the sun, illumined them all. Scattered rays of the luminary come down to us on earth. And eagerly seeking these scattered rays, we seize the reflection of eternal beauty.

Here too, Tolstoj's philosophy goes beyond the terrestrial world:

В беспредельное влекома
душа незримый чует мир.

Drawn to infinity, the soul senses the invisible world.

Tolstoj subscribes to a kind of vague Platonism but maintains that he can say nothing about other worlds in everyday language, which is too imperfect. Philosophical and religious motifs run through all his lyric poetry.

Tolstoj's ballads make up a large group of his poems and are mostly on themes from Russian and Slavic history. Typically, he rejects the old Russian absolutism. His ballads are almost too melodious and have little in common with his gentle lyric poems.

Some of Tolstoj's verse narratives have romantic themes, such as the love of a young man for a portrait that has come to life, an alchemist, and an episode from Italian history (told in terza rima in imitation of Dante). Two of Tolstoj's epics are on religious themes. One of them, *Ioann Damaskin,* tells how a father of the church was forbidden by his abbot to write religious songs and how he violated this order. The theme allows Tolstoj to remark on the calling of the poet:

Над вольной мыслью Богу неугодны
насилие и гнет:
Она, в душе рожденная свободно,
в оковах не умрет!

Despotism and suppression of free thought are displeasing to God.
Thought born free in the soul will not die in chains.

Despite its narrow plot, *Ioann Damaskin* is among the most important works of Russian religious poetry. It is a hymn on the basic
teachings of Christianity and is without equal in Russian
literature, in the opinion of D. A. Šaxovskoj, Bishop Ioann.

9. Tolstoj was a master of humorous poetry and attacked with
remarkable virtuosity the radical nihilists and the Russian
bureaucracy. His famous poem *Dream of the Councilor
Popov* is in pretty octaves and tells of how, in a dream, Popov
appears without trousers before a minister and is accused by the
secret police of being a political criminal. The poem contains a
vaguely liberal speech by a minister as well as references to practices of the political police, about whom no one dared speak at
the time. The *Dream* came out in 1878, in Berlin; it was not
published in Russia until 1882 and could not be read there before
an audience until 1915.[6]

10. Several other poets of the period were respected and are
still remembered, but we can discuss them only briefly.

Jakov Petrovič Polonskij (1819–1898) studied at Moscow
University at the same time as did Fet. Polonskij thought of himself as a poet "by profession," and, from the 1840s on, volumes
of his poetry came out almost every decade. He also wrote novels
and novellas, but he was primarily a lyric poet. His main theme
is restlessness of the heart, as B. M. Èjxenbaum points out. Some
of his lines have become popular sayings (such as *"pogibšee, no
miloe sozdanie"* ["a lost creature, but dear"], of a fallen girl);
several of his poems have been set to music and are well known
as songs. Polonskij was in touch with the great Russian writers
L. N. Tolstoj, Turgenev, Tjutčev, and Fet; and the lyricism of
his poetry influenced the early work of Blok. He wrote a long
verse narrative on his college friends of the 1840s.

Apollon Aleksandrovič Grigor'ev (1822–1864) was a fellow student of Fet and Polonskij and, like them, he was a lyric poet.
His "difficult" philosophical lyrics—he was a follower of

---

6. The humorous poems of "Koz'ma Prutkov" and Tolstoj's verse plays are discussed in section 11, below, and in chapter X, section 13.

Schelling—and his love poems, permeated with profoundly tragic melancholy, are especially effective. He introduced forms based on gypsy songs and wrote verse narratives with autobiographical motifs. His work expanded the Russian poetic vocabulary. He is still valued as a translator of Masonic songs, Goethe, Heine, Béranger, and others. In his last years, Grigor'ev contributed critical and theoretical articles to the magazines of the Dostoevskij brothers. He too had an influence on Blok and other symbolists.

Apollon Nikolaevič Majkov (1821–1897) was well thought of in his time. He wrote careful, chiefly anthological poems, in which he praised the beauty of the ancient world. Later, he turned to modern Italy and, with vaguely Slavophile views, to Slavic and Western European history. He also wrote the lyric play *Three Deaths* (1859), which deals with the struggle between the classical and Christian views of the world. His work is traditional in form.

Nikolaj Fedorovič Ščerbina (1821–1869) was of Greek descent and made a place for himself in Russian literature with philhellenic poems on the beauty and sensuous pleasure of ancient Greece. He also wrote pointed epigrams on contemporary writers. Soon after his death, he was all but forgotten.

Ivan Savvič Nikitin (1824–1861) also avoided literary schools. The son of a Voronezh merchant, Nikitin was forced to help his father in his business. He began publishing late; from 1859 on, he ran a bookstore and a lending library. His education was limited—he attended a seminary for a few years—and his poems are on the wrongs that fate has done him and on peasant life. His models were folk songs and the works of A. V. Kol'cov. In several epic poems, Nikitin portrays characters who, like him, have a burden to bear. His poetry was formally good and was respected, partly because he was thought to be a poet of the people, a somewhat incorrect notion.

From the early 1860s until the 1880s, some poets went beyond the limits of realistic themes and presentation. Among the earliest of them were K. K. Slučevskij, V. V. Krestovskij, and A. N. Apuxtin, to be discussed later.

11. Another poet of the second half of the nineteenth century should be mentioned. Koz'ma Petrovič Prutkov was supposedly born in 1803 and died while a high official in 1863. He was a happy invention of Count A. K. Tolstoj and his friends the

Žemčužnikov brothers, Aleksej Mixajlovič (1821–1908), Vladimir (1830–1884), and Aleksandr (1826–1896). The works that they ascribed to Prutkov fall into two forms that are a permanent part of literature but are seldom considered by literary historians. These forms are the literary parody, that is, the humorous exaggeration of a writer's stylistic, thematic, or compositional peculiarities, and the free humorous poem, which usually remains within the family or a circle of friends.

The collaboration of Tolstoj and the Žemčužnikovs, who were all young, wealthy, aristocratic, and intellectual, may have begun with works of the second kind, free humorous poems. In 1850, Tolstoj had already written works of this kind—in Russian, they might be called *ozornaja poèzija*—and some of them were poetry of the absurd. In 1851, the friends produced their bizarre play, *Fantazija,* at the Imperial Theater. Tsar Nicholas I happened to attend the performance, and the play was banned at once. In his review of the play, Apollon Grigor'ev noted the parody on the vaudevilles of the period, although this parody is not conspicuous. Tolstoj and the Žemčužnikovs recognized the opportunities that parody offered them, and they wrote parodies on the fable, a dying form, and ascribed them to Prutkov, as they imagined him, a confident official of scant education in the Bureau of Weights and Measures. From 1854 to 1863, the friends parodied the romantic poets, especially the epigones. The themes of the late romanticists are satirized:

> Кто всех презирая, весь мир проклинает,
> в ком нет сострадания и жалости нет,
> кто с смехом на слезы несчастных взирает,
> тот—мощный, великий и сильный поэт.

He who despises everyone and curses the world, knows no sympathy or mercy, and looks on the tears of the unfortunate with a laugh is a great and powerful poet.[7]

Tolstoj and the Žemčužnikovs parodied the various genres of the period. They wrote a ballad without a plot; the "wishes of

---

7. [The poem from which this stanza is taken was never published and is quoted here from a proof sheet. The punctuation is that of D. Čiževskij.—EDITOR].

a poet," who would like to be transformed into all sorts of things, such as a tulip, an eagle, a cloud, and a wolf; a parody on the "incoherent" impressionistic poems of Fet; several parodies on the philhellenic poetry of N. F. Ščerbina, with its naive cult of beauty—here Tolstoj and the Žemčužnikovs use Greek words as stylistic ornaments; a "wish to be a Spaniard"; a parody on the Russian translations of the Cid romances; parodies on the Russian imitators of Heine and on Byronic poets, such as A. V. Timofeev and the bold, turbulent stylist V. G. Benediktov; and parodies on scholarly prosaims in philosophical poems, such as those of A. A. Grigor'ev. They also made fun of individual poems that were not exactly typical, such as some by Polonskij. Although Koz'ma Prutkov generally satirizes second-rate poets, such as the Slavophile A. S. Xomjakov, Ščerbina, and the Russian imitators of Heine, greater poets loom behind these parodies (Lermontov, Heine himself, Schiller's "Ritter Toggenburg," and others). Some of the Prutkov poems border on the absurd, such as *Junker Schmidt*:

> Вянет лист. Проходит лето.
>   иней серебрится . . .
> Юнкер Шмидт из пистолета
>   хочет застрелиться.
> Подожди, безумный, снова
>   зелень оживится!
> Юнкер Шмидт, честное слово,
>   лето возвратится;

The leaves fade. Summer passes. The hoarfrost is silver. Cadet Schmidt wishes to shoot himself with a pistol. Wait, madman, the leaves will come alive again. On my word of honor, Junker Schmidt, spring will return.

No one has found a Russian or German poem that *Junker Schmidt* parodies. Actually, the poem is not a parody but a variation on a piece by Heine, a clever adaptation of one of Heine's jokes:

> Das Fräulein stand am Meere
> und seufzte lang und bang,
> es rührte sie so sehre
> der Sonnenuntergang.

> "Mein Fräulein! sein Sie munter,
> das ist ein altes Stück;
> hier vorne geht sie unter
> und kehrt von hinten zuřuck."

The girl stood by the sea and sighed long and deep, so touched was she by the sunset. Young lady, there's nothing to worry about. It's nothing new. It goes down here and comes up back there.

As has been mentioned, Tolstoj and the Žemčužnikovs liked to parody the self-centered late Byronic poets:

> Когда в толпе ты встретишь человека,
>   который наг;
> чей лоб мрачней туманного Казбека,
>   неровен шаг . . .
> Кого язвят со злобой вечно новой
>   из рода в род;
> с кого толпа венец его лавровый
>   безумно рвет: . . .
>   знай—это я! . . .
> В моих устах спокойная улыбка,
>   в груди—змея!

If, in a crowd of people, you meet a man who is naked, whose forehead is darker than the foggy Kazbek, whose gait is unsteady, whom every generation wounds with its new malice, whose laurel wreath the crowd tears madly off: . . . Then know, I am he. On my lips a calm smile, in my breast a snake.

Besides literary parodies, Prutkov also wrote nonsense verse, such as the epigram:

> Вы любите-ли сыр? спросили раз ханжу.
> «Люблю», он отвечал: «я вкус в нем нахожу».

"Do you like cheese?" a hypocrite was once asked. "I like it," he answered. "I find it tasty."

Sometimes the title of a poem is a joke, such as *To an Old Woman of Ancient Greece if She Were to Sue for My Love.*

The absurd prosaic anecdotes of Prutkov's grandfather are jokes. But Prutkov's aphorisms contain sharp satire on the police state of Nicholas I.[8] The following lines show how truth, beauty, and happiness were to be achieved in this state:

"Only in the service of the state do you find truth."

"If you want to be handsome, join the hussars."

"I shall compare the heavens strewn with stars to the chest of a meritorious general."

"If you want peace, do not charge sadness and unpleasantness to your own account but rather to that of the state."

Finally, Prutkov sets down the principle of the police state:

"Zeal conquers all!
Sometimes zeal conquers even understanding."

Prutkov's *Project for the Introduction of Like-mindedness* ("*edinomyslie*") is in the same style and still pertinent in Russia. Prutkov left behind several plays: a parody on the romantic mysteries—*The Relationship of World Forces*—and two works of the theater of the absurd—*The Overhasty Turk or Whether It Is Pleasing to Be a Grandchild,* perhaps deliberately published as a fragment; and *Ljubov' and Silin* (names of characters).

Koz'ma Prutkov is still popular. Since most of the works he parodies have been forgotten, his poems are now often thought to be simply playful.

8. For a discussion of the era of Nicholas I, see D. Čiževskij, *Russische Geistesgeschichte,* II (Hamburg, 1961), 62 ff., 85 f.

X

The Drama

1. Aleksandr Nikolaevič Ostrovskij (1823–1886) was a Russian realist who devoted himself entirely to the theater. Although the themes of his approximately fifty plays[1] differ from those of Shakespeare, Schiller, and Gogol' in that they scarcely touch on universal problems, and although the subject matter of his plays has little to do with present-day Russian life—let alone that of the West—they are often performed in the USSR and are becoming popular in the West. This favor attests to the theatrical quality of Ostrovskij's plays, though theatrical and literary excellence are not necessarily the same thing.

Ostrovskij was born in Moscow in 1823, the son of a court magistrate who married a wealthy woman. Ostrovskij attended Moscow University but did not graduate. In 1843, he began serving as a clerk in Moscow law courts. In 1847, he started publishing comic scenes and sketches in a Moscow newspaper. After his first comedy was produced, in 1851, he devoted himself to literature. He traveled through Russia and later through Western Europe. In 1852, he made friends with a group of young Slavophiles who had been enthusiastic about his early plays. He devoted his entire life to the stage, but not all his works could be produced. After plays had been approved by the regular censor, they had to be submitted to a theatrical censor. One such censor required Ostrovskij to revise his patriotic drama *Koz'ma Zaxar'ič Minin-Suxoruk* (1862) according to the censor's suggestions, even though the Tsar had thanked Ostrovskij and given him a present for the play. Ostrovskij complied, and in 1866 the piece was put on. Other

---

1. In addition, Ostrovskij worked on the translation of more than thirty plays by Shakespeare, Calderon, Lope de Vega, Goldoni, Gozzi, and others and finished about twenty of them.

works were also held up and could not be produced until long after they had been published.

Gradually, Ostrovskij acquired a pre-eminent reputation. In 1865, the Moscow Actors' Circle (*Artističeskij kružok*) was formed, and Ostrovskij worked closely with outstanding actors and influenced their art. In 1881, he began work on a committee to review the regulations of the excellent Imperial Theater. In 1886, he was appointed director of the Moscow Theater but was able to fulfill his duties for only half a year before his death.

2. Ostrovskij's plays are quite varied in theme. He first became known for his comedies and dramas on the merchant class, which was at the time hermetic and culturally backward. In these plays, there are also civil servants, who play leading parts in other dramas of Ostrovskij. Educated, intellectual Russians remain in the background. Some of Ostrovskij's works are about actors, whom he portrayed as they were at the time and as they had been in the early Russian theater. He also wrote several historical plays.

Ostrovskij occasionally collaborated on plays. Once he worked together with a historian; his other partners were well-known playwrights of the time. There is space here to discuss only a few works of each type.

3. Among the most notable of Ostrovskij's plays on the merchant class is *Svoi ljudi—sočtemsja* [All in the Family] (1846–1850), a comedy about swindlers. The merchant Bol'šov intends to get rich by going bankrupt. Instead of using his fortune to pay his debts, he signs it over to his son-in-law, Podxaljuzin. When Bol'šov is faced with making a partial payment on his debts or going to prison, he realizes that his son-in-law and daughter are indifferent to him and unwilling to help him pay. Ostrovskij has taken the old plot of the defrauded fraud and given it an impressive new setting. The language of the characters (besides the ones mentioned, Mrs. Bol'šov and a matchmaker play important parts) is perhaps the best example of Ostrovskij's linguistic art. It is the sharp, vigorous idiom of Muscovite merchants.

In his other plays about merchants, the *"samodur"* (an unusual word that Ostrovskij seems to have popularized), a hardheaded eccentric, plays an important part. *Poverty Is No Crime* (1854), a play as well liked as *All in the Family,* has a happy ending.

The *samodur* Torcov is reconciled with his poor, degenerate brother and permits his daughter to marry a poor young man. He yields because the rich merchant Koršunov, whom he has selected to marry his daughter, has angered him. In other works by Ostrovskij, the *samodur* is less innocuous and is reminiscent of a similar type in Goldoni, as in *I Rusteghi* [The Four Brutes].

The Storm was conceived as a serious tragedy; it takes place in a town on the Volga. The principal female character, Katerina, is married to a loving husband, who is weak and dependent on his tyrannical mother. While he is away, Katerina has an affair and feels that she has freed herself from the prison of married life. After he returns, she is frightened by a storm and confesses what she has done. She dreads the reaction of her mother-in-law, realizes that infidelity is a serious sin, and commits suicide. The other characters range from a semieducated inventor of perpetual motion to Katerina's frivolous sister-in-law, who is partly to blame for her trouble. These characters are so well portrayed that the play makes excellent theater. But it is difficult to understand how Dobroljubov could have said that Katerina was "a ray of light in the kingdom of darkness" merely because she enjoyed herself several evenings with a friend (*"guljala,"* she calls it).

Ostrovoskij's other plays, serious and amusing, on the merchant class almost all go well on stage. Some of his types, such as the *samodur,* his obedient wife, and the matchmaker, at once clever and stupid, are recurrent (see sec. 7, below).

4. Ostrovskij's plays on "educated" people are of various kinds and deal mainly with civil servants, landowners, and avaricious swindlers. Typical Russian intellectuals (*intelligenty*) do not appear.

Among the plays in this group are *Na vsjakogo mudreca dovol'no prostoty* [Enough Stupidity in Every Wise Man], *Bešenye den'gi* [Easy Money], and *Pozdnjaja ljubov'* [Late Love]. In the first of these, Glumov, a sly, unscrupulous young man, obtains a good government job. He sets down in his diary his low opinion of his superiors and benefactors. These remarks are accidentally made known, and he appears to be in a hopeless situation. But an unexpected turn comes when he tells his indignant patrons that they will have to keep him because they need such men, with practical ability and unscrupulous cunning. No one contradicts him, and apparently he will be retained.

In *Easy Money*, Ostrovskij portrays a new type: a businessman-landowner from the provinces, Vasil'kov, who marries a beautiful girl from the capital. She does not love him and soon leaves him. But when she learns that he is about to become a millionaire, she is willing to return on humiliating terms—she would rather be his companion than his wife. She and her friends recognize the importance of money: "Money has got smart; it goes only to good businessmen"; "Money used to be stupid"; "Money that you make by working is smart money." Actually, Vasil'kov's work consists of successful speculation, and he needs a socialite to help him with his connections. The enterprising, conscientious Vasil'kov is contrasted with lazy, unproductive noblemen who merely enjoy life.

Late Love (1874), a comedy with tragic overtones, was especially well thought of by Gončarov. The play is about the family of a lawyer, who is much like Ostrovskij's civil servants. His aging daughter falls in love with a man who seems to intend to defraud her father, but there is a happy and unexpected ending. The part of the daughter is outstanding; it carries the play and is an example of Ostrovskij's mastery.

5. The best known of Ostrovskij's plays about actors is *Les* [The Forest] (1871), in which two actors visiting an estate turn out to be morally better than the noblemen and businessmen who live and work there. The actors cleverly resolve traditional comic complications and help a young married couple. The situations are not unusual, but the play is one of Ostrovskij's best, mainly because of the original roles of the actors—they are quite different on and off the stage.

The plots of other plays on actors range from the fate of a talented young actress, who is thought by men to be fair game and yields to temptation (*Talents and Admirers*, 1882) to the melodramatic meeting of a great actress with her illegitimate son, whom she has lost track of and who has become an actor *Bez viny vinovatye* [Guilty But Innocent] (1884). Ostrovskij knew the world of actors thoroughly, but the plots of his plays about them are generally primitive. The popularity of these plays is often due to good acting.

6. Ostrovskij wrote a historical comedy in verse, *Komik semnadcatogo stoletija* [The Comedian of the Seventeenth Century] (1873), about the beginnings of Russian theater in 1672. More important are his historical plays on the interregnum of the late sixteenth and early seventeenth centuries; they came out in 1862 and were revised in 1866; two plays were added in 1867. Despite their patriotism, some of these plays ran into trouble with the censor. *Vasilisa Melent'eva* (1868) treats one of the many marriages of Ivan the Terrible. *Voevoda* [The Governor] (1865; extensively revised in 1885) portrays a corrupt high official of the late seventeenth century. All these plays were based on thorough research. Like many contemporaries, Ostrovskij made use of the Shakespearian technique in Puškin's *Boris Godunov,* and his historical plays have much in common with those of his contemporaries and make similar demands on the actors. Although simple persons and the masses are sometimes important, the high theatrical style of the plays is unmistakable. Historical processes are interpreted as the deeds of great men or as acts undertaken for private interests. The theatrical qualities of Ostrovskij's historical plays have led composers to set them to music. The best-known example is Čajkovskij's *Voevoda* [Dream on the Volga], composed in 1868.

The most interesting of Ostrovskij's plays in the historical style is pseudohistorical. In *Sneguročka* [Snow Maiden] (1873, also set to music by Čajkovskij; in 1881, Rimskij-Korsakov based a composition on a revised libretto), the story of the fairy tale is changed and set in the prehistoric Slavic period. Slavic gods appear in the work and are influenced by the romantic folklore of scholars such as A.N. Afanas'ev. These folklorists misunderstood the Slavic gods and interpreted them according to their own notions. Snow Maiden's father is Frost, his patroness is Spring, and there is a forest sprite named Lešij. Snow Maiden appears in human form in this peaceful, happy prehistoric realm but dissolves when she falls in love with a mortal. The play is set against a background of popular scenes with songs and games. Other examples of this genre are Gerhard Hauptmann's *The Sunken Bell,* set in the present, and *Lisova pisnja* [The Forest Song] by the Ukrainian poetess Lesja Ukrajinka.

7. Ostrovskij's plays are interesting in form and style and con-

tain desirable roles. Occasionally, he wrote plays for particular actors. By the 1870s, actors were training for roles typical of Ostrovskij.

Ostrovskij's works have received much attention but have not been really well investigated. He started writing in the Natural School. His first published works were sketches in the form of reports; he called them scenes. Some features of this writing carry over into his later work. All his comedies, dramas, and historical chronicles include two elements, a particular walk of life and sharply defined characters. Most of his works are extremely concentrated. Often they have only five or six changes of scenery; and the number of characters is usually limited to ten or less. Only in the four chronicle plays do many secondary characters appear, and these plays have from thirty to fifty. Ostrovskij did not study Goldoni for nothing; in keeping with the old tradition, some of his characters are definite types, despite all their individuality—of course, different types from those in Italian comedy. Among Ostrovskij's types are the crude, tyrannical merchant paterfamilias; his wife, who is continually terrified; his children and in-laws; and the help, who all resist the father in some way; eager, dishonest officials; and matchmakers. Some of these types, such as officials and matchmakers, appear in the grotesque art of Gogol'. But in Ostrovskij, these characters are never schematic; with few exceptions, they are realistic.

Despite the few characters in his plays, Ostrovskij gives a broad picture of the period, through the characters, the information that they convey, and their past lives, as suggested in the play. Groups of characters usually form a whole, and the play is advanced through comparison and contrast of characters and their actions. Similar or opposing characters are often paired. Characters who may appear superfluous, such as those in the chronicle plays and in *The Storm*, inform us about the environment (*sreda*) of the principal characters.

Ostrovskij's plays are concise, with no unnecessary scenes or speeches. His thorough knowledge of the theater and his careful revision of his manuscripts enabled him to achieve brilliant effects with a minimum of characters and scenery. The action is always unified and well plotted, and it usually begins without preparation. The content of a play is often suggested by the title.

Ostrovskij found proverbs particularly appropriate as titles, as in *Poverty Is No Crime;* but titles such as *Wolves and Sheep* achieve the same effect. All Ostrovskij's plays were written to be performed; there are no closet dramas among them.

The curtain rises on realistic scenery and everyday conversation. Gradually, the scope broadens; and one puts together the antecedent action, which is conditioned by environment. As in *The Storm,* the action is usually well advanced when the play begins. Situations are often resolved by a kind of surprise. Ostrovskij seems to believe that even characters who appear immutable, as in *Poverty Is No Crime,* are capable of sudden, profound change. These abrupt decisions and changes of heart are not always adequately motivated, but they are effective on stage. Ostrovskij said that he was not interested in original plots. His turning points are seldom complicated. He uses few devices to awaken interest, as though he were indifferent to stirring curiosity, as B. V. Tomaševskij indicates. These features of realistic drama are all the more interesting since Ostrovskij had studied the European baroque theater.

8. The details of Ostrovskij's language are original. His contemporaries noticed this; but it was his literary remains that showed how much he had been concerned with the speech of those around him. He often writes about language in his letters, and he left extensive notes on vocabulary. For his historical plays, he gathered material from chronicles, documents, and historical works. As a result, he employs vulgarisms, dialect, and words from the idiom of manual laborers, fishermen, card players, merchants, actors, and others. He is sparing in his use of dialect; for instance, in *Easy Money,* he suggests that a character is from northern Great Russia through four or five words and expressions in the appropriate dialect. In his works, he uses only a small part of his *Material for a Dictionary of Vernacular Russian ("narodnyj jazyk").* Occasionally he emphasizes that a character has used jargon or dialect when another character does not understand him. He does not limit the use of proverbs to titles; his characters use large numbers of them. There are many other examples of popular languages in his works: simple everyday expressions, such as *"bežat' slomja golovu"* and *"carstvo nebesnoe";* unusual and local expressions, such as *"gol' saratovskaja";* prover-

bial expressions, such as *"kak ne kraxmal'sja, a vse-taki ne barynja"* ["no matter how much starch you use, you still won't be a lady"]; and "incorrect" words and sentence constructions that identify the speaker as uneducated or from the lower classes. In some cases, Ostrovskij overlooks linguistic boundaries and attributes words of one dialect or class to persons from another, a practice that may or may not be deliberate.

Ostrovskij attempts to suit language to the personality of his characters. Especially typical is the variation in speech among members of the merchant class. A tyrannical paterfamilias and his wife, who knows her power, speak differently from a dependent son, a young woman, or a zealous employee. Naturally, there are differences in language between generations, as between the old mother-in-law, Kabanixa, and the two young women, Varvara and Katerina, in *The Storm*. Ostrovskij gave some of his characters his own favorite turns of phrase; and actors liked the practice so much that they repeated the expressions, mostly original, in other plays. The language of the chronicle plays is full of archaistic and historical words. Among Ostrovskij's peculiarities is a tendency to use unusual or studied proper names; the name of a police official, "Tigrij L'vovič," is based on the words for *tiger* and *lion*.

9. The ideological content of Ostrovskij's plays does not match their linguistic and theatrical quality. Tolstoj and Dostoevskij teach and preach; one finds food for thought in Turgenev, Gončarov, and Grigorovič; the works of the radical "friends of the people" (chapter V) give vent to sociopolitical indignation; but Ostrovskij achieves nothing of the sort. Whether he intended to does not matter. Soviet scholars attempt to show, if not the revolutionary, at least the revolutionizing character of his plays. Naturally, his objective portrayals reflect Russian life as it was, and his appropriate reward is an objective presentation of the Russia of his time.

Ostrovskij observed and mirrored developments in Russia between 1840 and 1880, but his depiction of society cannot be compared with Turgenev's in importance. Unlike Turgenev, Ostrovskij did not set himself the task of acting as literary historian. Although there is little ideology in Ostrovskij's works, it is wrong to charge, as Ščerbina did in an epigram, that he was the "Kotzebue of the marketplace" ("*gostinodvorskij Kocebu*").

10. Many important Russian writers of the late nineteenth century wrote plays. There are dramas by Turgenev, Leskov, Pisemskij, and L. N. Tolstoj, the curious sketches (written between 1856 and 1861 and reminiscent of the Natural School) of Saltykov-Ščedrin, the vaudevilles of V. A. Sollogub, and the historical plays of L. A. Mej and A. K. Tolstoj. Nevertheless, Aleksej Antipovič Potexin (1829–1908) and Aleksandr Vasil'evič Suxovo-Kobylin (1817–1903) were the only writers, besides Ostrovskij, who wrote primarily for the theater. Many of Potexin's plays were popular in his time but are now forgotten, despite their considerable merits, perhaps because they are not very original.

11. By contrast, Suxovo-Kobylin's dramatic trilogy, his only work, is quite original. He was from a family of wealthy, enlightened noblemen. During the 1840s, Suxovo-Kobylin frequented intellectual circles in Moscow. He had completed his work at the University in 1838 and, like many of his contemporaries, was fascinated by Hegel. He worked all his life on a translation of Hegel into Russian. Unfortunately, this translation as well as his own philosophical work was lost in a fire, and nothing is known of his interpretation of Hegel. As a young man, Suxovo-Kobylin planned a work for the stage, but his trilogy was not completed until much later, between 1855 and 1869. In 1850, his French mistress was found murdered in Moscow. He was charged with murder or with instigating the murder. At the time, all cases in Russian courts were official proceedings, and the public was not permitted to observe. During the seven years of his trial, he grew more and more isolated. When acquitted, he emigrated.

The first part of his trilogy, *Krečinskij's Wedding*, was produced in 1855 and published in 1856; the second part, *The Affair*, was published in 1861; the third part, *Tarelkin's Death*, butchered by the censor, in 1869. The second part of the trilogy was not produced until the 1880s, the third part not until the early 1900s. The parts of the trilogy are loosely connected but give a uniform picture of the Russia of officials and swindlers.

In the trilogy, the impoverished landowner Krečinskij seeks to marry well, but he is frustrated by the police. The emphasis of the play is less on the schemes of Krečinskij and his accomplice,

Raspljuev, another impoverished nobleman, than on the characterization of individual types, of the swindlers and of Muromskij, the father of Krečinskij's bride.

The second part of the trilogy deals with the trial. Krečinskij's bride and her father become involved when they appear to know something about Krečinskij's fraud. They are caught up in the machinery of Russian justice, before the reforms of the 1860s; and it is only through death that the unfortunate Muromskij is released. The persons of the play are passive objects or mere wheels in the bureaucratic machinery. *The Affair* is hardly a realistic play. As in Gogol', the characters are symbols, more effective for the grotesque improbability of the plot.

The third play is dominated by grotesquery. The swindler Tarelkin, who has appeared in the second part, dies for official purposes, that is, he has a dummy buried in his place, acquires new papers, and continues his previous practices. The grotesquery is fantastic and anticipates the symbolic theater of fifty years later. Among the important features of the trilogy is an extraordinary variety of language, also reminiscent of Gogol'. When the trilogy was finally produced, it was apparently too original, for it was not very popular with audiences.

12. Producing historical plays in Russia involved so much trouble with censorship that they often remained closet dramas. Puškin's *Boris Godunov* was held up because, among other things, it was not permitted to show, on stage, tsars of the ruling dynasty, clergymen, usurpers, or rebels. Sacred scenes, such as religious services, and sacred objects, such as icons, were also banned.

L. A. Mej (see chapter IX, sec. 5) wrote two plays on sixteenth-century themes. *Carskaja nevesta* [The Tsar's Bride] deals with Ivan the Terrible's third wife, who, according to legend, was poisoned and died only a few days after their wedding. The story of *Pskovitjanka* [A Maid of Pskov] was freely invented by Mej; Ivan the Terrible meets a young princess who bravely resists him and commits suicide when he disregards her efforts to save Pskov and orders an attack on the defenseless city. Both plays are well constructed and exciting. The language is natural, with only moderate use of archaisms. The plays are good examples of Russian historical drama but acquired their popularity as operas by Rimskij-Korsakov. Since a large cast would have complicated an opera, Rimskij-Korsakov replaced Mej's text with a libretto of his own. Mej's plays are based on serious study of sources and of scholarly literature, although his emphasis is more on personal tragedy than on historical events and his dramas can be called historical only with reservations.

13. Far more important are the plays of A. K. Tolstoj (see chapter IX, sec. 6).

Tolstoj wrote five plays, three of which were produced rather late; one of them is very good indeed. In *Don Juan*, Tolstoj attempts to give this character new meaning. Like Goethe's Faust, Don Juan is the subject of a wager by Satan and the good spirits (naturally, no Russian playwright could present God or God's voice on stage). Don Juan's amorous adventures are interpreted as his search for a human ideal, one that he finds in Donna Anna. Through his love for her, Don Juan comes to believe in God and, in the original version of the play, decides to live out his life as a monk in a monastery. In a separate edition of the work, in 1867, Tolstoj omits this scene and concludes the play with the appearance of the Commendatore's statue and Don Juan's death. The play was not produced until 1905, with deletions. Several passages were made into songs by Čajkovskij.

Tolstoj's other plays are on historical subjects and include a trilogy. The first part of the trilogy, *The Death of Ivan the Terrible*, was finished in 1864 and revised several times. The second part, *Tsar Feodor Ioannovič,* treats the reign of Ivan's pious son; the third part, *Tsar Boris,* the rule and death of Boris Godunov. In style, the trilogy is dependent on Puškin's *Boris Godunov,* but Tolstoj's plays contain the traditional five acts. For *The Death of Ivan the Terrible,* Tolstoj turned to Karamzin and other sources, including Prince Andrej Kurbskij, an enemy of the Tsar. Tolstoj put together events in Ivan's last days to make an exciting tragedy that goes well on stage. Tolstoj was opposed to Muscovite absolutism, and used Kurbskij's letters and history and the speeches of several boyars. Boris Godunov appears early in the trilogy, and Tolstoj emphasizes his ambition. In the German translation of Karolina Pavlova, the play was successfully produced in Weimar in January 1868. After the première of a censored version, in 1867, the play was seldom performed in Russia until the Art Theater took it up at the end of the century.

The second part of the trilogy, *Tsar Feodor Ioannovič* (1868) was particularly successful. Here, Boris Godunov's ambition is contrasted with the gentle Tsar Feodor, who is weak-willed and cannot manage the affairs of state but is a good, almost saintly man and attempts to reconcile Boris with his enemies. According to tradition, Feodor was not only weak-willed but perhaps weak-minded.[2] Tolstoj follows Karamzin and allows Boris to have Dmitrij murdered—Dmitrij is not yet of age—in order to claim the throne himself, as the brother-in-law of the tsar. (It has since been shown that Boris did not abet the murder.) The theatrical censorship found that the presentation of Tsar Feodor encroached on his dignity, and it was not until the time of the Art Theater that the play could be put on, in an abbreviated version. Nevertheless, audiences understood Tolstoj's wish to portray a just, almost saintly tsar with sympathetic features. The role of Tsar Feodor is coveted in the Russian theater.

The third part of the trilogy, *Tsar Boris,* is based on Karamzin, Puškin's *Boris Godunov,* and independent research. Tolstoj emphasizes the conflict in Boris's conscience; but despite his great art in portraying the contradictory Boris, his play is overshadowed by Puškin's. Tolstoj's work was first produced in 1881, on a private stage, and has not been put on often since. Karolina Pavlova's German translation of the trilogy received the benefit of Tolstoj's suggestions but is now almost forgotten.

Tolstoj's last play, *Posadnik* [The Governor], is unfinished. It was to have been a "human drama." "A man commits an apparently base act (*'podlost'*) in order to save a city." The act is said to have been performed by a *"posadnik"* of Novgorod in the thirteenth century. More than in Tolstoj's other plays, the "human drama" of the hero is connected with his social environment. In 1876, the work was allowed on stage, with certain changes.

In contrast to some primitive Russian patriotic plays of the nineteenth century, the historical dramas of Mej and Tolstoj are works of art. But it was not until the twentieth century that they could be staged in the provinces.

2. In this respect, much has been made of his ability to play chimes, an interest interpreted as a sign of imbecility. Playing chimes is a musical art practiced in France until the nineteenth century and still practiced in England. A man who possessed this ability was, in any case, a gifted artist.

XI

Other Realistic Prose Writers

1. The only great realistic writer who can be called unreservedly a consistent, deliberate realist is Gončarov. There are other prose writers who reveal more distinct features of the realistic style than do Turgenev, Dostoevskij, and Leskov. These writers, to be discussed briefly, are still treated by literary historians, reprinted, and read; but they have had little influence on modern literature in Russia or abroad. They are overshadowed by the enormous influence of L. N. Tolstoj, by the late realists Čexov and Gor'kij, and by Turgenev, Dostoevskij, and Leskov.

Some of the prose writers to be discussed here sought to follow in Turgenev's footsteps and portray contemporary life and intellectual currents. To some extent, they dealt with the same period as Turgenev, but from a different point of view. Other writers undertook to explore areas that Turgenev and the other great prose writers had overlooked. It is only in *The Possessed* that Dostoevskij commits himself on the questions of the day; in his later novels, he seldom speaks out on current issues. There is even less about current conditions in Gončarov's *Precipice*; and Leskov deals with nihilists in only two atypical novels.

2. Aleksej Feofilaktovič Pisemskij (1821–1881)[1] was regarded as an equal by the most important writers of his time. He is, incidentally, one of the few outstanding writers from Northern Russia, from Kostroma Province.

From 1840 to 1844, Pisemskij studied mathematics at Moscow University, but spent most of his time reading Russian and Western European literature. He considered himself a student of Gogol' and of the critic Belinskij, both of whom he thought of as consistent realists. He worked for years as an administrative official in his

---

1. The date often given for his birth, 1820, is apparently wrong.

native province; and his first novel was not passed by the censor, but Pisemskij never gave up his literary ambitions. A. N. Ostrovskij helped him publish his first book, a short novel (*povest'*) with the curious title *Tjufjak* [The Mattress], which came out in 1850. In 1854, Pisemskij moved to St. Petersburg, where he wrote more novels, among them *Tysjača duš* [A Thousand Souls]—that is, a thousand serfs—which was well received. He also wrote tales and plays, among them *Gor'kaja sud'bina* [A Bitter Lot]. In 1863, he published an "antinihilistic" novel, *Vzbalamučennoe more* [The Troubled Sea], and added pointed articles in newspapers. The result was a setback similar to that suffered by Leskov (see chapter VIII, sec. 1). Pisemskij was odious to progressives, and for a long time his work was ignored. His later novels, *The Men of the 1840s, The Freemasons,* and *Meščane* [The Petty Bourgeois] were considered by such contemporaries as L. N. Tolstoj, Turgenev, and Leskov to be skillful portrayals of Russian life. These writers thought equally well of Pisemskij's plays and novellas, among them the cycle *Russian Liars*. Later, Čexov had a high opinion of Pisemskij.

Pisemskij attempted to tell the truth and is more merciless than any other realistic writer. He does not elicit sympathy for his characters, even when they fail. His first novel, about a fallen woman, was not passed by the censor. The work, *Is She Guilty?*, lacks the sentiment of Herzen's novel on a similar subject (see chapter II, sec. 8) and of the writings of the Natural School. There is no sentiment either in Pisemskij's novellas on the same theme as Turgenev's *Sportsman's Sketches*: the immorality of serfdom. Pisemskij mercilessly describes the divisions among the peasants and the exploitation practiced by some rich peasants.

In Pisemskij's first published novel, *The Mattress,* with which he made a name, a spineless man submits to everyone else's will, including that of his wife, whom he has married "by chance." He is a literary relative of Oblomov but lacks the latter's intelligence and moral purity and does not ultimately find a happy family life (although Gončarov views that life as a spiritual decline) but ends in the filth of rural life. He is surrounded by the vulgarity that Russians call *pošlost'* and is released only by an early death.

In his more important novels, Pisemskij portrays eras in the intellectual life of Russia. The central character of *A Thousand*

Souls (1858), Kalinovič, is a contemporary of Pisemskij, a man of the fifties. He is a success as a young official, receives an important position, marries well, and acquires a thousand souls. But, in an effort to be just, he goes against his society and is ultimately defeated. The only one who remains true to him is his friend Nasten'ka, whom he has abandoned to further his career and to whom he returns when he sees that he has failed. She is the only positive character in the novel; Kalinovič's struggle with society is a result of his ambition, and he is defeated because he is on the same level as his enemies.

In *The Troubled Sea* (1863), Pisemskij portrays the next generation, that of the sixties, from an antinihilistic point of view. His picture of political radicals is weak, as it is in similar novels by other writers. He presents the radicals as wicked schemers, stirred up and led by Poles, who fought against Russian rule in 1863, and by revolutionary emigrants, such as Herzen. They are contrasted with bureaucrats, businessmen, who have just established themselves as a social group and are gradually acquiring influence, and landowners, who still lead idle lives. But bureaucrats, businessmen, and landowners are the physical and, to some extent, intellectual fathers of the "new men," the nihilists.

In *Meščane* (1877), a late novel, big businessmen no longer run into opposition with their financial schemes; the aristocracy is on their side. An honest man can only flee from this avaricious society with its mania for satisfying its baser instincts through wealth. Nekrasov presented society in the same light in his "contemporaries" (see chapter VII, sec. 6).

Pisemskij's novels *The Men of the 1840s* (1869) and *The Freemasons* (1880) are about idealists of the forties and of the twenties and thirties. The first book is essentially a roman à clef on Pisemskij's experiences at college; he shows the moral enthusiasm and the shortcomings of his contemporaries. The second novel describes the defeat of the Freemasons of the twenties and thirties, men portrayed as pure idealists.

3. Pisemskij's novels are conceived as genre paintings. The plots center on schemes and adventures. The stories are developed skillfully. There is almost continuous suspense; the many secondary characters appear only when called for and do not disturb the action.

Benz   Bx 320.2
                    ,B413
         (O C S)   Luntgramma
Bx 485   ladnik -
  ,F4   Aizetmuller
                491.
)   8,7013 glossary
              Leškich - Altkirch
PG 619
  ,L8

2) 710   Slovoobrazovanie

Peškovskij -
        P6 2361
           ,P37

Pisemskij uses various narrative techniques. He prefers to present his characters in conversation but often seems to resist dialogue and go over to narration, at which he is less successful. His "villains" and petty bourgeois speak strong, colorful language, but Pisemskij does not render idealists well, even when they are as limited as Kalinovič. All too often his idealists deliver bland sermons or merely tell what they are about to do. Pisemskij employs the old narrative device and indicates the inner life of his characters through their words and actions. This method is a kind of literary behaviorism and is inadequate for complicated situations, all the more so since Pisemskij's contemporaries, such as Turgenev, L. N. Tolstoj, Dostoevskij, and Leskov, had developed psychological studies to a high art. In Pisemskij, even a murder (as in *Russian Liars*, VIII, "The Handsome Man") seems almost accidental.

One finds in Pisemskij a primitiveness of language that prompted Čexov to call him "crude and without problems" and "naive" (*prostovatyj*, which is not the same thing as simpleminded). It is often not until we get the total picture of a work that we are impressed, when we take the author at his word. That may be why Pisemskij, who gave the most complete account of any realist of his characters' backgrounds, had little influence on the development of realism and why, despite reprints of his works, he is little read today.

4. Pisemskij's play *A Hard Lot* (1858) got little attention when it came out because of the reaction to his antinihilistic novel, but it was later well received. The interesting situation is apparently taken from a work by the Polish novelist Ignacy Kraszewski. A peasant returns to his village from his job in St. Petersburg and discovers that his wife is the mistress of his master. He kills the child she has had by his master and is arrested. There is much popular language in the play. Pisemskij shows how the crime is judged by different groups and how no one thinks to blame the master. From time to time, the play has been successfully produced and then almost forgotten. Several of Pisemskij's other plays are good theater, and he himself was an excellent actor.

5. Dmitrij Vasil'evič Grigorovič (1822–1899) was briefly popular, but he is now almost forgotten. The son of a landowner

and his French wife, Grigorovič began writing in the style of the Natural School, and his novel (*povest'*) about peasant life, *Anton Goremyka* [Bad-Luck Anton] (1847) was popular. His early tale *Derevnja* [A Village], which is almost as long as his first novel, and his later novel *Rybaki* [Fishermen] (1853) were widely read. Grigorovič had talent; and it is to his credit that he recognized the merit of Dostoevskij's *Poor Folk* and called his friends' attention to the work—he and Dostoevskij had studied together at a school for military engineers. Toward the end of the century, he seems to have prompted Čexov, whom he did not know, to work on more serious things; Grigorovič recognized the promise in Čexov's humorous novellas. Grigorovič was long one of the old guard of writers of the 1840s and 1850s. From the late 1860s on, he wrote, with little success, about Russian art and art education.

Derevnja tells of a peasant woman who is forced to marry by her landowner-master and who leads such an unhappy life that she dies young. The novella is a physiological sketch of the Natural School, but it differs from typical sketches in the pretty scenes of nature and the positive characterization of the peasant woman, a sentimental dreamer who has little in common with her surroundings. By contrast, Anton, the principal character of Grigorovič's first novel, is distinguished by his boundless patience and obedience. When he attempts to do something about the unjust steward of his village and submit a complaint to the landowner, he is put in jail. *Fishermen* is an almost folkloric account of that occupation.

In his early short novellas and in his later works, all of which were received coolly, Grigorovič portrays landowners and poor artists. His later works contain a new, satirical note that should have appealed to his contemporaries.

The main features of almost all Grigorovič's work are good language, with much popular speech, and a conspicuous use of sentiment that reminds one of Dostoevskij's *Poor Folk*.

6. Pavel Ivanovič Mel'nikov (1819–1883) used the pseudonym Andrej Pečerskij. He was known as *homo unius libri,* since his two long novels, *V lesax* [In the Forests] (1871 ff.) and *Na gorax* [In the Mountains] (1875 ff.) form a single work with the same characters.

Mel'nikov was from Nizhni Novgorod. In 1837, he finished his studies at Kazan University, intending to become a professor of Slavic languages and literatures. But a remark he made at a student party proved offensive, and the eighteen-year-old was sent under police escort to teach in a small town in Perm Province, in northeastern European Russia. He began at once to make a study of the region and, from 1839 on, published his impressions in magazines. Soon afterward, when he was transferred to Nizhni Novgorod, he met the historian M. P. Pogodin and the ethnographer V. I. Dal'. In 1847, Mel'nikov was made an official for special assignments in Nizhni Novgorod, and in 1850, in St. Petersburg. One of his tasks was to investigate Old Believers,[2] who were considered unreliable and were persecuted. Subsequently, he reported to the Department of the Interior in 1866: "In my view, the Old Believers are the mainstay of the future of Russia."

In 1840, Mel'nikov published a story in which he anticipated the style of the Natural School and was perhaps influenced by Gogol's early novellas and *The Inspector General*. It was not until 1852 that he published another novella; there followed a series of novellas (*rasskazy* and *povesti*) that are well told, have clever, concise plots and little stylistic embellishment, and are distinguished by their pure, excellent language. These novellas were well received by critics, who especially liked the satirical tone, but they were later forgotten. After his essays on the Old Believers, Mel'nikov published, in 1866, a novella that proved to be the first part of *In the Forests*.

Both of Mel'nikov's novels treat the life of the Old Believers in northern European Russia. There, far from administrative centers, with the aid of the bribery that took the sting out of harsh laws, the Old Believers had created their own culture. Mel'nikov's work runs to more than two thousand pages and has a large cast of characters and various story lines. At the center of the work are the Old Believers, particularly the members of the rich merchant family Čapurin. There are other merchants, as well as members of the Orthodox Church, officials, sectarians, and members, some of them noblemen, of the ecstatic *xlysty*,[3]

2. See D. Čiževskij, *Russische Geistesgeschichte*, II (Hamburg, 1961), 30 ff., 46 ff., 107 f., 134 ff.
   3. On sects, see D. Čiževskij, *Russische Geistesgeschichte,* II, 47 f.

whom Mel'nikov dislikes. The wives of the Old Believers play an important part in the community, and enjoy much independence of thought and action. Among the women, the nuns in the Old Believer hermitages are noteworthy, since they rear the daughters of the community. There are also peasants, who are not serfs, but who work for the state or in factories and live in village communities administered by officials.

Mel'nikov recognizes that there are various classes of Old Believers. His sympathy is probably with the "modern" merchants who have dispensed with the traditions of everyday life and put aside old-fashioned dress. He knows that, in the mountains, there are Old Believer merchants who are more rigid and, at times, merciless. Nevertheless, Mel'nikov likes the Old Believers, who, despite the hardships they have suffered for a hundred and fifty years, have created a culture of everyday life that they consider Christian and wish to preserve. Mel'nikov's community merchants are quite different from the willful Moscow eccentrics whom Ostrovskij was portraying at the time (see chapter X). Mel'nikov's merchants are honest and strict but fair with their subordinates. They do not tyrannize their families, and they are religious, but not fanatical. There is no substance to the charge of some Soviet scholars that the home life of the Old Believers in Mel'nikov is reminiscent of *Domostroj*. (*Domostroj* is a guide to domestic life written in the sixteenth century. Its ideal is an egoistic, hermetic family and devotion to the tsar. There is nothing of this ideal in Mel'nikov.) Mel'nikov did not think that the Old Believers found it natural to live in a kind of exile. The principal character, Čapurin, believes that he will someday be able to live in the capitals of Russia, and he is motivated in his dreams, not by ambition or greed, but by a desire to serve his country.

There are also love stories in Mel'nikov's work—for instance, about "Mother Manefa," who is deserted by her lover when she is young and becomes a nun and later an abbess; about Flenuška, Manefa's daughter, who has also had an unhappy love affair and who confronts her former lover as the stern nun "Mother Filagria"; and about other girls, such as poor Nastja, who is bitterly disappointed by her husband; and a girl married against her will to a hypocrite. Women in the Old Believer communities seem not to have been as subject to man's will as in other parts of Russia.

But it would take an extensive study to determine whether Mel'nikov has given a true account of the Old Believers.

Mel'nikov's language is notable. Lexically, it is akin to the speech of the Old Believers; but when expressing his own thoughts, Mel'nikov sometimes reverts to the vocabulary of routine literary language. The most typical feature of his language is rhythm, which is reminiscent of the rhythmical language of folklore, bylina rhythms, and the subtle rhythms of fairy tales. The following example of Mel'nikov's style comes from the legend of the city of Kitež, which sank into a lake.

Цел тот город до сих пор — с белокаммеными стенами, златоверхими церквами, с честны́ми монастырями, с княжескими узорчатыми теремами, с боярскими каменными палатами, с рубленными из кондо́вого, негниющего леса домами. Цел град, но невидим. Не видать грешным людям славного Китежа. Сокрылся он чудесно, божьим повелением. . . . Подошел татарский царь ко граду великому Китежу, восхотел дома огнем спалить, мужей избить либо в полон угнать, жен и девиц в наложницы взять. Не допустил Господь бусурманского надругания на святыней христианскою.

This city is still undamaged—with white stone walls, churches with gold domes, and venerable monasteries, ornate princely castles, the stone palaces of the boyars, and houses of hard wood that never rots. The city is undamaged, but it cannot be seen. Sinful men cannot behold the famous city of Kitež. It vanished miraculously, at the behest of God. . . . The tsar of the Tatars came to the great city of Kitež, intending to burn the houses, kill or enslave the men, and make concubines of the girls and women. But the Lord did not permit the desecration of Christian shrines by the infidels.

When Mel'nikov considers it necessary, he places stress marks over words, as with *čestnými* and *kondóvogo,* above. In describing everyday activities, his language differs little from that in our example. He scatters quotations from songs and legends in his stories and sets down long catalogues of objects and activities. In some passages, there is anaphora and rhymed prose.

Mel'nikov's account of the life of the Old Believers is often regarded as a good source of folklore. Besides quotations, he introduces supposed remnants of pre-Christian popular religion and mentions the pagan Slavic gods. But his sources are dubious. He relied on the romantic folklore literature of his time, especially the three-volume work *The Slavs' Poetic View of Nature* (1866–69) by A. N. Afanas'ev, to which he turned for the pagan story of creation (according to Mel'nikov, the "geocosmic love affair between heaven and earth"). Mel'nikov presents all the features of the mythological theory of folklore advanced by Afanas'ev and Max Müller. Mel'nikov's symbols—the earth washing its face with dew and drying with the towels of clouds, lightning as the arrow of a deity, and so forth—also go back to Afanas'ev. For popular superstitions, such as the symbolic meaning of plants and flowers, predicting the future, and magic, Mel'nikov used Afanas'ev, Saxarov, Tereščenco, and others, who also furnished most of his quotations for songs, legends, and incantations. These sources explain why his folklore comes from other parts of Russia—even the Ukraine—rather than from the Far Northeast. Mel'nikov's Old Believers are a little like a princess clothed by a scholarly romantic tailor. Mel'nikov's Slavic mythology is as much a creation of the nineteenth century as is that in Ostrovskij's *Sneguročka* (see chapter X, sec. 6).

All that was presented within a framework of realism. Impressive descriptions of popular festivals, a sleigh race at night, the virgin forests, a nun taking the veil, and the like, show in memorable scenes the exotic quality of life deep in Russia and are Mel'nikov's most important contribution to Russian literature.

7. Gleb Ivanovič Uspenskij (1843-1902) was of a younger generation than Mel'nikov. His family were officials in Tula. Uspenskij studied at St. Petersburg University and joined the populists. He began writing in the tradition of the Natural School, which by that time was largely forgotten. He drew away from literary narration toward physiological sketches, which had greater variety and complexity than those of the 1840s. In his later work, Uspenskij combined imaginary encounters and conversations with descriptions of real people, long-winded observations, statistics, and pages from diaries—in short, things normally thought of as journalism.

Uspenskij presents no landscapes, even when he describes the land; his scenes are gloomy and reminiscent of the Natural School. He first treated the petty bourgeoisie and artisans in city slums, as in his sketches *Nravy Rasterjaevoj ulicy* [The Manners of Rasterjaeva Street] (1886 ff.; the name *Rasterjaeva Street* sounds pejorative but has no particular meaning; it is derived from the verb *rasterjat'*, "to lose gradually"). The characters are poor and some of them degenerate. Uspenskij sensed emerging capitalism. But when he got to know the Volga peasants better, he lost some political and social illusions, in particular his belief in the socialistic tendency of the peasants within the *mir*. In describing peasant life, in his series *Vlast' zemli* [The Power of the Land], he seeks to excuse economic egoism, moral crudity, and cruelty on the grounds of the conditions in the villages. Uspenskij realizes that peasant businessmen and factory owners from outside the village have achieved a breakthrough. He often uses the metaphoric word *čumazyj* ("dirty," "smudgy," the smoke and soot from factories) for capitalism.

The development of capitalism seems to Uspenskij dark and tragic. He views capitalism as a disease that infects the whole country, a monster that devours it. Few of his characters are important; they are impersonal, are intended only to represent types, and are portrayed with bitter irony.

From 1892 until his death ten years later, Uspenskij was insane.

8. The professional man of letters Petr Dmitrievič Boborykin (1836–1921) was also of a younger generation. He studied science in Dorpat and wrote novels, plays, and lengthy memoirs. In a sense, he continued the work that Turgenev had begun by writing a "chronicle of Russian life" in the 1870s. Boborykin did not attain Turgenev's mastery, but he did supply writers on intellectual history with rather authentic material. His novels, some of them romans à clef, present typical persons, groups, and tendencies of the period. Scholars who regarded literature as a reflection of history found much material in Boborykin (men such as D. N. Ovsjaniko-Kulikovskij, who wrote a history of Russian literature as a history of the intelligentsia).

In his novel *Dr. Czybulka,* a Slavic, presumably Czech, teacher living in Russia is interested only in personal success. In *Vasilij Terkin* and *Kitaj-Gorod* (the business section of Moscow),

Boborykin describes critically and satirically but with less bias than Uspenskij the advance of Russian capitalism. In other novels, he notes the rise of Marxism (*Po-drugomu* [Different]) and of the proletariat (*Tjaga* [The Driving Force], 1898) and the beginnings of the symbolist school of literature. Boborykin's style is simple and good; he was a well-rounded writer, familiar with European culture, and he wrote convincing works that are still of interest and have made something of a comeback. He also began a history of the European novel but finished only the first volume, in 1900.

The "current" vocabulary that Boborykin uses is interesting. He seldom coined his neologisms, but got them from his contemporaries, particularly journalists. These words add life to his writing and are an untapped source of information on literary and vernacular Russian.

9. Several other realistic prose writers should be noted briefly.

The beginnings of the Russian psychological novel can be seen in the late work of A. F. Vel'tman (1800–1870) and in some of the novels written in Russian in the 1850s by the Ukrainian P. A. Kuliš (1819-1897, one of the first Gogol' scholars and the editor of his letters). Examples of this trend are particularly apparent in Vel'tman's recently reprinted *Adventures Drawn from the Sea of Life* (ca. 1850), which V. F. Pereverzev considers a direct predecessor of Dostoevskij's psychological novels.

Nadežda Dmitrievna Xvoščinskaja (1825–1889) wrote under the pen name V. Krestovskij, chiefly about women.

Boleslav Mixajlovič Markevič (1822–1884) was branded a reactionary by his contemporaries and largely ignored, especially since he was involved in a bribery scandal. Nevertheless, he was well regarded as a novelist by some, including A. K. Tolstoj. He also wrote on questions of literary theory. His unfinished trilogy, on the period from the 1840s to the 1870s and his own life, has been wrongly neglected. The first part, *A Quarter Century Ago,* about the forties, is particularly interesting. The second part of the trilogy is tendentious and antinihilistic.

The Ukrainian Marko Vovčok, the pen name of Marija Markovič (1834—1907), wrote more in Russian than did P. A. Kuliš. In the 1850s, she published sentimental novellas about peasants in good "Turgenev" style.

Vsevolod Vladimirovič Krestovskij (1840–1895) wrote much prose and poetry and is remembered for his adventure novel *Peterburgskie truščoby* [The St. Petersburg Slums] (1864 ff.), which combines a description of the slums with an exciting adventure story. His other prose works, including an antinihilistic novel, are unimportant.

Sergej Nikolaevič Terpigorev (1841–1895) wrote rather monotonous novellas on landowners before and after the emancipation of the serfs. His pseudonym is Sergej Atava.

Dmitrij Narkisovič Mamin (1852–1912) was born on the Siberian border, wrote novels and novellas about his native region, and later dealt with European Russia as well. He used the pseudonym Sibirjak.

Aleksandr Ivanovič Èrtel' (1855–1908, descended from Germans named Oertel) was interested in philosophy and wrote novels about the peasants' view of the world. His long, important novel *Gardeniny* [The Gardenins] makes a study of a family, through which he tries to picture all of Russian society.

Besides A. K. Tolstoj, Daniil Lukič Mordovcev (1836–1905) wrote historical novels, with varying success. Mordovcev wrote in Ukrainian and Russian and was unfairly criticized by his friend the historian N. I. Kostomarov, who remarked, "Our authors of historical novels are often accused of having a poor knowledge of history. Mr. Mordovcev is an exception; he knows no history at all." In contrast to Mordovcev, who stressed human interest, Count Evgenij Andreevič Salias de Tournemir (1840–1908) based his novels on historical sources. This practice was more successful in the hands of Vsevolod Sergeevič Solov'ev (1849–1903), son of a Moscow historian and brother of the philosopher Vladimir Solov'ev. Solov'ev's novels give a broad picture of the not-too-distant eighteenth century.

10. Oddly enough, Sergej Timofeevič Aksakov (1791–1859), who payed homage to late classicism as a young man and later admired Gogol' and whose sons, Konstantin and Ivan, were mainly influenced by romanticism, was one of the most important Russian realists. His best work came out after 1845.

Aksakov was born in Ufa, in extreme eastern European Russia. He grew up on the family estate in Orenburg Province, went to high school and college in Kazan, became a government official, retired in 1839, and lived in Moscow. As a young man, he was attracted to the "archaistic" classicists, wrote in the classicist style, and translated Boileau and Molière. The literary interests of his sons and his acquaintance with Gogol' led him to resume his writing, a realistic rebirth of the classicist style. Aksakov shows that the new realism is related to classicism, a kinship with few other examples.

In his reminiscences of fishing (1847) and hunting (1852), his excellent, even style suits the subject matter, dispenses with burdensome Church Slavonicisms, and is, by and large, a model of realistic prose. From 1856 on, Aksakov published novels that could be grouped under the title of the first of them, *Semejnaja xronika* [Family Chronicle]. These novels are autobiographical or semiautobiographical works of the kind that Herzen, L. N. Tolstoj, Korolenko, Gor'kij, Belyj, and F. A. Stepun were later to write, works that combine truth with fantasy. All in all, Aksakov seems to have stuck to the truth and to have changed only names (for instance, "Aksakov" becomes "Bagrov"). His novels cover the period from the last third of the eighteenth century to the beginning of the nineteenth century and include much that he must have heard from his parents or surmised. He describes nature, as he had done in his brilliantly clear recollections of fish, birds, and other animals.

An example is his treatment of the partridge:

> How beautiful his motley, dark, reddish-yellow, brown, and light green feathers are! How symmetrically, roundly, and firmly he is built! How alive, quick, dexterous, and handsome all his motions are! ... He is distinguished by the speed with which he runs and by his swift, straight line of flight. He takes off quickly and noisily and can startle a person who is taken unawares.

His descriptions of other animals are equally vivid.

In his autobiographical novels, Aksakov brings to life diverse landscapes and characters. His vocabulary is rich, as in his many designations for colors, and it contains local words from Aksakov's region, as well as technical words on farming, fishing, and hunting. After a brief introduction, characters are often allowed to reveal themselves through their speech and actions. Usually, little is told about their innermost thoughts; the reader is left to deduce these thoughts from the characters' behavior. Aksakov portrays his grandfather by showing him in various situations, on a good day, on a bad day, and so on. Aksakov narrates chronologically, and one must wait to decide what kind of person a character is. Despite the many characters, one does not lose track of them; and Aksakov, unusually objective even for a realistic writer, seldom judges them. Persons are treated much as are birds and fish. Although the pike is not very likable, it is described with the same poetic love as other animals. Aksakov was sometimes reproached for his objectivity; but the reader learns at least as much from his objectivity as from the satirical, tendentious, and ideological works of the time. It is especially interesting that Aksakov was able to describe his early literary enthusiasm for works such as the epics and didactic novels of Xeraskov, works considered unbearably dull since the 1830s, in such a way that readers of a later day feel close to them. This ability accounts for the importance of Aksakov's *Literary Reminiscences,* which grew to a long series of sketches.

A *Family Chronicle* has no plot; it has, rather, several compositional lines. Aksakov's grandfather is an old-fashioned landowner, often unjust and cruel; but through the influence of his daughter-in-law, Aksakov's mother, he eventually mends his ways. She has married Aksakov's (Bagrov's) father for love, an act that strikes the grandfather as incomprehensible and reprehensible. She seems a stranger to her husband's relatives, since she is from a family of officials in the city, and conditions in the country are repellent to her. Aksakov shows how she brings about a change in his father and has a healthy effect on those around her. He does not praise her excessively but does show how she is able to rise above conditions in the country, though she is herself simple and provincial. In a sense, *A Family Chronicle* is a Russian *Entwicklungsroman*; and Aksakov traces his intellectual development more convincingly than do L. N. Tolstoj and Herzen in their literary autobiographies, for, as they write, they are unable to leave their present stage of intellectual development and put themselves completely in the past.

XII
Saltykov-Ščedrin

1. The satirist Mixail Evgrafovič Saltykov (1826–1889), who used the pseudonym N. Ščedrin, has a special place in Russian realism. The son of a landowner in Tver Province, Saltykov attended the Lyceum at Carskoe Selo, where Puškin, Del'vig, and other writers had gone, and wrote poems there, which he later omitted from his works. The task of Carskoe Selo was to educate boys to become high officials; and in 1844, after finishing school, Saltykov went to work in the Ministry of War. He learned the ideas of utopian socialism but was only briefly a member of the Petraševskij circle (see chapter VI, sec 1. Petraševskij was a fellow student of Saltykov at Carskoe Selo). In 1847–48, Saltykov published his first novellas, in which the Minister of War found ideas already "shaking Western Europe." As a problem case, Saltykov was transferred to Vyatka, where Herzen had lived in exile. Saltykov was not allowed in the capitals of Russia until after the death of Nicholas I. On his return, he became Deputy Governor of Ryazan, and later of Tver. In 1862, he was forced to resign because of friction with landowners. After two years with the radical magazine *Sovremennik,* he went back to the government, to the Ministry of Finance. In 1868, he left government service for good and went to work for Nekrasov's *Otečestvennye zapiski.* After Nekrasov's death, Saltykov was editor-in-chief of the magazine until it was banned.

Saltykov wrote novellas, many of which he included in the two cycles *Gubernskie očerki* [Provincial Sketches] (1856-57) and *Pošexonskaja starina* [Old Times in Pošexonie] (1887–89), a novel, *Gospoda Golovlevy* [The Golovlev Family] (1875 ff.), satirical "fairy tales" (1886), and the grotesque *History of a City* (1860 ff.). He also wrote semijournalistic sketches, which make up the greater part of his work. He gave these sketches titles that often tell little about the content, such as *Present-Day Idylls* (1883),

Motley Letters (1884–86), and *Pis'ma k teten'ke* [Letters to Auntie] (1882). The reason these sketches are "motley" is that Saltykov often wished to discuss current issues and devoted articles to topics that had little to do with other articles in the series.

Not all Saltykov's contemporaries thought well of his semijournalistic work; many of them, including those who agreed with his views, found his style crude and his humor superficial.

2. Saltykov's description of conditions in Russia, especially of serfdom in Pošexonie—"Podunk"—is terribly gloomy. The corrupt bureaucracy and inhuman landowners differ from related types in the literature of the day in that they have no positive features at all. The only characters in Saltykov with some attractive features are the peasants in his early novellas, peasants somewhat akin to Turgenev's. Saltykov thought that there was something positive about the peasants' feeling for religion but had nothing good to say about the Old Believers or religious sects (*raskoly*). The many urban types in his novellas are all negative. In his later novellas, he turns again to serfdom and finds hardly a ray of hope. He thinks that emancipation has been a failure, since the liberated serfs seem as badly off as before.

Saltykov's novel *The Golovlev Family* was begun as a series of separate novellas and was brought out in book form in 1880. It hardly differs in tone from his other novellas. The aristocratic Golovlevs are all unfeeling egoists, unscrupulous, caring only for their material well-being. Eventually, they are undone, with the exception of the worst of them, Iuduška [Little Judas], who operates with hypocrisy and cunning and is, in the end, the apparent victor. His success cannot stave off madness; and after his mother's funeral, he becomes deranged, goes out into a blizzard, and freezes to death.

3. *The History of a City* is a bitterly ironic caricature of Russia in the eighteenth and nineteenth centuries, an account of fantastic events in a city of blockheads (the name of the city is Glupov, from *glupyj*, "stupid"), ruled by the incompetent and cruel. The men who govern the city have various features of Russian tsars, tsarinas, and statesmen, and reflect Russian history. Saltykov characterizes each governor in a register in which attempts to improve conditions or education appear senseless, such as "introduction of mustard and the laurel leaf," for which war was

waged against those who resisted. The governors are portrayed as sentimental ("He could not hear the black cock's mating call without weeping") or licentious ("He almost doubled the population of Glupov"). They come from families of clergymen (a reference to M. M. Speranskij, codifier of Russian law) or have been elevated from low stations by the tsar and made governors (as was a "former stoker in Gatchina," the site of a palace of Paul I, who had conferred nobility upon his footman and barber). The appalling episode of the battles of the "six women governors" is a wicked caricature of the five empresses who ruled Russia from 1725 to 1762. Occasionally, fairy-tale motifs are introduced into the realistic satire. One governor has in his head a machine that repeats "I will not put up with that" and "I will destroy it" ("*Ne poterplju*"; "*Razzorju*"); another has, in place of a head, a pastry that the marshal of the nobility eats from time to time. The *History of a City* ends as one governor destroys the old city and builds a new one on another site, and another governor "rode into the city on a white horse, burned the high school building, and abolished learning." But the citizens are no better than their governors; they are incapable of offering resistance, and their rebellions are confined to fighting and murdering each other.

Saltykov's "fairy tales" were written between the 1860s and the 1880s and are actually fables in prose, often animal fables. The persons and animals in the fables are symbols of the same types as those in his novellas; bureaucrats, incompetent authorities, oppressed, timid, and long-suffering citizens, vacillating liberals incapable of action, and patient, hard-working peasants who do not resist injustice. One type is the idealistic carp who tries to preach virtue to a pike. The astonished pike takes a breath, draws in water, and, almost without noticing, swallows the optimistic carp. This tale shows that Saltykov is content to appear to be a hopeless pessimist. Actually, he considered socialism a way out of the intolerable situation; but, of course, he could not write about that.

4. In his essays, Saltykov does not always speak in his own name. He is fond of talking through a fictitious author and is a master of stylization. He seldom writes directly about matters at hand; it was only through the masterful use of allusion that he was able to publish, for his audience knew how to read between

the lines. He treats Russian life under cover names. For example, government officials concerned only with fulfilling selfish aims are called "Pompadours," in the series *Pompadury i pompadurši* (1873); and when Russians sought to get rich in Russian Central Asia, Saltykov portrayed a new type, the Tashkenter, named after Tashkent. Tashkenters carry "culture" to Central Asia because "Tashkent is a classic land of wethers that can always be sheared and that grow wool with astonishing speed." The progovernment or venal press to which Saltykov is hostile is given imaginary names, such as the newspaper *Čego izvolite?* [What Is Your Pleasure?] and *Pomoi* [Dishwater]. At a time when the secret police had feelers everywhere, Saltykov described an international congress of statisticians in Russia, at which all "foreign" participants are police agents with assumed names of well-known Western European statisticians; the story anticipates the theme of Chesterton's *The Man Who Was Thursday*. Saltykov even dared write about the Secret Society, alluding to the *"Svjaščennaja družina"* or "Holy Guard" formed in high government circles in 1881, after the murder of Tsar Alexander II, to combat revolutionaries.

In his essays, Saltykov uses names of well-known characters in Russian literature. Griboedov's insignificant Molčalin becomes a malicious, criminal civil servant in Saltykov's hands. In some sketches, Saltykov draws sarcastic caricatures of conditions in Russia. He denounces the lack of respect for human dignity and designates a "going rate" for assault and battery. A statute assigns the Academy of Science the task of "suspending harmful learning, and, if no remorse is evident, of forbidding it altogether," since one can separate the kinds of learning into the "useful and the harmful." Saltykov also takes a stand on the supervision of the police and the censorship of culture. The persistent traditions of the police state, which go back to Nicholas I, prompt Saltykov to write his *Rules for Proper Cake Baking* in the best legal language; the final point is that, when the cake is baked, the middle part must be cut out and taken as a gift to the official in charge; only someone who "does all that may eat" (an able parody on many pages of Speranskij's legal code.[1] Much of Saltykov's grotes-

1. See D. Čiževskij, *Russische Geistesgeschichte,* II (Hamburg, 1961), 63 f.

query has lost its meaning, since he treats long-forgotten events, scandals, and court trials. Without commentaries, his satires could be taken for a collection of jokes and anecdotes.

A trip to Western Europe prompted Saltykov to write his series of sketches *Na čužbine* [Abroad]. He found very little abroad that he liked. The reader comes away with the idea that modern society should be torn down to make way for a new system. The difference between the West and Russia is illustrated in the conversation between a Western "boy with pants" and a Russian "boy without pants". The Western boy confesses that he sold his soul to the devil for a penny; the Russian boy simply gave his soul to the devil. This devil is money, or capitalism, which was thriving in the West but just beginning to make headway in Russia. Like D. I. Fonvizin a hundred years before, Saltykov overlooked the accomplishments of Western arts and science and dealt with French literature in a maliciously uninformed caricature.

5. What distinguishes Saltykov from his realistic contemporaries and makes his satire unique in Russian literature is his language and style. He wrongly thought of himself as a follower of Gogol', though, like Gogol', he went beyond the norms of literary language and enriched his vocabulary with countless words and expressions from different linguistic strata, including argot. In this respect, Saltykov's satirical essays and the *History of a City* are especially notable. In his novels and novellas, he adheres more to literary norms.

In many ways, Saltykov's innovations continue those of Nekrasov, although Saltykov is less indebted to the vernacular and to the speech of the landed gentry. He uses expressions that even the common people would have considered vulgarisms, such as invective and the language of drunks and crooks.

Most of Saltykov's nonliterary words came from judicial language and the legislative language that was already beginning to sound archaic. The use of this vocabulary in his primarily satirical works cleverly suggests that the parasites, extortionists, and shady dealers portrayed are somehow connected with the authorities, since they all speak in the same way. Saltykov employs the epithet *administrative* with words such as "forgery," "slap in the face," "efforts," "cheap taverns," "kiss" (in the sense of "Judas kiss"), and "enthusiasm." He makes suggestive use of *arxiv, pravo, zloumyšlenie,* and *pravomernost'*.

Many of these words are foreign or Church Slavonic and, in Saltykov's context, they sound ironic and hostile to the Church. The Church Slavonic *sonmišče,* "group," is used in combinations such as *"sonmišče staryx dev,* " "group of old maids," and *"sonmišče èlegantnyx molodyx ljudej,"* "group of elegant young people"; and *žrecy,* "priests," appears in combinations such as *"žrecy kanceljarij,"* "priests of the law office," and "high priest of literary gossip." Saltykov makes similar use of *stogna, vesi, vertograd, vopijat', peščis',* and *predrekat'*.

The satirical use of these and economic, technical, and scientific words consists in Saltykov's making new complexes of phrases in which the exalted, archaic words are debased and the words used with them appear ironic. Interestingly, Saltykov goes back to the use of grotesque names, which were popular in the eighteenth century and occur in the work of Gogol'. Sometimes these names are given to swindlers, sometimes to ordinary characters for the sake of humor.

Saltykov uses neologisms, but obvious ones, mostly formed by adding such Church Slavonic suffixes as *-ost', -stvo, -nie,* and *tel'*.

Many expressions that Saltykov introduced have become popular sayings in Russian, such as "administrative enthusiasm," describing pointless or harmful administrative measures carried out with great enthusiasm. There were no worthy imitators of Saltykov; writers who tried to follow him were capable only of dull invective. More than any other Russian writer, Saltykov had the gift of viewing reality with merciless sarcasm.

Various Kinds of Realism

1. From the treatment of prose writers in the preceding chapters, it should be clear that there was as much leeway in realism as in romanticism and that realists were not required to adopt a particular view of the world. It was not until later that socialist realists attempted to find a common denominator for writers of the old variety of realism. Although non-Russian theoreticians, such as the Hungarian G. Lukács and the Pole S. Morawski,

have put forward more convincing cases than have contemporary Russians, they have left too many questions unanswered and have resorted to paralogisms to force nineteenth-century Russian realistic writers into their own narrow definitions.

2. Dostoevskij and Leskov differ from most recognized Russian realists in that they are not content to portray typical characters of a period, country, or class. They are more interested in borderline cases, in men who are "worse" or "better" than average. Such men may have sunk to the level of criminals or animals, or they may be angelic and saintly; they may be eccentrics or dreamers, social outcasts, pilgrims, beggars, drunks, madmen, or prisoners. Dostoevskij and Leskov also present empty characters, men with nothing to them, no interests and no desires.

Almost all these types occurred in romanticism. But Dostoevskij and Leskov, the two realistic writers interested in borderline cases, used romantic poetics far less than did other realists. It was during the 1860s that Dostoevskij began writing his major works and Leskov, his first works, when the romantic tradition had all but died out. Some characters who could be considered atypical appear in works by survivors of the Natural School, such as I. I. Panaev. Both Dostoevskij and Leskov prefer extreme situations, thoroughly unusual ones. That could be considered a legacy from the romanticists, who were fond of paradoxical plots. But despite the still strong influence of the great romanticists, Dostoevskij and Leskov hardly borrowed their situations from them.

In most respects, Turgenev is closer to romantic poetics than are Dostoevskij and Leskov; and S. Rodzevič is right in calling him the "romanticist of realism." But Turgenev, Pisemskij, Boborykin, Gleb Uspenskij, and many other realists attempt to present typical or average characters and situations and to write a literary chronicle of the time.

3. In style and composition ǀ the Russian realists go different ways, and these ways become more apparent in the late realism of Čexov and Gor'kij, to some extent, and their followers. The naive theoretical basis of realism was that literature should describe reality. In Russia, it was thought possible to represent reality exactly, although the old interpretation of mimesis had long since been refined. There was discussion, of course, about rendering the "typical" and the "characteristic"; but the goal was to portray

reality, to present as many characteristic features of reality as possible in a work of literature. Realists sought to depict precisely landscapes, characters, cities, and living quarters. But Dostoevskij seldom describes characters and gets around describing cities by selecting well-known ones.

Since an exact portrayal of the real world and real people is impossible, it is natural that a presentation was found that may be called impressionistic. Realistic writers wish to convey the impression that what they describe is credible. It is not enough, however, to reproduce typical features of reality in order to create impressive characters and scenes. It is often necessary to note individual traits of personality, features of a face, details of landscapes and surroundings, and the way a man moves or walks. Portrayals of extreme situations are based on details. But in literature, the impressionistic style is properly limited to that of those writers who make deliberate use of individual strokes and touches that raise their characters above the typical and impress them on the reader. These individual touches may appear to be accidental or superficial and may be condemned by consistent realistic critics.

In their grotesquery, the romanticists often employed impressionistic devices. Among realists, L. N. Tolstoj was the writer who made the most conspicuous use of these devices, a practice at first criticized by Turgenev and K. N. Leont'ev. It was not until later that these devices were understood, and even then they were used sparingly. In late realism, impressionistic descriptions became a recognized stylistic device. Nevertheless, impressionism was seldom dealt with theoretically and was long considered by critics a literary flaw.

4. I have used the word *impressionism* in connection with Afanasij Fet. In keeping with the demands of poetry, Fet, who wrote primarily miniature poems, used the compositional, lexical, and syntactical devices discussed in Chapter X. For the broad, complex purposes of prose writers, impressionistic devices merely sharpen and polish individual scenes. It was not until short prose forms became popular that impressionistic devices were emphasized, a practice obvious in Čexov and, to some extent, in V. M. Garšin. Tolstoj's use of impressionism is deliberate but limited.

XIII

L. N. Tolstoj

1. Like Dostoevskij, Lev Nikolaevič Tolstoj (1828–1910) is a writer of international renown and an important figure in the intellectual history of Russia. In his works, he speaks his mind more directly than does Dostoevskij on Russian and Western European culture; and he was an important influence in his own lifetime. To discuss his creative work adequately, one should first review the main events of his life. Tolstoj now appears a monolithic giant, but he wrote differently at various times and underwent an ideological change. In his work, he usually tries to render reality objectively; but more than any other Russian writer, he expresses his opinions openly and, at times, obtrusively, by developing his mutable ideas quite consistently in his characters and stories.

Tolstoj's works are didactic, but they are essentially different from the equally didactic works of Dostoevskij, who is an eternal seeker and takes the reader on his search. Like his ever-changing authorities, Tolstoj deals almost exclusively with developed thoughts and systems of thought designed to convert the reader. Surprisingly, this passionate stubbornness in proclaiming truths that he has discovered does not diminish the aesthetic value of his literary work.

2. Although the vicissitudes of Tolstoj's long life may explain much about his approach to literature, in my opinion biographical explanations are not a proper part of literary history. Nevertheless, one must do more than give an outline of Tolstoj's life; one must go more thoroughly than usual into his changing views.

Lev Tolstoj was born in 1828 on the estate that he made famous, Jasnaja Poljana, near Tula, in southern Great Russia, the region of which Turgenev, Fet, and Leskov were also natives. When

Tolstoj was two, his mother died; when he was nine, his father; and Tolstoj was reared by relatives. In 1844, he enrolled in the department of Oriental languages at Kazan University, with the intention of becoming a diplomat; later, he studied law. In 1847, he left Kazan and went to St. Petersburg, where he hoped to take his university examinations. After he had already begun them, he changed his mind, went back to Jasnaja Poljana, and opened a school there for peasant children, where he did some of the teaching. In 1851, he joined the army and fought against the mountaineers in the Northern Caucasus. There he planned a number of works and completed *Detstvo* [Childhood], which came out in 1852; and *Otročestvo* [Boyhood], which came out in 1854. Although he had no close literary connections, these works along with several novellas made him one of the most respected writers in Russia. His psychological descriptions were considered remarkable (by Nikolaj Černyševskij among others).

In 1854, Tolstoj secured a transfer to the Army of the Danube, which was fighting the Turks. During the Crimean War, he was in Sevastopol during the siege and wrote reports in the form of novellas, the *Sevastopol Stories*.

When the war and the era of Nicholas I were over, Tolstoj went to St. Petersburg, where he met the best-known writers of the day, Turgenev, Grigorovič, Nekrasov, Družinin. In 1857, Tolstoj published the third part of his "autobiographical" trilogy, *Junost'* [Youth]. The entire trilogy is a mixture of truth and fiction. He planned to write a fourth part, but never finished it. *Utro pomeščika* [The Morning of a Landowner], published in 1856, was probably to have been part of it.

3. It was clear that Tolstoj did not feel close to the other Russian writers of his day. All the others were, in one way or another, the products of the intellectual atmosphere of the 1840s. Leskov was no exception, although he had a different social background. In his fierce egocentricity, Tolstoj sought to see everything from his own point of view and adhered to writers such as Rousseau, Voltaire, Swift, and Sterne, who were considered passé. Tolstoj had little interest in the intellectual sources of his contemporaries, romanticism and the philosophy of the German idealists, from Kant and Schiller to Hegel. As a result, he had to find his own authorities. They proved to be influential Western thinkers and

currents of thought (he "discovered" Schopenhauer and, through him, the Orient and Schopenhauer's interpretation of Kant; later, Tolstoj was interested in social reformers of the turn of the century and in liberal Protestant theology) and isolated Russian philosophers and sects. Occasionally, Tolstoj's path crossed that of other Russian writers and thinkers, though generally he went his own way. Some of his contemporaries, such as N. N. Straxov and Leskov, were drawn to him but had reservations about his ideas.

4. In 1856, Tolstoj left the army and took a trip to Europe. After his return, in 1857, he lived alternately at Jasnaja Poljana and in Moscow. He was very much interested in the reforms being worked on, especially in emancipation. In 1859, he published the novella *Tri smerti* [Three Deaths], in which didactic motifs are obvious. His interest in education was reawakened; and he took a second trip to Europe, to study European schools. He had a low opinion of them, especially of German ones, but came home with many ideas on education, gained not from educators but largely from the writer Berthold Auerbach and the Munich historian Wilhelm Riehl, now regarded as a sociologist. Tolstoj did not agree with the leading Russian educators, who had begun to go in new directions.

In 1861, the emancipation of the serfs was proclaimed; and Tolstoj took an active part in carrying out reforms in his district. He worked as a mediator (*mirovoj posrednik*) in conflicts between peasants and landowners, but he soon resigned because of friction with landowners.

Tolstoj's marriage to Sof'ja Andreevna Bers, in 1862, was the main turning point in his life. Once married, he withdrew to Jasnaja Poljana, and afterward his life was closely connected with his estate and his growing family.

He soon turned again to literature. He wrote the novella *Kazaki* [The Cossacks] and the peasant novella *Polikuška* (a proper name). Both of these works came out in 1863, and Tolstoj then started work on his major novels. He planned a novel about Russia from 1812 to 1825—that is, about the Decembrists—and he wrote a family novel, *1805,* that later served as the first part of *Vojna i mir* [War and Peace], completed in 1869, in which he presents his philosophy of history. He collected material for a novel on the period of Peter the Great, but put it aside. Returning to education, he wrote a primer (*Azbuka*) and short tales to be used in Russian class. He carried on a polemic on educational questions and again could not agree with Russian educators.

In 1873, Tolstoj began work on a new novel, *Anna Karenina*, which came out from 1875 to 1877 and was evidently even less appreciated than *War and Peace*. Around this time, he went through a religious and philosophical crisis that held sway over the rest of his life and found expression in his extensive religious and philosophical writing.

The first evidence of this crisis was his "folk tales." Then came his didactic literary works, such as his "folk drama" *Vlast' t'my* [The Power of Darkness] (1886), the novella *Smert' Ivana Il'iča* [The Death of Ivan Il'ič], and the novella *Krejcerova sonata* [The Kreuzer Sonata] (1889). In 1899, Tolstoj brought out his last major novel, *Voskresenie* [Resurrection], which had to be published abroad, in a not entirely authentic version.

In 1898, Tolstoj published his treatise *Čto takoe iskusstvo?* [What Is Art?]. Most of his other theological and moralistic treatises had to be published abroad. Like the anticlerical passages in *Resurrection,* they led to an open conflict with the authorities of the Russian Church; and, in 1901, Tolstoj was excommunicated by the Holy Synod.

Around 1891 and 1898, Tolstoj took part in famine relief; this act, along with his social and political views and a letter to Tsar Alexander III, brought about a conflict with the civil authorities. Only Tolstoj's worldwide reputation prevented the government from taking action against him. He continued openly to condemn the government's policies, such as the execution of political opponents after the revolution of 1905.

Although Tolstoj tried to give up literature, his creative urge was so great that he was compelled to keep writing. His late works, among them the play *Živoj trup* [The Living Corpse], were published posthumously in three volumes.

Tolstoj's death came as tragic evidence of his break with those close to him. For a long time, his family had not sympathized with his ideas; and, as early as 1884, he had planned to leave home. In the fall of 1910, he left Jasnaja Poljana and several days later was found ill in the railroad station at Astapovo, where he died on November 7. His flight from the orderly circumstances of his home moved his contemporaries. But the government was opposed to doing him homage, and public mourning was forbidden. When students demonstrated, the universities were closed. The government proceeded against the press, organizations, and individuals with arrests and reprisals. And all that was repeated a year later on the anniversary of Tolstoj's death.

5. With his moral, religious, and social writings, Tolstoj won many followers in Russia and abroad. Some of these followers formed groups of "Tolstojvians" (*tolstovcy*), which resembled sects, and attempted to put Tolstoj's ideas into practice. Whenever these groups acted, they were subject to persecution by the police. Even Russians who did not agree with Tolstoj considered him a kind of conscience of Russia.

In Russia and abroad, opinions differed on Tolstoj's work and ideology. Some saw in his ideas a "Russian view of the world." Others thought that his ideas were utopian and were doomed to failure or might be harmful. Boris Èjxenbaum is right that, in its sources, Tolstoj's "is the least Russian work of any Russian writer," since he came to literature as a "stranger," stood apart from the literary currents of his time from about 1856 on, and blazed his own trails. Tolstoj did not at first have much influence on literature, but he was unquestionably one of the great Russian writers. His expulsion from the Church and the government's disapproval of his work did not prevent many in authority from respecting and admiring him. Some theologians found Tolstoj's unorthodox religiosity a vital force. One professor of theology spoke well of Tolstoj as a religious and ethical seeker—and was dismissed from his position.

6. Apart from characters who represent Russian types, there are in all Tolstoj's works individual characters who reflect some aspect of his real or imaginary personality. It is true that none of Tolstoj's works is purely autobiographical; but in his trilogy, *Cossacks* and *Morning of a Landowner*, there are autobiographical features. Characters such as Nikolen'ka Irten'ev (*Childhood, Boyhood, Youth*), and Olenin (*Cossacks*) speak Tolstoj's language. And Levin (*Anna Karenina*) is particularly close to him.

All these characters tend to observe and analyze themselves. The novels of the trilogy consist partly of scenes accompanied by extensive psychological commentary. The analysis is at first concerned with the central character's search for security, in his family and, later, at college, among people from a completely different background. The central character's awareness that he is different from his brother and from other students at college and his efforts to draw close to people seemed even to sympathetic readers, such as Apollon Grigor'ev, hardly worthwhile describing in a work of literature. But the art of Tolstoj's psychology and the perfection of his writing won over men such as Černyševskij who had nothing in common with him.

Tolstoj's typical novel technique comes out in his trilogy. He concentrates on Nikolen'ka but does not neglect other characters. There are several parallel lines, typical of Tolstoj's "decentralized" composition in *War and Peace* and *Anna Karenina*; in some novellas, such as *Two Hussars* and *Three Deaths,* these parallel lines develop into comparisons and contrasts of human types.

Autobiographical motifs are most evident in *The Cossacks*. The principal character, Olenin, has an "aversion to well-traveled paths." As Tolstoj had done, he observes the Cossacks fight against the mountaineers in the Northern Caucasus. Tolstoj pays particular attention to his relations with the Cossacks. The old Cossack Eroška, the young Mar'jana, with whom Olenin falls in love, and his rival in love, Luka (Lukaška), are represented as "natural people," in contrast to Olenin. The opposition between "civilized" and "natural" men is emphasized when an acquaintance of Olenin comes to the village (*stanica*), where Olenin has become attracted to Cossack ways. Gradually, Olenin realizes that he cannot become a Cossack. He sees that Mar'jana can never love him, and he leaves the village. The problem treated in *The Cossacks* is much the same as in Puškin's *Gypsies.* The best drawn "natural" character is Uncle Eroška. With an art all his own, Tolstoj portrays but does not idealize him. Eroška is coarse, cruel, and egoistic; but he has those human features that Olenin and civilized men have lost. (Another of Tolstoj's "natural" men is Platon Karataev in *War and Peace.*)

Rousseau's influence on Tolstoj has often been stressed; but the two were similar only in that they contrasted "civilized" and "natural" men. It was not until later, in his criticism of modern "civilized" society, that Tolstoj used Rousseau's arguments, which he had learned in his youth.

In other stories, Tolstoj carries the motif of *The Cossacks* further and contrasts "civilized" man with subhuman life, as in *Three Deaths,* which was written in 1858, during the slow work on *The Cossacks,* and explores the theme that the two levels of society cannot understand each other. These levels are "natural" men, who have preserved their inner freedom, and those men who have been changed, or corrupted, by civilization. Civilized men are contrasted with peasants and with animal and plant life. *Three Deaths* does not tell outright whether mutual understanding is possible between natural and civilized man. Three deaths are described: that of a lady, a coachman, and a tree. The lady appears first at a posting station on her way abroad, where she hopes to be cured, and later in her apartment in Moscow, where she dies. She clings to life desperately. Her husband and doctor no longer believe that she can be cured, but they pretend to believe, and they lie to her. She is surrounded by deception. At the posting station where the lady has stopped, a coachman is dying, and he divides his modest belongings and warm place on the stove among the other people who live in the house. His death is quiet and simple. The third death is that of the tree that a friend of the coachman chops for a cross to put on the grave. The tree dies tranquilly. Birds continue to sing; the branches of the other trees "move slowly and solemnly over the dead tree." Tolstoj explains the basic thought of the work in a letter to A. A. Tolstaja, May 1, 1858: "The lady is sick and disgusting; she has lied all her life and lies again just before her death. The peasant (coachman) dies peacefully; his religion is nature, with which he lives. The tree dies peacefully, honestly, and beautifully."

The story *Xolstomer* (the name of a horse; the piece was written around 1863 and published in 1886) contrasts the life of a racehorse with the dishonest and corrupt life of man. The "noble horse" had been a subject for reflection by cynics in the classical period and by Jonathan Swift, in *Gulliver's Travels.*

7. Tolstoj's interest in education diverted him for a time from literature, for he was convinced that the peasant children could write better than he or any other major Russian writer. He

defended this "discovery" with his usual passion and later wrote excellent children's stories and "folk" tales.

Toward the end of the 1850s, Tolstoj attempted to describe the life of the peasants as it was "in reality." While abroad, he had read the peasant tales of Berthold Auerbach and Jeremias Gotthelf. He acquired several educational ideas from Auerbach and found in Gotthelf (whose collected works he took back to Russia) the model for the merciless gloom of his own peasant novellas, as B. M. Ejxenbaum points out.

In some of his peasant novellas, Tolstoj acknowledges that there are people who have nothing in common with people of his own cultural level. He believed at the time that Russian literature was alien to the common people. "There are works of Puškin, Gogol', and Turgenev," he writes and then mentions the best-known magazines, "and all these magazines and works are unfamiliar to the common people. The common people do not need them (*nenužny*) and derive no benefit from them (*nikakoj vygody*)." But Tolstoj continues to write about the common people, not for them.

The most typical of Tolstoj's peasant novellas is *Polikuška* (written in 1859–1860, published in 1861). It tells of the peasant Polikej, who lives before emancipation, at a time when landowners control the destinies of their serfs and decide who must serve in the army. Military service is for twenty-five years, virtually the rest of one's life. The landowner in the novella is an apparently well-intentioned but moody woman. She must choose someone for military service, and Polikej is a candidate. He is said to have been a thief. Since he has supposedly reformed, she sends him to the city to pay a large sum of money. He loses the money and hangs himself, leaving behind a wife and five children. His youngest child also dies, and his wife is distraught and goes mad. In the end, the money is found by another peasant, and the landowner gives it to him. His family must also put up someone for the army. They use the money to buy a substitute, a permissible practice. And no one seems to care about Polikej's family.

The opening lines and other passages in the novella indicate that Tolstoj intended to show the power of fate over the life of the peasant and the attitude of the peasant to his fate, which was quite different from that of cultured people. Later, Tolstoj discovered other basic features of peasant life. *Polikuška* is the darkest picture of serfdom in Russian literature.

8. Tolstoj's great work *War and Peace* developed out of plans to write a novel on the Decembrists. He rightly thought of the generation of the Decembrists as his intellectual ancestors. In writing a novel set in 1805, he meant to deal with events that led up to the Decembrists. The first scenes take place in a Petersburg salon, where much French is spoken. The Napoleonic Wars are going on, and war is the subject of several chapters. The important families of the work are introduced (Tolstoj did not decide on the title *War and Peace* until later). The lives of the principal characters are tied together, and the many secondary characters help to set the time and place. These secondary characters include historical persons, although the principal characters are fictitious. The first part of the novel, which appeared as *1805,* presents the families of Prince Bolkonskij and of Count Rostov. Several characters are emphasized: Prince Andrej Bolkonskij, the childlike Nataša Rostov, and Pierre, Count Bezuxov's illegitimate son, who has been reared abroad. These characters are carefully, clearly drawn. The preliminaries to the novel and the detailed account of the time and setting show the metonymical (see chapter I) nature of *War and Peace,* a feature that K. Hamburger has called "decentralization." Important characters are generally described in detail. Tolstoj makes consistent use of description that could be called impressionistic, since it emphasizes certain features but neglects an over-all depiction. Turgenev considered this method an innovation and rejected it.

The composition of *War and Peace* is cohesive and depends on a contrast between historical and personal events, between conventional and unconventional people. In war scenes, those who believe in plans of battle are grouped together; actually, it is only vain, ambitious officers who pretend to believe in such plans. Opposed to them are soldiers and officers who make decisions practically, according to the situation at hand. The hostess of a Petersburg salon seeks to manipulate her guests as the "manager of a weaving mill" manipulates workers and machines. Like a maitre d'hotel, she "serves up" distinguished visitors. But in Moscow high society, there are persons such as Pierre and Andrej, as well as eccentrics and children, who do not observe the conventions. Similarly, in battle, there are those who cannot grasp the disposition of troops but who may decisively influence the course of the fighting. Among these is the enigmatic Russian commander-in-chief, Kutuzov, who remains curiously passive and takes things as they come.

Tolstoj makes no effort to conceal the tendentiousness of his writing. He lays bare hypocrisy and stupidity, a practice acquired from his boyhood reading, particularly of Voltaire and Swift. Exposing these qualities does not prevent Tolstoj from creating convincing, memorable, individual characters.

Tolstoj's impressionistic devices include stressing features that typify the build, face, movements, and habits of his characters, identifying them for the reader. For instance, Prince Andrej Bolkonskij's pretty wife has down on her somewhat narrow upper lip, as Tolstoj frequently points out. Andrej Bolkonskij is lean and has, one is often reminded, "small white hands." Of the three Mamontov sisters who keep Count Bezuxov company, one has a "long and dry waist" and another, a birthmark on her face. The diplomat Bilibin has the habit of wrinkling his forehead. This art of emphasizing certain physical features prompted D. S. Merežkovskij to call Tolstoj a "clairvoyant of the body." But Tolstoj also stresses features of his characters that reveal their souls. He often mentions the "shining," "radiant," "lovely" eyes of Andrej Bolkonskij's unattractive sister. The expression on Andrej Bolkonskij's face—at times bored, at times energetic—and the interest of his father, an eighteenth-century man, in geometry and working with his hands tell more about the spiritual aspects than they do about the physical side of their lives. Tolstoj emphasizes spiritual qualities in the same impressionistic way in which he accents physical qualities. There is the balanced calm of the egocentric Prince Boris Drubeckoj, the awkward unconventionality of Pierre Bezuxov, and so on. Tolstoj uses peculiarities of speech to distinguish characters. By the end of the first part of the novel, the principal characters, and others, such as Prince Kuragin and his three attractive but soulless children, have come to life.

A great deal happens in the first part of the novel. There is a dispute over the millions that Count Bezuxov leaves behind, and the inheritance falls to Pierre. Pierre marries the beautiful Hélène Kuragin. Boris Drubeckoj and Andrej Bolkonskij take part in the unsuccessful Russian campaign against Napoleon in Lower Austria and Moravia. During a Russian retreat, the seriously wounded Andrej Bolkonskij is taken prisoner by the French. Tolstoj writes as openly about the moral depravity of Russian society as about the sincere patriotic enthusiasm of soldiers and officers for a war they do not really understand. Old Prince Kuragin attempts to steal Count Bezuxov's will; his daughter Hélène prompts the rich Pierre to marry her; ambitious officers succeed and fail on the battlefield.

Subsequently, scenes of characters' personal lives alternate with scenes of war. Andrej Bolkonskij is not dead, as supposed, but returns to the family estate as his wife is dying from giving birth to a son. Pierre's marriage has been unhappy, as one might have expected; after a duel with the man he believes to be his wife's lover, he leaves Hélène. With a seriousness unusual in Russian historical novels, Tolstoj concentrates on the inner lives of his characters. Andrej Bolkonskij takes part in efforts at reform and comes into contact with the Tsar's well-known assistant M. M. Speranskij; and the unfortunate Pierre finds solace in the moral and social endeavors of the Freemasons. Eventually, both Andrej and Pierre realize that they have not found ultimate truth and that their spiritual search is unsatisfied.

Various scenes deal with the Rostov family and the Russian army in Europe—Tsar Alexander I and Napoleon have appeared in the first part of the novel. The action shifts from high society to the Christmas festivities of young aristocrats and the estate of an old-fashioned nobleman. When Nataša Rostov turns sixteen, Andrej Bolkonskij falls in love with her, and they are engaged. At the request of her father, the marriage is postponed for a year. Nataša succumbs to the handsome Anatol Kuragin; and it is only by chance that he is prevented from abducting her. Her engagement to Andrej is broken. The great decisions of all the characters still lie ahead of them.

Gradually, the line between true and false is less sharply distinguished than at the beginning of the novel. But Tolstoj retains his impressionistic devices. The face of Andrej's wife is described in the same way till her death, and her sister-in-law's "shining" eyes are often mentioned. Speranskij is introduced and is identified by his "long face" and "plump white hands." Tolstoj was fond of "unmasking" the emptiness and pointlessness of "culture" and, in his detailed description of Nataša's first visit to the opera, he represents everything as "strange and curious." What happens on stage is made to appear a series of senseless movements and songs with unintelligible words (nothing is said about the story of the opera), that is, the opera is "affected," "unnatural," and "ridiculous." Tolstoj carries out his attack on false culture with special devices apparently derived from Swift and Voltaire (see sec. 9 below).

Tolstoj uses more impressionistic devices in his psychological portrayals. He concentrates on obscure and seemingly unmotivated experiences and actions, the sources of which are in the depths of the soul, without entering the consciousness of his characters. For instance, Nataša's mother and Andrej's sister envy Nataša when she is engaged; and Pierre simultaneously hates and admires the unscrupulous and uninhibited way in which Anatol Kuragin deals with people and, himself a married man, almost abducts Nataša.

9. Tolstoj recognized that his experience in the Crimean War was not sufficient for him to describe the War of 1812, although his *Sevastopol Stories* are the basis of episodes in the Austrian campaign in *War and Peace*. He therefore did what he did on other occasions and made an extensive study of memoirs and histories. Among the historians he consulted was the old M. P. Pogodin, whose circle at the time included the Slavophile Jurij Samarin and the independent scholar and eccentric S. S. Urusov. In 1864, Tolstoj met with these men; and his exchange of ideas with them was evidently of importance to him, just as was a short work of Pogodin, *Historical Aphorisms* (1836). While abroad, Tolstoj had met the French journalist and politician Pierre Joseph Proudhon and was much impressed with his book *La guerre et la paix* (1861; translated into Russian in 1864), on which various articles were written in Russia, as B. M. Ejxenbaum notes. In 1866–67, Fet called Tolstoj's attention to Schopenhauer; and Tolstoj was immediately enthusiastic. But these different interests did not prevent Tolstoj from developing consistent story lines in *War and Peace*.

After brief observations on the philosophy of history, Tolstoj continues his novel with the French invasion of Russia. With respect to historical events, he makes a sharper distinction between the genuine and the false. Persons are no longer judged strictly according to these categories, but Tolstoj distinguishes between events as they were and the false interpretations attributed to them. He first suggests and then maintains that the true historical process is predestined, although it "does not appear sensible or intelligible" to men, who pursue their own goals. His contention lacks ultimate clarity.

Tolstoj makes gradually more use of a device acquired from Swift and Voltaire, that of rendering apparently meaningful things meaningless by looking at them through "noncomprehending eyes." Instead of calling things by their usual names, he relies on an ancient device and notes only aspects of them that are not meaningful.[1] This device can also be applied to long descriptions and scenes. Some simple examples are Tolstoj's surprise that Murat has been named King of Naples, his report that in the Russian victory at Krasnoe "twenty-six thousand prisoners, hundreds of cannon, and some sort of stick (*kakuju-to palku*) that is called a marshal's baton were taken," and general remarks, such as victories are judged by how many "scraps of material attached to poles"—banners—are captured from the enemy. It is not just victories that are made to appear unimportant and ridiculous, but all the attainments of culture as well. Doctors are disposed of: "Although he was treated by physicians . . . , he recovered."

Characters are still treated impressionistically. Mrs. Bolkonskij has passed on her upper lip to her son; Bilibin, who appears in one scene, wrinkles his forehead; and Mar'ja Bolkonskij's eyes continue to shine to the end of the novel. A new feature is Napoleon's "little tummy," a detail taken from descriptions of him in exile.

Tolstoj tells what is happening to his characters on the home front. Andrej Bolonskij is mortally wounded at the Battle of Borodino and is reconciled with Nataša, who nurses him while he is dying. His father dies; and, when French troops approach, his sister is forced to flee the family estate. Pierre Bezuxov remains in Moscow when it is occupied by the French, is taken prisoner

---

1. See D. Čiževskij on Comenius in *Harvard Slavic Studies,* I, 117 ff., and Erich Auerbach, *Mimesis,* 1946, p. 356 ff.

by them, and is forced to accompany them on their retreat until
he and his fellow prisoners are set free by partisans. Meanwhile,
his wife, Hélène, dies.

The idyllic epilogue features two happy couples. Pierre marries
Nataša, who has lost her animation and is content with family
life; and Mar'ja Bolkonskij marries the older son of the Rostovs,
Nikolaj, who has played a modest part in the novel. Tolstoj
describes the experiences of these two couples with intensive
psychological analysis. The experiences of the principal characters
are generally presented on two levels. Thoughts and feelings
originate in the irrational depths of the unconscious and finally
come to light; and one is surprised at the turn one's soul has
taken.

Military events are treated in great detail, and new characters
are introduced. Here the principal characters are Napoleon, Field
Marshal Kutuzov, and a fellow prisoner of Pierre, Platon
Karataev, who is a professional soldier from the peasant class
and appears on only a few pages. The events of the war are presented on two levels. The heroic deeds of the Russians are not
overlooked but are not extolled. Tolstoj can hardly be thought
to have written an *Iliad,* something his philosophy of history
would not have permitted. He shares the Russian patriotic
enthusiasm of 1812, but his main thesis is that every man lives
for himself and uses his freedom to achieve personal goals, goals
far removed from those of the historical process. Therefore, Tolstoj
describes in detail episodes that lead one to expect anything but
the destruction of Napoleon's great army. Many Russians have
surprisingly little to do with historical events, as one sees in
the descriptions of St. Petersburg society, Hélène Bezuxov's sensa-
tional love affairs, and people in Moscow before and during the
French occupation. Pillaging is a problem, not only in occupied
cities but in the heroic combat units of both armies, and repeatedly
cost an army certain victory. At the command level, there are
men in both armies who frustrate their victories because they
act according to the dictates of military theory or personal
ambition. That is demonstrated in a series of scenes in which
humor, rare in Tolstoj, plays a major part.

In the beginning of the account of 1812, there are observations
on the philosophy of history in which the words *fate* and *hand*

of God occur. The literary level is far above these vague, incautious terms. It is important to note that Tolstoj's historical characters are quite different from historical accounts of these persons. Napoleon seems a man destined to ultimate failure. A participant in the Austrian campaign has seen Napoleon in the presence of "eternal nature," a sky with clouds hanging far away, and found him to be a "vain and petty man." During the Russian campaign, Napoleon's vanity and his poses are emphasized; everything he thinks, writes, and does is made to appear false (an interpretation certainly influenced by Proudhon). Napoleon is shown in this light in many scenes, for which Tolstoj uses documents (this is not the place to ask whether Tolstoj's is the real Napoleon). Napoleon is contrasted with the Russian commander-in-chief, Kutuzov, who has the mysterious ability to sense the direction history is to take and who sees his mission in meeting the demands that historical necessity has presented (we need not ask whether this is the real Kutuzov). But in the end, one remembers Tolstoj's word *fate* and its milder synonyms and recognizes his tacit assumption that Napoleon's defeat and the Russian victory were predetermined in the historical process. Tolstoj's philosophy of history seems to have been a rather complicated synthesis of Urusov's and Schopenhauer's.

Perhaps the most important character, the modest Russian soldier Platon Karataev, is a type that Tolstoj was to concern himself with later. Karataev does not make a major contribution to the Russian victory, and he saves Pierre Bezuxov from a spiritual crisis, not through anything he does, but just by being himself. It is Karataev's *being* that enables one to overcome the grim idea of historical fatalism. Karataev seems to exist almost entirely outside the historical process, to be an "eternal personification of the spirit of simplicity and truth." That is Pierre's view of him and, presumably, Tolstoj's. The principal features of Karataev's character are humility and love. His humility consists in having the same attitude in his private life that Kutuzov does as commander-in-chief. He demands nothing of life and passively accepts the good and the bad. He has no egoistic interests and presumably believes in Providence (although Tolstoj does not say so). The active feature in his make-up is love, which has little in common with Pierre Bezuxov's idea of love or that of any other cultured person. Karataev's love is not directed at individuals or objects but is universal—cosmic, as one writer has said. It is not restricted to individuals or things; and nevertheless, or perhaps for this reason, one can never doubt it and can always rely on it as a brotherly gift. Tolstoj thought that Karataev was typical of the Russian national character. But he is merely an indication of Tolstoj's later moral views.

War and Peace is a truly powerful book. The literary impact is not diminished by Tolstoj's tendentiousness and debatable philosophy of history. Scholars have been struck by his ability to draw on many sources; Victor Šklovskij is not wrong in calling some pages of the novel "montages." Tolstoj borrowed, almost in toto, whole sections of historical works and memoirs, changing only details of expression and turning this raw material into the gold of his novel. He put this same ability to use in later works.

Tolstoj revised *War and Peace* after its original publication, starting with the first part. Subsequent publications reveal a number of changes, primarily those pertaining to his philosophy of history. In the epilogue, there are allusions to the futures of the main characters; and one suspects that Pierre Bezuxov and the young son of Andrej Bolkonskij will become Decembrists. Apparently Tolstoj had given up his plans to write a Decembrist novel. Instead, he started collecting material for a novel on Peter the Great but decided not to go ahead with it. He also set aside other plans, such as those for a *bylina*-novel. After some hesitation, he did begin a work, and, despite interruptions, completed it. It was his second great novel, *Anna Karenina*.

10. *Anna Karenina* is great in a different way from *War and Peace*. It is set in Tolstoj's own time and deals with contemporary problems; it is a social novel. Among the problems discussed in detail are the reforms of the period, particularly the judicial reforms and the consequences of the emancipation of the serfs; the decline of the landowning class; the attitude of Russian society toward the 1877 Slavic war of liberation; and all sorts of new currents, from Pietism to spiritualism. The characters and sometimes the author express their opinions on modern art and music, education and economy, labor questions and the emancipation of women. In the drafts of *Anna Karenina,* there are references to other problems not treated in the finished version.

Against this complicated background, Tolstoj deals with Anna's adultery. The principal characters are by no means limited to the triangle formed by Anna, her husband, Aleksej Karenin, and her lover, Count Vronskij. The landowner and farmer Konstantin Levin is another focal point, and his marriage to Kitty Ščerbackij is an important contrast to the love affair between Anna and Vronskij. The two couples are linked through a good friend of Levin, Anna's brother, Stiva (Stepan) Oblonskij, who is married to Kitty's older sister. Konstantin Levin's two brothers also play a part, the sick, degenerate Nikolaj and the scholarly Sergej. Despite the many important characters in the work and the large number of problems treated, *Anna Karenina* is not "decentralized," as is *War and Peace*. The structure of the novel with its three focuses—contemporary problems, Anna and Vronskij's love affair, and Levin and Kitty's marriage—is so extraordinarily artistic that the reader never loses track of the two couples, though they are connected almost exclusively through Oblonskij and his wife. All the characters are presented with Tolstoj's typical clarity.

Since the romantic period and the novels of George Sand, the theme of adultery had been dealt with repeatedly in second-rate Russian literature. Perhaps *Anna Karenina* is Tolstoj's answer to critics such as Belinskij who condemned Tat'jana's fidelity in Puškin's *Evgenij Onegin*. Tat'jana declines to leave her husband to live with Evgenij, whom she loves (see Ludolf Müller on this subject). Later, Čexov responded to *Anna Karenina* with his *The Duel*. Criticism of marriage was one of the liveliest problems in the literature of the day. In *Anna Karenina*, Tolstoj again presents the class that he knows best, high society. In addition to the wealthy landowner Levin, almost all the other characters are princes and counts, or at least officers in guards regiments and high government officials. In Tolstoj's time, many critics rejected the novel because the characters were from high society. It was a tribute to Tolstoj's art that the novel was, nevertheless, soon recognized as a jewel of Russian literature.

The plot of *Anna Karenina* is rather simple. Anna has been married for a long time to a dry, distant, but not unintelligent husband. They have an eight-year-old son, but it seems that Anna and her husband see each other only in society and in bed. Anna is courted by the dashing guards officer Count Aleksej Vronskij, experiences her first real love, and yields to him. In contrast to the many flirtations going on around them, Anna and Vronskij's love is portentous. She is forced to give up her son, and Vronskij must leave the service. Since Anna's husband is unwilling to grant a divorce, she and Vronskij break with society and see each other on Vronskij's estate and abroad. In time, their passions cool; and their unconventional "free" marriage is shaken at the point where normal marriages begin. Anna has doubts about her relations with Vronskij and misinterprets some of his remarks and actions. In despair, she commits suicide by throwing herself under a train. Her death ruins Vronskij's life.

Levin's idyllic love and marriage is not without problems. Once married, he continues his religious search and struggles with ultimate questions; and, in the end, it is only suggested that he is nearing a firm belief.

The characters in *Anna Karenina* are not so one-sided as those in *War and Peace*; they combine various human traits. Vronskij regards his affair with Anna as a real marriage and has a rather good mind but is so class-conscious that he judges his fellow soldiers by their family backgrounds and not by their intelligence. His interest in art is not deep, and his work on rural self-government is prompted at least in part by vanity. Anna cannot overcome her passion, which Tolstoj thinks is far removed from real love. Her concern about public opinion is in Tolstoj's view a doubtful instance of vanity and contributes to her ruin. Neither Levin nor Kitty is idealized or infallible. In the beginning, Oblonskij is presented as a man of the world, negligent of his family but basically likable. In his dealings with people, he is a little forward and frivolous; but he tries to be helpful, and he has none of Vronskij's class-consciousness or Levin's proud disdain of businessmen. Even the unattractive Karenin is occasionally shown to be thoughtful and sensitive.

The spiritual fermentation that began in Tolstoj around 1874 left few traces, all in all, in *Anna Karenina*. The contemporary problems that he treats in the novel reveal little about his later views. In *Anna Karenina,* one is struck only by his rejection of the organization of the state, which can be interpreted as criticism of the present condition of the organization, and by his occasional criticism of militarism.

In *Anna Karenina,* Tolstoj still uses impressionistic devices, but he relies on them less than in his earlier works. The first chapters are particularly reminiscent of the simplicity of Puškin's style, which is by no means realistic (one is reminded of drafts of Puškin's works published as fragments); and, in style and language, *Anna Karenina* is a model of Russian prose. Portraying the human psyche, especially in the second part of the novel, Tolstoj employs new devices. Early in the novel, experiences of the characters are presented rather clearly; but later, the reasons for experiences and actions are relegated to the irrational depths of the soul. That is particularly true of Levin's marriage and the last hours of Anna's life. The moods behind Anna's actions are apparently unmotivated and vague, but they often lead to lucid false conclusions.

First, there is an unimportant quarrel. Anna's "irritability had no apparent cause," since she has no one to be jealous of. When one of her suspicions proves false, she "seeks a new reason to be angry" with Vronskij. Some of Vronskij's thoughts and feelings are also indefinite. He does not understand the intensity of Anna's experiences, especially when she is angry about words that he "has spoken only in her imagination" but that she "can no more readily forgive him than if he had actually said them." Anna is moody for a long while. She has a "vague thought that she cannot summon to mind (*soznat'*); she wishes "to inflict pain on Vronskij," and when this desire grows less keen, "she was startled that she had given up her intention"; she is also surprised at her own wish to forget, to console herself. Then everything becomes seemingly obvious: "It's clear—he's in love with someone else"; "she saw it plainly—it was not merely a suspicion"; "she knew that he would not return," and so on.

That is the way she perceives everyday sights as she drives to Mrs. Oblonskij's, where she will meet Kitty. Groundlessly, she senses that both of them consider her an "immoral woman," and she thinks that she is justified in despising them. Her mood goes on: "Everything is wretched (*gadko'*)"; "we all hate each other"; "everything is false, everything is a lie, everything is deceptive, everything is evil." Suddenly, Anna is shaken and recovers from her vague mood, from her half-conscious daydream. When she throws herself under the train, her last thoughts are, "What am I doing? . . . What for?"

Compositionally, Anna's suicide is well foreshadowed. Early in the novel, she learns that a railroad worker at the Moscow station has been run over by a train. Later, she is often troubled by an ugly dream, in which an old man "speaks unintelligible French words" and "pounds on iron." Just before she commits suicide, she notices a railroad worker striking the wheels of the cars to check them; and she is reminded of her dream. This series of apparently chance events determines her course of action. Like other images, such as a snowstorm and a dying candle, these omens serve a symbolic function. One could say that, in *Anna Karenina,* Tolstoj uses symbols consciously, as B. M. Èjxenbaum and Ulrich Busch indicate.

Tolstoj had various things to say about the meaning of *Anna Karenina,* but one cannot help being skeptical about his later remarks. The motto of the novel (from Paul's Epistle to the Romans xii:19 and Epistle to the Hebrews x:30—it is a quotation from the Pentateuch v, xxxii:35) is probably intended to mean that adultery will be requited in some way. Neither the published novel nor Tolstoj's drafts reveal whether he had in mind God's vengeance. But we know that, instead of a quotation from the Bible, he originally planned to use a similar motto from Schopenhauer.

One of the factors in Anna's death is Karenin's refusal to grant her a divorce. It is doubtful that Anna would have committed suicide if she had been able to obtain a divorce and marry Vronskij, and her death seems merely the result of a chain of events. But that does not diminish the artistic merit of the novel any more than do the tendentious motifs.

11. When Tolstoj finished *Anna Karenina,* he intended to write no more fiction; but he soon realized that works of art were as suited to propagating his views as were his "theoretical" writings. Among the works of art designed to publicize his views is his last novel, *Voskresenie* [Resurrection], begun in 1889, completed in 1899.

In 1887, Tolstoj had heard from the prominent lawyer A. F. Koni the story of a juryman who found that a prostitute on trial for theft was a woman whom he had seduced years before and led astray. She died in prison, although the juryman had offered to make good his guilt and marry her. Tolstoj tried to persuade Koni to put the story in literary form and later used the material himself.

Tolstoj revised *Resurrection* a number of times, and various versions were published. It appeared, with many censored deletions, in the popular illustrated magazine *Niva,* in a not entirely authentic form abroad (in Russian and in translation) and, later, in its final version. Tolstoj changed Koni's story by having the accused woman, whom he called Katja Maslova, sent to Siberia, because of a legal error, instead of to prison and by showing her and her seducer, Prince Nexljudov, in Siberia.

There is almost no "decentralization" in *Resurrection*; the focus is on the two principal characters, especially Nexljudov. Maslova's thoughts are revealed mainly in conversation with Nexljudov and others. In comparison with Tolstoj's two other novels, *Resurrection* is short and its composition simple. The first part describes the trial at which Nexljudov recognizes Maslova. The verdict of the court, which Nexljudov tries to have annulled, is based on a misunderstanding. The pardon comes too late; Maslova is transported to Siberia, and Nexljudov follows her. In Siberia, she is pardoned and allowed to settle there. She repeatedly declines to marry Nexljudov, for several reasons. She has been rejected by society; she and Nexljudov are from different stations in life; and he wants to marry her only to vindicate himself morally, and she resents his motives. She decides finally to marry a political exile whom she has met on the long journey to Siberia. The brief conclusion to the novel consists of Nexljudov's thoughts on reading the Gospels, after he has given up Maslova. His observations take the form of short commandments that reflect Tolstoj's views at the time.

Resurrection is an almost purely didactic work. Tolstoj's skill makes the novel seem a work of art despite its tendentiousness. He frequently resorts to a device that he has used often before, exposing social institutions and people who serve them. Among these people are prisoners and guards, lawyers and jurymen, officials and churchmen, and Nexljudov's friends and relatives, to whom he turns for help. Tolstoj does not expose institutions merely by looking at them in the fashion of Voltaire, with uncomprehending eyes. He also preaches his views straight out. A typical example is his description of a church service (I, chapter 39 f.). His treatment of communion best demonstrates this kind of criticism.

It is assumed that the priest "has eaten a portion of the body of God and drunk a swallow of his blood." "Afterward, the priest drew the curtain [that separates the altar from the nave—D. Č.], opened the middle door [the so-called 'emperor's gate'—D. Č.], took a gilded cup [the chalice—D. Č.] in his hands, went out through the middle door with it, and invited those who, like him, wished to partake (*poest'*) of the body and blood of God, which were in the cup."

In the following chapter, Tolstoj says that this church service has nothing to do with the real teachings of Christ; he is astonished that neither the priest nor the congregation notices. The persons to whom Nexljudov turns for help are portrayed similarly, whether they reject him, are indifferent to him, or sympathize with him. Tolstoj's aim is to criticize lawyers and the aristocracy. All the characters are well presented, and all seem vain and empty.

The composition of the novel joins two different lines. Nexljudov is shown to be obsessed with a single idea. All his actions are aimed at one goal; he is indifferent and at times rude to others, even to those who sincerely try to help him. On the other hand, Katja Maslova undergoes a change brought on by her new surroundings, especially by the political prisoners. Nexljudov's resurrection does not seem to have a definite effect on her. It is uncertain whether Tolstoj intended that it should.

On his journey to Siberia, Nexljudov meets a new world of criminals. Tolstoj attempts to vindicate them in part, particularly the political ones, by showing that they are no worse than their judges and jailers. He thinks that these political prisoners have gone about correcting society the wrong way but that they oppose the same social institutions he does. He does not overlook the morally depraved and the egoistic political criminals. But Simonson, who wants to marry Maslova, is particularly decent and noble. Tolstoj's characterization of positive and negative types among the convicts and political exiles is one of his greatest achievements.

Tolstoj does not neglect landscapes and nature in *Resurrection*. He describes a spring day in the city:

The evening before, the first warm spring rain fell. Everywhere that there was no pavement the grass suddenly turned green. The birches in the gardens took on green fuzz. The buckthorns and poplars bent straight their long, fragrant leaves, and in the houses and shops people took out windows and washed them ... In the streets, which were cool and damp on the left side in the shade, but which had already dried off in the middle, heavy wagons kept rumbling by, cabs jingled, and horse-drawn streetcars rang. All around, the air shook with sounds of various kinds and with the din of church bells. . . . People in their finery were going to their churches.

In *Resurrection,* Tolstoj makes little use of his impressionistic devices. But even in this tendentious, didactic work, his artful language stands him in good stead.

12. Among Tolstoj's works after his religious and moral conversion are a number of novellas, some of which he published, some of which were published posthumously.

In 1884, he began work on the novella *Smert' Ivana Il'iča* [The Death of Ivan Il'ič], published in 1886. Ten years before, he had undergone a conversion as a result of a strong awareness one night that since death destroys all, it renders life senseless. *The Death of Ivan Il'ič* shows this awareness in an average man and reveals the man's emptiness by subjecting his normal, happy life to a perhaps too strict examination. In 1891, Tolstoj published the novella *Krejcerova sonata* [The Kreutzer Sonata], on which he had been working since 1887. The original title, *How a Man Killed His Wife,* is a brief summary of the plot. The novella takes the form of a confession of a man who has murdered his faithless wife. It scrutinizes the marriage traditions of cultivated society and sex in general as severely as *The Death of Ivan Il'ič* does the life of an average man. *The Kreutzer Sonata* has become widely known, more for its theme than for Tolstoj's narrative art.

Starting in the mid-1880s, Tolstoj wrote a number of "folk tales," stories or artistic, tendentious works disguised as fairy tales, that are intended for the masses and for children. In these tales, he uses language that is popular in vocabulary and phrasing. All these folk tales are sermons on his religious and moral views,

on love, nonviolence in combating evil, and the harmful effect
of civilization. The tales continue the series of short novellas that
he began earlier and published in his primer and in his *Russian
Readers,* which came out before 1875. From time to time, Tolstoj's
folk tales demonstrate his incomparable art of literary montage
(see sec. 9, above); he revises entire folk tales and succinctly adds
his own views.

In 1896, Tolstoj began work on his novella (*povest'*) *Xadži-Murat,*
published posthumously. The novella deals with an episode in
the Caucasus, the tragedy of a mountaineer leader who surrenders
to the Russians in 1851. In *Xadži-Murat,* the contrast between
natural and civilized man is more pronounced than in *The Cossacks,* a related story; Tolstoj had meanwhile decided that modern
culture should be rejected totally. All his other novellas and fragments of novellas are didactic in some way.

13. Tolstoj also wrote plays. Besides the unfinished antinihilistic
comedy *Zaražennoe semejstvo* [The Infected Family] (1864) and
his satire on educated people's interest in spiritualism *Plody pros-
veščenija* [The Fruits of Enlightenment] (1890), Tolstoj wrote two
other plays.

The darkness referred to in *Vlast' t'my* [The Power of Darkness]
(1896) is moral, the power of evil, and not intellectual ignorance.
The play is set in a peasant milieu and is obviously designed
to produce a moral effect on a peasant audience. It was at first
strongly opposed by the theatrical censorship and was then passed
to be produced only in large cities.

Like *Polikuška,* this play is a gloomy picture of Russian peasant
life. It is about the struggle of good and evil for the soul of the
young peasant Nikita; good and evil are represented by his mother
and father. Nikita works for a rich, sickly peasant, who is poisoned
by his wife with the help of Nikita's mother. The widow then
marries Nikita. He has already seduced one girl and seduces his
wife's stepdaughter. On the advice of his mother, he murders
the child the girl bears. Afterward, his conscience begins to bother
him, and he heeds his father, who has warned him against his
evil ways. Nikita confesses his crime to a number of guests and
is arrested. His father is not preachy, but he stammers his admoni-
tions in barely intelligible words. He is a symbol of the conscience
that is in everyone, even in Nikita. Although the work is full

of gloomy, repellent scenes, the ending produces a catharsis; and, in this respect, *The Power of Darkness* is reminiscent of Sophocles.

Tolstoj's other play, *Živoj trup* [The Living Corpse], was published posthumously and not entirely revised. The principal character, Fedor Protasov, a good but weak man, senses that he cannot give up his licentious life and pretends to commit suicide to set his wife free. When he is found out, his wife has remarried and is considered a bigamist and brought to trial. Protasov shoots himself when he realizes that she will not be acquitted. *The Living Corpse* contains well-constructed scenes and a number of impressive characters. Apart from satire on Russian marriage law, there is little moral tendency in the work. *The Living Corpse* lacks clarity of over-all construction and requires a large cast of characters—at least fifty—but it has enjoyed an extraordinary success on the Russian stage, a success now being repeated abroad.

All Tolstoj's plays bear witness to his great literary art.

14. Tolstoj's long creative career, almost sixty years, makes it impossible to set down basic characteristics of style that hold true for all his works. A further difficulty is that his philosophical and literary sources were largely foreign to Russian literary tradition, as B. M. Ėjxenbaum points out, somewhat exaggeratedly.

In any case, Tolstoj certainly intended to be a consistent realist. In his *Sevastopol Stories,* he writes, "The hero of my narrative, whom I have tried to render in all his beauty and who was, is, and will always be beautiful, is truth (*pravda*)." Tolstoj is akin to other realists in his efforts to portray human types and in the metonymical quality of his style. A typical peculiarity is his literary egocentricity, which allows him to create uniquely individual characters resembling Tolstoj in their tendency toward introspection. Tolstoj characterizes his types primarily through dialogue and impressionistic strokes; but his eccentrics are distinguished by their penetrating self-analysis, reminiscent of that in Tolstoj's diaries and *A Confession*. Sometimes, one is not told how these eccentrics look (for example, Levin), and that contradicts D. S. Merežkovskij's theory that Tolstoj proceeds from a description of external traits of his characters to their thoughts. One could hardly say that his descriptions of his characters' appearance are typical of him. It is his *dynamic* portrayal of character that is striking.

His characters are compared and contrasted with one another, even in the early works—*Childhood, Boyhood, Youth,* and *The Sevastopol Stories*—where the characters contrasted are members of the same family. To achieve these contrasts, Tolstoj uses various devices, primarily linguistic. The principal characters are inter-related in various ways: Stiva Oblonskij and Anna Karenina are brother and sister, for example, and Kitty and Mrs. Oblonskij are sisters.

15. Tolstoj's stylistic devices are more numerous than his com-positional patterns.

A typical feature is his extraordinarily rich language, which varies considerably from person to person and work to work. His linguistic devices range from the popular, awkward language of some of his peasants and clumsily mixed languages (Russian and French or Russian and English), which members of high society speak, to the even language of his "folk tales" and his own lan-guage, particularly in *Anna Karenina*. The "motley language" of Gogol' and Leskov was alien to Tolstoj, and he remarked that he did not care for it.

Another typical feature of Tolstoj's language is the art of "montage" (see sec. 9 above), with which he creates the illusion of verisimilitude.

One is struck by the objectivity with which Tolstoj portrays people and events. But he cannot always clearly combine the good and bad features of a character, and at times his didactic tendency interferes. He is merciless to his favorite characters, not only in his negative portrayal of the dying woman in *Three Deaths,* but in the presentation of such characters as Sonja in *War and Peace,* who is an "empty blossom" from the beginning and has a hard life, and Nataša, who becomes faded and listless after her marriage to Pierre. During her stay at Bad Soden and after her marriage to Levin, even Kitty is somewhat effaced.

Tolstoj was prompted to take this merciless attitude by two of his philosophical and stylistic masters, Rousseau and Voltaire. His growing aversion to civilization and culture led him to blacken all those who did not sympathize with naturalness and "natural men" and who were not critical of culture. He is merciless and somewhat unfair to Ivan Il'ič, to many lesser characters in *Resurrection*, and to the Russians around the captive Xadži-Murat.

With the aid of the technique of unmasking (as K. N. Leont'ev calls it) learned from Voltaire, Tolstij portrays various individuals and aspects of culture as trivial and empty (see sec. 9 and sec. 11 above).

The impressionistic aspect of Tolstoj's style includes the artistic emphasis of certain features, which distinguish characters (in *War and Peace*, the emphasis is on external features; in *Anna Karenina*, on the inner lives of the characters), and the omission of essential features of reality, a device he uses in his early and middle period, to the time of *Anna Karenina*. Later, he combines impressionistic devices with unmasking.

It has been mentioned that Tolstoj often uses symbols, frequently as omens for the development of the action. His symbolic scenes (as Anna's happy lover, Vronskij is a "murderer";[2] perhaps his accident in the horse race is an omen and symbol; his attempted suicide could be considered foreshadowing; see sec. 10 above) are an involved means of replacing the almost totally absent metaphors. Tolstoj is important as a forerunner of the Russian symbolists.

16. We have already touched on several aspects of Tolstoj's view of the world. Starting in the 1880s, he published philosophical and theological writings. In 1880, he began work on *Ispoved'* [A Confession] and a theological treatise. In 1883, he presented his religious views in *What I Believe*. Later, he published shorter works on the same subject and the aesthetic treatise *What Is Art?* (see sec. 4 above).

We shall not be able to deal with these works here. The rejection of all organized authority led Tolstoj to adopt views that could be called anarchistic; but his anarchism was free of politics and of the violent means anarchists sometimes used.[3]

Tolstoj's philosophy of religion is a rational, moralistic doctrine, very much influenced by Protestant "liberal theology," as Ernst

---

2. *Anna Karenina*, chap. II, sec. 11.
3. See D. Čiževskij, *Russische Geistesgeschichte*, II, 127 ff.

Benz indicates. This system determines Tolstoj's interpretation of the Gospels and the religious motifs in his later works.[4]

The ethical conclusions that Tolstoj drew from his social and religious philosophy are important to his imaginative works. In contrast to his consistently rationalistic social, political, and religious views, the main thought of his ethic is the irrational demand that man be dissociated from all historical realities and morally regenerated by declining to make decisions that would require the use of force. Tolstoj finds arguments in the Gospels to support his view that one should not resist evil. This doctrine, which Tolstoj considered the essential ethical thought of the Russian people, led to a tangle of contradictions that even he could not resolve. He rejects culture as a corrupting force (here he is influenced by Rousseau but has a great negative pathos of his own) and seeks the return of "civilized man" to his "natural state," in which there is neither science nor technology (in the full sense of the word, from railroads to medicine and even obstetric care) and in which the art of the civilized world would be rejected. He decides that the enjoyment of aesthetic pleasure prevents men from doing good. In his treatise on the essence of art, he maintains that the taste and level of understanding of the broad masses should be the criterion of beauty in art.

Tolstoj's attitude is peculiar, to be sure, and is usually considered inexplicable, a curious aberration on his part. When his aesthetic treatise appeared, its thesis was rejected and has been rejected ever since. The most that anyone has said for Tolstoj in this respect is that there are historical parallels, in particular Plato's condemnation of poetry in *The Republic*. Actually, Tolstoj's views are not at all inexplicable, though they may be misguided.

Works of literary art have a definite aesthetic form and are directed at a community of readers. The form should make works accessible to the community. Very aesthetic, formalistic works are intended for a small community; and writers who aim at a maximum aesthetic effect may find no community of readers at all and may merely hope to create one. Writers of this kind

4. See G. Florovskij, *Puti russkogo bogoslovija,* 1937, pp. 282 ff. and 402 ff.; see also V. Zen'kovskij, *Istorija russkoj filosofii,* I, 1948, 391 ff.

have usually produced obscure works; in Russian literature, the futurists are an example.

Tolstoj believed that he should set aside aesthetic considerations to acquire as large a community as possible—the entire Russian people—and, theoretically, all mankind. In his treatise on art, he addresses himself primarily to literature but intends that his remarks should pertain to all art forms. And that is the sense of Tolstoj's "inexplicable" aesthetic views. Here, he is in agreement with Plato, who is concerned with the state as a total community and is therefore sceptical of poerty.

In his personal life, Tolstoj put his nihilistic aesthetic criterion into practice as seldom as in his literary works. Despite his merciless treatise, he continued to listen to classical music and play it himself. He revised his works with the same zeal as before. He could not bring himself to allow his nihilistic views to triumph over beauty.

XIV

Signs of a Crisis

1. The 1880s brought a change in the mood of Russian intellectuals, a change that influenced Russian literature for two
reasons. Intellectuals were the "consumers" of literary production
and, to a large extent, the subjects of literary works. Literature
was a pulpit for political, social, moral, and religious sermons
because it was best able to break the silence prevalent in Russia.
The censorship responsible for the silence made it impossible to
discuss many pressing problems.

In the 1860s and 1870s, political radicalism was the dominant
mood of Russian intellectuals. In the 1880s, the picture changed.
This change has been described in different ways, and there are
different interpretations of the new mood. There was talk of a
skeptical young generation, unwilling to heed the utopian pro-
grams of the political radicals. The tasks that this new generation
took on were referred to as "minimalism." People were content
to limit themselves to "small deeds" (*malye dela*); they recognized
that the heroism of the revolutionaries, who had risked imprisonment, exile, and death, was gone. The skeptical attitude of the
new generation was explained by the failures of the old. The
ambitious goals of the radical intellectuals seemed out of range.
It was said that the political reaction of the 1880s, which
encroached on the reforms of the 1860s and was a considerable
force, had caused intellectuals to turn away from politics. Others
said that the new generation was more realistic and preferred
simply to live and not to struggle for ambitious, unattainable
goals. None of these explanations does more than describe the
symptoms; and none of them takes into account all the causes
for the change in mood. The new intellectual climate made new
demands on literature. New attitudes had to be described and
new interests satisfied, and there had to be less of the preaching
that the new generation no longer wanted.

2. Most of the populists had died or been exiled in the 1860s; and around 1880, many other prominent writers died: Nekrasov, in 1878; Dostoevskij and Pisemskij, in 1881; and Turgenev and Mel'nikov-Pečerskij, in 1883. Gončarev wrote no more after 1869, when his third novel, *The Precipice,* came out. From 1880 on, Tolstoj went his own way, although a number of his adherents followed him. Some realists did live on and continue to write; but Ostrovskij, who died in 1886, was hardly an ideological leader; and Leskov, who died in 1895, remained a lone figure in Russian intellectual life. Saltykov-Ščedrin, who died in 1889, was the only writer who retained his militant attitude. But he had lost many once-loyal readers. The crisis was intensified, but not brought on, by the death and silence of older writers.

Saltykov-Ščedrin called the era one of the "triumphant swine," but he was not heeded as he had once been. The younger populists (see chapter VI, sec. 11) were less read than in the sixties and seventies. The more important writers of this considerably modified school were N. K. Mixajlovskij (1842–1904) and G. I. Uspenskij (1843–1902); but they were unable to create the kind of didactic literature so typical of Russia. Mixajlovskij was a journalist and was forced to treat so many subjects allusively that only the initiated understood him. Gleb Uspenskij drifted from his purely literary work and developed a journalistic style before his career was cut short by madness. The prose writer V. M. Garšin (1855–1888) and the poet S. Ja. Nadson (1862–1887) introduced new elements of style. V. G. Korolenko (1853–1921) and A. P. Čexov (1860–1904) enjoyed longer careers.

Then and later, this period was called a *bezvremen'e,* which means a "gray," "indistinct" era, in which nothing important happens and which has no real substance. But the human soul has an eternal need for art, and for literature in particular; and the new literature satisfied this need with new form and content.

3. In the continuation of this work, we shall see how the new literature came about. It met the demands of a new community of readers, who wanted to be entertained rather than instructed and who resented didacticism. These new readers also read the works of the older and younger populist writers, insofar as these works were reportage, and insofar as the satirical and humorous aspects of them were entertaining.

This period "without substance" produced men whose interests were no longer limited to sociopolitical problems or for whom these problems were not the focal point of their interests. There were not yet many of these new men; but, as had been the custom in the first half of the nineteenth century, they turned to the intellectual life of Europe, to European literature and science, which were gradually freeing themselves from the fetters of materialism and positivism. The writers of this small group went off in different directions. Some returned to the philosophical tradition of the 1840s, to older periods of philosophy, or to religious problems. Others went the way of modern European fine arts (few were drawn to impressionism; more were attracted to the predecessors of the young "modern" style); in literature, writers turned to Western drama, prose, and verse.

4. The new is always appealing, except in times when views prevail that have or appear to have a ready answer for everything. In the 1860s and 1870s, Russia had experienced a "fortunate" era of this sort, content with itself, but unproductive and unable to achieve its ideals. When belief in the fundamental views of this era was lost, there arose a strong interest in everything new. The old faded away and lost its appeal, even when, objectively speaking, the new was not as good. A disenchantment with the old, not always justified, was a strong force in driving people to make often dubious "discoveries." In this phase, the works of Dostoevskij were almost lost sight of by the searching new generation. In literature, the "new realists," such as Garšin, Korolenko, Čexov, and Gor'kij, came on the scene first and were followed by the really new men, who created a new literary style and introduced new themes.

Index